For Bert, Ren and Chomsky, my three Saving Graces.

And for my beloved mother, Alice Wharton, who did this three times over without the aid of a computer.

Contents

About the Author

Wiz Wharton was born in 1969 and had her first publishing success at the age of 13 as co-illustrator of the children's book, *Never Trust A Camel.*

A post-graduate of the National Film and Television School, she has gone on to become an award-winning scriptwriter with success both at home and abroad. *How To Have A Baby on eBay* is her first non-fiction book – the result of a year's self-imposed sabbatical which also saw the birth of her son, Ren.

Having first stumbled across the site in 1999, she now regards herself as something of an eBay veteran and divides much of her spare time between buying too much and having to sell it again.

She lives in London.

Acknowledgements

My very grateful thanks to all at Harriman House for their encouragement and hard work in getting this project realised. In particular to my editor, Philip Jenks, for his wonderful input and discreet corrections! Philip, you always give great email...

Thank you, too, to all the manufacturers and experts whose input has been so instrumental in the more technical aspects of this book and to eBay Inc. for allowing me to use its materials so wantonly. Only kidding.

As all new mums know, it's pretty damn hard to write anything, even a shopping list, with a demanding baby in tow, so a big shout must also go out to those people in my life who have made the late nights possible. In particular to Josie Logan, child entertainer extraordinaire, Elaine Marney, whose text messaging kept me going through many a lonely period and all the staff at Newpin, who have been an incredible lifeline for us through some tough times.

Huge hugs are also owed to the many friends and relatives who have allowed me to bend their ears, borrow their children and become an eBay bore, including Angie, Janet, Hannah at *Oh Baby London*, Gidd, Harriet, Ben, Caroline, Ian and Sue. Also to the many strangers that I accosted with my own strange brand of market research who were never less than generous in their feedback and advice.

Finally, love and thanks to Bert Logan for making me do this, even if it was after I had made the dinner. Your belief that there is life after birth has hopefully now been proven.

Introduction

Since its launch in 1994 eBay has been the subject of so many 'how-to' books that it has almost created its own genre. There are basic guides for beginners, detailed handbooks for experienced traders, manuals for computer hackers, and, of course, the ubiquitous 'how to make a million' titles. This book is none of those.

My aim is to be more entertaining and realistic than any of these, instead focusing on a very specific but sizeable section of the population: parents and parents-to-be. In doing so I hope to show them how to utilise the phenomenon that is eBay to its full, practical advantage.

My first encounter with eBay

Although I didn't know it at the time, the inspiration for this book began in 1999 when my personal circumstances were a world away from where they are today. For a start, I was younger, thinner and childless. Money, then as now, was a priority as I prepared to move into my first flat, a dingy basement in South London. Faced with a long list of expenses and a meagre £500 budget I stumbled, quite by chance, on the concept of online auctions.

Still in its early stages, and a far cry from the retail giant it is today, eBay was nonetheless the most intriguing of this new breed and soon became a fertile hunting ground for anything and everything that I needed. My particular passion then, as it is now, was vintage furniture, the sort of stuff from the 50s and 60s which the rest of the world seemed to be getting rid of in their droves. At that time, I was able to pick up pieces for a song and soon had a front room that resembled a cross between a stage set from Steptoe and Son and Brighton Flea Market on a rainy Sunday.

As the general consciousness of eBay grew so did the awareness of its potential, and soon I was bidding not against myself as in the old days but against professional dealers with the tenacity of terriers and deep pockets to match. Having satisfied my immediate need, my eBay habit was put on hold for a while, and I gave little thought to when I might use the site again.

Necessity is the mother of invention

That day came when, at the beginning of 2005, I was suddenly taken ill. Admitted to hospital with what I thought was some kind of disorder, I was discharged a few hours later with a diagnosis of impending motherhood.

For almost any other occasion in life, ten months seems a long time to prepare but the normal rules just do not apply where having a baby is concerned. Parenthood is not a one-off event but rather a (sometimes frightening) learning curve that has an immediate permanence the moment your baby arrives. And despite coming from a fairly large family, including two sisters with four children between them, I was no threat to Penelope Leach; in fact, it is fair to say that I had *no idea* what having a baby involved except that it could be very, very expensive.

"For every parent who wants, needs and can afford the latest designer offering there are countless others who cannot."

For women of my generation the rights and wrongs of parenthood are learned less from our parents and grandparents than from the media. And its relentless message seems to be that our children will somehow be lacking if they don't receive the best products that money can buy.

Yet for every parent who wants, needs and can afford the latest designer offerings there are countless others who cannot, and some who cannot but will buy them anyway in the belief that this will in some way benefit them or their children even if it means getting into serious debt. Yet, as recently as one generation ago babies were happily bathed in sinks, wore hand-me-downs from relatives, and played with toys fashioned from household items. Few who grew up in that earlier time appear to have suffered from the experience.

Nevertheless, it is unrealistic to expect a modern mum to adopt a mindset of 1940s frugality. I know I couldn't. When I was a mum-to-be, I spent many happy hours compiling wish lists of items. My problem was that although there were some items that I genuinely needed and could afford, there were many others that I *wanted* but which were financially out of my reach.

The solution to this dilemma came to me quite quickly. Remembering how valuable eBay had been, I wondered if it could once more come to the rescue.

In my absence the little site with big ambitions had swelled to mammoth proportions. Now with an inventory of 25 million items and close to 158 million users worldwide it is fair to say that there is very little that *can't* be found on eBay these days.

Second hand, but not second best

One of the criticisms often leveled at eBay is that it has cannibalised the trade of charity shops, jumble sales and antique fairs, I disagree. Far from damaging these businesses, it has in fact done them an enormous favour by removing the stigma of buying second hand. Using charity shops used to be a sign of desperation; now it is normal – *fashionable* even – to buy second hand goods from merchants on eBay. The smarter charities have recognised this and are themselves big sellers on auction sites. eBay has made it easy for them to reach millions of potential buyers and actually invigorated their trade.

Neither do you have to be 'skint', 'desperate' or 'mean' to shop at eBay; the money that I have saved on baby goods has been used to fund activities and experiences for my son that he might otherwise not have been able to enjoy.

Also, the short-lived use of baby goods means that when you do buy second hand they often arrive in nearly new condition – one reason why the yummy mummy brigade in search of designer bargains is a keen forager on eBay.

> "I estimate that having my baby on eBay has cost me less than £500 for an almost identical inventory."

A friend recently bemoaned the fact that she had spent over £4,000 in a well-known baby superstore in order to kit out her new son, and by all accounts this is not unusual. I estimate that having my baby on eBay has cost me less than £500 for an almost identical inventory.

When I told friends and relatives that I intended to write this book, there was immediate interest. Although nearly all of them had heard of eBay most of them had either never used it, or had used it only sporadically. I set out to provide definitive answers to all their questions and then some; from what to buy, to how to buy it and, finally, how to resell it when your little one has grown.

What to buy, what *not* to buy

The workings of eBay are only a part of this book's remit. The other crucial part is concerned with exactly what you should be looking to buy for your baby.

When I first faced decisions of the 'which cot?' and 'which pushchair?' variety, I was overwhelmed by the choice. What I really wanted was a definitive one-stop guide to everything that I needed but none seemed to be available. Although there were (and are) some excellent monthly magazines which carry out consumer testing, the information they contain can be selective. And, of course, you have to buy the magazine every month to be sure of getting the survey you want. Armed with a year's worth of these magazines, a good six month's research on the internet, and liaison with various manufacturers, I have put together the Buyer's Guides which form Part 2 of this book. They should give you what you need to make an informed decision.

This is not a child-care manual, though you will find amongst its pages some advice about safety awareness and sensible precautions. Neither is it a book about how to make a fortune on eBay since its emphasis is more on saving money than making it. Rather it is something of a hybrid: part consumer guide, part eBay primer. It assumes no previous knowledge and requires no investment other than a commitment of time and energy. I am not an expert, but I am a parent and that is, perhaps, the greatest qualification of all for reading and using this book. I hope that you enjoy what you find, and find what you enjoy.

How to use this book

This book is primarily aimed at first-time parents and parents-to-be. Although I hope that it will help any parent looking to save money I am guessing that those who are adding to their existing family will have a lot of the equipment and knowledge to see them through their subsequent arrivals.

The book is divided into four parts which follow on logically from each other and are best read chronologically.

- Part 1 focuses on providing new parents with the information they need in order to make informed buying choices for their pregnancy, birth and beyond.

- Part 2 consists of eighteen Buyer's Guides – detailed guides to the products parents are likely to need, and how to choose between them.

- Part 3 deals with the mechanics of buying on eBay, from learning to navigate its pages, to searching its inventory, to having the confidence to bid and buy, to different payment options. It also includes tips on how to avoid the most common internet scams, and how to bag the best baby bargains.

- Part 4 shows how you can recoup some of the money you have spent by selling items on eBay. Whether you use this revenue to fund future purchases for your baby or to treat yourself and your family is up to you!

Unlike many of the books on eBay, this one doesn't promise to make you a million; rather, it was written from my own experiences of bringing up a baby on a limited income. Its emphasis is therefore on learning to *save* money, whilst hopefully having some fun along the way. It was also written as an antidote to the modern epidemic of mass consumerism and disposal. Even in this day and age, beset with the constant search for the newest and the brightest, I hope there is room for the idea of re-using our commodities.

To all the countless friends, strangers and relatives who have asked me how I had my baby on eBay, this is for you.

So You're Going
To Have a Baby

So you're going to have a baby
What do I do and when?
Your pregnancy calendar
What do I really need?
Sources of help, support and advice

So you're going to have a baby

There's an old joke which defines parenthood as "having a picture in your wallet where your money used to be". Actually, it's not always a laughing matter.

According to the number crunchers at a particular credit card company new parents can expect to spend in the region of £40,000 – £50,000 on their little darling in the first five years of its life. £7,000 of that will be in the first twelve months alone. Add to this the fact that the rate of multiple births has increased by 20% in the last decade and suddenly the words 'captive' and 'market' take on a frightening relevance.

So what, you may ask, is the good news? Well, with the help of this book I want to tell you that it is perfectly possible, with a little creativity and effort, to have a baby and raise it from 0-5 on *much, much less.*

When I discovered that I was pregnant, a little under a year ago, I was living in rented accommodation with no regular income. What I lacked in finances, however, I made up for in ingenuity, eventually managing to buy all of my son's purchases from 0 to way beyond 3 for about £500, including all my own maternity items. Best of all there is no secret formula to how I managed it; it just took lots of preparation, research and a little bit of discipline. Oh, and the largest online auction in the world: eBay.

If you find yourself in the position of being cash-rich and time-poor you're probably reading the wrong book. I wrote this mainly for people who have both the time and the commitment to do a bit of legwork, and dedicate half an hour two/three times a week to trawling the internet. You can do it on less, but in order to get the best bargains I think you really do need to put in that amount of time. It's not hard to find, especially if you have no other children at the moment; simply browsing whilst watching just one episode of the weekly soaps is a wonderful place to start.

I said just now that this probably isn't the book for you if you are cash-rich, but that's not strictly true. Most of us would like a little more disposable income, whether it be for a little luxury now and then, or more practical purposes. By using the tips in this book you will find that your money will go further, allowing you to splash out on something special or to boost your

Child Trust Fund – in my opinion, one of the best government initiatives of recent years.

The other positive aspect of eBay, to my mind at least, is that it instructs us all in the benefits of recycling. We live in a vastly wasteful society where perfectly usable items are discarded when they still have years of good life left. All of the items which I bought as a second user from eBay had at least another baby's life span in them and probably much longer. Clothes, especially, are so infrequently worn before they are outgrown that many of the things I bought could easily have passed for new. I know some people are superstitious about buying second hand for a baby, and of course, it's always nice to have something new for immediately after the birth, but after that you will soon be lost in such a swathe of washing and wearing that you will lose track of what is new and what isn't. Similarly, equipment is now manufactured to such a high safety standard that most items have a longevity way beyond the time that they are needed.

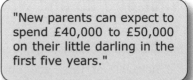

"New parents can expect to spend £40,000 to £50,000 on their little darling in the first five years."

Of all the considerations which may have prompted you to read this book, however, I am guessing that the strongest is financial. I know it was for me, and I make no apologies for that. More and more women and men are now bringing up children on their own and trying to do so either on a single income or, in many cases, not even that. We are so caught up in the have-it-now, regret-it-later culture that by the time we are into our thirties, when more of us are now having our first child, many of us have accumulated a frightening amount of personal debt.

With credit now so easily available we don't think twice before handing over plastic to pay for things, with scant regard to how we are going to repay the debt. But credit has implications not just for ourselves but for the way in which its message is translated to our dependents as they are growing up. If our children learn that they are able to have anything they want when they want it they, too, will grow up with the impatient mindset that keeps the credit card companies in business and ourselves indebted to them. In time, your children will have financial decisions of their own to make; you owe it to them to have a healthy attitude to money and its value.

Whilst I sincerely hope that this book will be of great help to you, at some time in the course of your parenting career, it's likely that you, your partner or family will need someone else to turn to for advice, be it practical, emotional or even legal. With this in mind I have included on pages 30 to 33 some of the great organisations/publications that can offer you this support. Many operate confidential helplines; others will be able to correspond with you via email. Refer back to this list whenever times get tough and you need to be reminded what a brilliant job you are doing. I have divided them into different categories for ease of reference.

What do I do and when?

One of the most comforting and useful things to have when you're pregnant is a timetable of what you can expect to happen during your 40-week journey – physically, medically and emotionally. What follows is a checklist to help you decide what to do and what to buy, at each stage. I don't advise that you try and buy everything at once. The reasons for this are twofold:

You will change your mind. In your excitement, you are likely to fall in love with a certain something – a pram that's been in the magazines or a changing bag that is the current celeb must-have – and rush to buy it there and then, only to find yourself falling in love with something completely different three months later. Take my word for it – this happens. I know of many parents (mums, especially!) who confess to being serial pram buyers, and a lot of their redundant purchases end up on eBay!

It's better to pace your expenses. Buying everything at once may seem like a good idea as it gets the big expenses out of the way, but as already mentioned, people in the real world are rarely that restrained – especially hormonally-charged mums-to-be. Somewhere along the line you are going to see something else that you just have to have.

Pacing yourself and buying only what you need when you need it means that you not only stagger the financial burden over the months, giving yourself time to play catch-up on the credit card bill, but you also have something to look forward to at each stage of the pregnancy.

Your pregnancy calendar

Weeks 1-4

Books

Weeks 1-4 are a time to buy or borrow books on pregnancy and parenting. There are a frightening number of titles on the subject these days, from whimsical journal-type books to in-depth instruction manuals and everything in between.

If you can get out for the day, go to one of the larger high street book chains where they allow you to sit with a coffee and peruse the books on offer. That way, you can get a feel for their style and whether they suit your own temperament or philosophies about pregnancy and child rearing.

Make a list of the books that you like and then, rather than buying them new, either borrow them from a library or check out the options on both eBay and Amazon's new and used 'Sellers' Programme'. The latter often offers books at bargain prices with little or no wear. Simply go to Amazon's website at www.amazon.co.uk and do a search for books by title or author. Any available will appear under the main listing as *New and Used From...*'. Don't forget to factor in postage costs which are currently about £2.50 per item, in order to work out whether this really is cheaper than buying directly from Amazon itself or, indeed, from the high street.

If you have a partner, consider buying books specifically aimed at them: though they may be loathe to admit it, they are facing an incredible journey of their own and can sometimes feel as overwhelmed as you!

Some of the books that my friends and I found most useful are listed on pages 41-42. Reviews for most of them can be found either on Amazon or one of the other book review websites.

Supplements

Start taking a daily amount of folic acid (current guidelines suggest a recommended dosage of 400mcg per day).

Habits

If you are a smoker consider cutting down, or, even better, stopping altogether. Even though this is easier said than done you may be lucky, as I was, and find that your morning sickness quickly overwhelms any desire to smoke (did I say "lucky"?!) By the time this abated, at about 16 weeks, I was over the worst of my nicotine cravings and managed to get through the rest of my pregnancy cigarette-free, albeit sometimes under duress.

Ask your GP or pharmacist for smoking cessation products and advice. For a confidential one-on-one you can also contact the excellent Quitline on 0800 002200 (www.quit.org.uk), or check out the options offered by hypnotherapy, acupuncture and other alternative therapies.

Medication

If you are currently taking medication for any pre-existing conditions do check with your GP to see if any are contra-indicated in pregnancy. Again, this may not simply be a case of stopping as you must discuss both the pros and the cons of no longer taking something which you may have relied on for some time, such as anti-depressants. NEVER come off any prescribed medication suddenly without advice, whether you are pregnant or not.

EDD

Your final mission for these first four weeks is to visit your GP to confirm your pregnancy if you have not already done so. You will also be able to ask them to calculate your Estimated Due Date, or EDD. Hurrah! Your wonderful journey has begun!!!!!

Weeks 5-9

Hospital and birthing centres

In weeks 5-9 you should get in touch with local hospitals or birthing centres to check out their facilities and the options available to you. You are not obliged to go to the nearest hospital, although hospitals out of your area may be unwilling to take you onto their books simply due to logistics.

Be aware that in the (hopefully, unlikely) event of an emergency during both pregnancy and labour you will be taken to your local hospital by default. Don't feel pressured, however, by purely geographical considerations and if you feel particularly strongly for or against a certain institution's facilities or reputation make a strong case for moving to an alternative location to your GP or midwife.

> "The longer you spend on research the less likely you are to make a mistaken purchase."

If you think you may need or want specialist drug relief such as an epidural, check the availability of anaesthetists during unsocial hours as at some locations you may suffer an unpleasant wait if your baby decides to make an appearance in the small hours.

At the time of writing the Royal College of Midwives has started a public debate regarding the issue of paying for epidurals for which there is no real medical 'need'. The cost being bandied around in these discussions is £500 for each procedure. I strongly believe that extreme pain equates to medical 'need' as much as a patient undergoing an operation would require anaesthesia, but maybe that's just me. All I know is that after labouring for 25 hours without success, the epidural was, for me, a definite necessity, medically legitimate or not. Anyway, I digress ...

You might also want to check out your chosen hospital's selection of other labour aids such as birthing balls, pools or TENS machines if this is something you would like to try. You should also research the feasibility of a home birth if this is what you've set your heart on, although bear in mind that whether or not you can have one will depend very much on the local availability of midwives. Many hospitals offer a tour of their birthing facilities to prospective parents and these are well worth taking if only to rehearse your journey to/from the hospital in preparation for D Day!

Baby equipment

Now is also the time to knuckle down and do some preliminary research on baby equipment. Nothing too heavy at this stage, although the longer you spend on research the less likely you are to make an impulsive, expensive or otherwise mistaken purchase.

Don't feel embarrassed to ask other mothers in the street where they got a particular item if you like the look of it. There is nothing better than first hand advice and my experience has been that most people are only too happy to tell you what you need to know. 'Real world' advice has saved me many a prospective purchase when I was told things like how heavy a particular buggy was to lift and fold on your own.

Other sources of research are internet search engines such as Google and specialist parenting sites such as Mumsnet which offer a ratings system for various items of equipment. Don't forget to ask friends and relatives' advice, too; you never know what you might be able to borrow or inherit!

Booking-in appointment

It's at about this time that you may have your booking-in appointment at home, hospital or your GP's surgery. The National Centre for Clinical Excellence recommends that this be carried out before 12 weeks gestation. The purpose of this appointment is to assess your individual needs and to ensure that you are keeping well, both emotionally and physically, and that your baby is growing healthily.

A thorough examination will be made at this time and detailed histories taken of both you and your partner's family, including any inherited diseases, early mortalities, etc. You will be asked for information about the date of your last known period, as well as questions about any previous pregnancies, whatever their outcome, and also about your lifestyle and where you want to have your baby.

Blood tests will be taken to check for immunity against Rubella as well as to ascertain your current iron levels, blood group and rhesus status (whether you are negative or positive). You will also be asked to consent to other blood tests to ascertain your status concerning HIV, Syphilis and Hepatitis B. You can refuse to take any or all of these tests although it is worth noting that much can now be done to assist your unborn child if you are found to be positive for infection.

You will also need to provide a sample of urine to test for early signs of pre-eclampsia, a potentially life-threatening condition, gestational diabetes and/or bacteria. Finally your blood pressure, weight and height will be noted and may be periodically checked throughout the coming months. Any serious health concerns/pre-existing conditions will be referred to a consultant obstetrician who you will continue to see on a regular basis throughout your pregnancy.

Morning sickness

You may want to start considering either conventional or alternative therapies to control morning sickness. Magnetic wrist bands that locate on your pulse points were quite helpful to me, as were recordings of sound patterns specifically aimed at tackling this unpleasant symptom of pregnancy. I believe the sound therapy works by targeting receptors in the ear which respond to particular rhythms, counteracting the sense of nausea.

If you are finding it hard to eat large solid meals, consider buying a food blender or dedicated smoothie maker so that you can stay healthy with juices and soups to keep your energy levels high. Finally, a rather unconventional tip from my own rather sad experience: always make sure that you carry some nappy sacks or dog poop bags in your pocket or handbag as you never know when the urge will strike or, indeed, what might trigger it!

Pregnancy classes

If you feel up to it, start thinking about pregnancy classes, including yoga and/or aquanatal sessions, or simply buy a low impact DVD or video for use in the comfort of your own home. Many women underestimate the great physical demands that both pregnancy and labour make on their bodies, which is why being as fit as possible is more important than ever.

Employment rights

If you are currently in paid employment, telephone or pay an online visit to an organisation such as Working Families to get advice on every aspect of parental leave, rights and benefits, as well as help on how to negotiate family-friendly working conditions following the birth of your baby. The legal position on these issues is constantly changing and they will be able to give you the most up-to-date advice on your particular situation. www.workingfamilies.org.uk.
Telephone: 0800 013 0313

Weeks 10-14

First scan

Sometime during this phase you will be offered your first scan which may be used to establish the date of your baby's expected birth. This date is needed if you are planning to have blood screening tests for Down's Syndrome and/or Spina Bifida. If you are over 35 some hospitals will routinely offer you a nuchal translucency screen which gives an estimate of the risk of your baby developing Down's Syndrome. Note that this will only be an *estimate* and that you will need to undergo other tests such as an amniocentesis to tell you for sure.

The amniocentesis procedure itself carries a small risk of miscarriage as it involves inserting a needle into the abdomen and extracting a vial of amniotic fluid for screening. For this reason, women who are not determined to be at high risk during the nuchal translucency screen are not recommended to go on for the diagnostic tests proper. In some areas of the country, nuchal translucency screens are not offered on the NHS, so if you want one, expect to pay about £70-£100.

Midwives

If you think you may want one, consider looking now for a Doula or private midwife as the popular ones are much in demand. The London Baby Directory is one of the manuals available from hospitals and GP surgeries that has a list of approved agencies. Alternatively you can do a search on the internet. You will need to call the individual agencies involved and ask for a list of suitable candidates.

Weeks 15-19

Maternity clothes

Your clothes may be starting to feel a little snug by Week 15, so think about ordering some of the maternity wear catalogues and researching what you may need for the months ahead. You will probably want to buy a few key pieces plus one or two items to cover special occasions such as Christmas, New Year, weddings, etc.

Antenatal classes

Now's the time to start booking antenatal/parenting classes as the popular ones get booked up very quickly.

Mid-trimester scan

Depending on your local health authority, you may be offered a mid-trimester scan sometime between 18-21 weeks which will enable you to see your baby in more detail. You will even be able to see some movements as long as your baby isn't asleep (!) and some hospitals will give you the opportunity to learn his or her sex. You will also be scanned for any foetal abnormalities.

Weeks 20-24

Exercise

Many women find their morning sickness starts to peter out at this stage and they begin to feel really great for the first time in their pregnancy. Now is therefore a good time to sustain your energy levels with some light exercise.

Basic baby equipment

If you are feeling particularly energetic, think about decluttering your home and buying things for the nursery. You may also want to buy some of the baby equipment that you haven't been able to borrow from friends/relatives, such as sterilisers, bottle warmers, monitors, etc.

The virtue of buying now is that you will have time to study the instructions and learn how to use the equipment before the baby arrives. Planning early also ensures that you can afford to wait for the real bargains on eBay rather than last minute panic buying where you will be competing against the majority of other parents-to-be!

Weeks 25-29

Last chance holiday

If you fancy one last holiday before your baby is born, now is the time to take it! Some airlines place restrictions on pregnant women travelling and may not allow you to fly after about 28 weeks. You should also check that any travel insurance policy you have covers pregnancy. Most will allow you to fly until you are up to to approximately 32 weeks gestation.

Discuss plans with your employer

If you are in work, think about what your plans will be regarding employment after the birth. You should already have had some preliminary discussions with your boss and human resources department regarding leave. You can take official maternity leave from your 29th week.

Childcare

If you plan to return to work soon after your baby is born you should sort out your childcare provisions now. Research all the alternatives, from nurseries to private child care, either full or part time. Don't forget to check that any prospective child care provider has the necessary qualifications and experience of dealing with very small babies. Don't forget, also, that the popular child care resources often have a waiting list of up to a year!

Weeks 30-34

Buy larger baby equipment

By now you should have researched and decided upon your larger baby items such as prams, cots and car seats (if you are not buying a complete travel system). Buy these early and learn how to assemble and use them whilst you have the time. Practise putting the car seat in and out of the car well before you are due to use it for real and don't forget that some items if bought new can take up to six weeks to be delivered.

Manage fatigue

You will find your first trimester fatigue returning with a vengeance now, so take the time to treat yourself. If you can find a practitioner with experience with pregnant women, a massage can be lovely, although they and you should be aware that the use of some oils is definitely contra-indicated in pregnancy.

Mementos

If the idea of a permanent memento of your pregnancy appeals to you, consider ordering specialist services such as lifecasting, body painting or pregnancy photography.

Prepare pets!

Get any pets in the house used to the idea of the new arrival by letting them investigate baby blankets and clothes. I used to carry a teddy around in a blanket so that our dog would get used to me cuddling something other than him! You can also try occasionally wearing baby lotion to gradually accustom pets to the soon-to-be familiar smells of the new arrival.

Weeks 35-37

Home birth

If you have decided on a home birth, organise all your materials now: birthing pool, TENS machine purchase or hire, birthing ball, massage oils etc. You should also start to buy in all those less-than-luxurious essentials such as breast pads and breast shields if you are intending to breastfeed, and bottles, teats and formula if you have decided to bottle-feed.

Prepare your labour bag

Buy or borrow a bag that will serve as your labour bag, and keep it packed by the door with your hospital notes. Take it with you whenever you leave home for an extended period – if you go to visit friends for the weekend, for example.

Weeks 38-40

Stock up on food supplies

Now's the time to stock your larder and freezer with batches of nutritious home-cooked food that can simply be taken out and reheated. Having some convenience foods to hand will stand you in good stead over the coming weeks, and it's no crime to keep a few takeaway menus within arm's reach!

Start ordering groceries online

If you haven't done so already, and assuming you have access to the internet, start ordering your groceries online. Fairly soon you won't have the time to make regular trips to the supermarket, or the energy to lift heavy bags out of the car boot, so the sooner you organise home delivery the better.

Stock up on pet food

Don't forget to stock up on pet food, too, and buy Rover or Tiddles an extra treat. If this is your first baby, your pet may feel pushed out and unwanted at this time.

Look after yourself

Put your feet up and relax! You probably already know that life will not be this peaceful again for some time.

PEANUTS and peanut products are best avoided both in pregnancy and whilst breastfeeding if you or close members of your family suffer from peanut allergies or allergic diseases such as atopic eczema, asthma or hayfever.

There are also other foodstuffs contra-indicated in pregnancy; for the full run-down and expert advice on nutrition at this important time visit:

www.eatwell.gov.uk/agesandstages/pregnancy/

What do I really need?

As with everything in life, what we would *like* to have and what we really *need* are totally different things. When it comes to preparing for a baby the considerations most often at the top of a parent's list are money and space.

One golden rule to remember is that babies want for very little aside from warmth, shelter and food. They have no preconceptions about the latest must-have consumer item, and no knowledge of whether their parents are rich or poor except in an emotional sense. Therefore there is no reason to feel obliged to provide them with the latest designer cot, pram or clothing when hand-me-downs and cheap high street alternatives will more than suffice.

I often think when it comes to having children that spending habits are guided more by vanity and the way parents wish to be perceived by those around them than by real need. As you'll find out, there's nothing like a mother and baby group to reinforce primeval feelings of competitiveness! Still, if you can rise above this, you can actually get by very nicely thank you with a few basic essentials.

If you have a large extended family or generous friends by all means make a list of the more expensive items that you would like but can't necessarily afford, and see whether they will help shoulder the cost. I cannot stress enough that having children will be one of the most expensive, albeit rewarding, experiences of your life, and good financial planning now will ensure that you are not storing up problems for yourself later on. Good habits will also send a message to your children later on in life that money is a valuable commodity and not something to be spent recklessly.

> "Babies want for very little aside from warmth, shelter and food."

That said, there are some things that simply must be bought. To that purpose I have compiled two checklists:

1. Items you will need during pregnancy.
2. Items you will need after your baby is born.

The other factor I mentioned earlier is that of space. If, like me, you live in a comparative shoebox in London, you may want to think twice about large items of nursery furniture such as a dedicated breastfeeding chair or a changing table. Although certainly nice, you will soon find that you are deluged in a swathe of other baby items that will have you desperately wishing you inhabited the Tardis.

Besides, although useful for storage purposes, a changing table is not really needed if you have a changing mat on the bed and, speaking from experience, I happen to think babies actually prefer the softness of a mattress to the sometimes cold, unwelcome surface of a cot top changer. For this reason some of the items have been listed as optional.

Okay, so what do you *really* need...? Read on for suggestions!

During pregnancy

- Folic acid supplements and, if required, an additional multi-vitamin and mineral supplement.

- A selection of maternity wear from about four/five months onwards, including maternity underwear.

- A selection of books or magazines on pregnancy, childbirth and childcare.

- A comfortable, dedicated maternity pillow to support your tummy and back in the later months.

Optional

- A selection of gentle fitness DVDs specifically targeted at pregnancy and beyond, such as yoga or pilates.

- A birthing ball or gym ball for relaxation and exercise.

In your labour bag

- Your Birth Plan.

- A pair of slippers and a couple of pairs of socks. Believe it or not, feet become very cold during labour, especially if you end up flat on your back during an epidural. For other women, slippers are a comfy alternative to shoes if you find yourself pacing the ward in order to kill time.

- An old nightdress or t-shirt for labour itself. Select something which you are not particularly attached to and do not mind discarding afterwards as it can become messy.

- Massage oils or lotions if you would like your birth partner to massage you during labour.

- A TENS machine if you have decided to use one.

- Lip balm. This is not a vanity thing! Entonox, or gas and air as it is more commonly known, makes your mouth extremely dry, as does all the huffing and puffing in the transitional stage!

- Bottled water.

- Snack foods. Pack something that is both nutritious and which releases energy slowly, such as dried fruit and nuts, rather than sugary foods which may not sustain you. You could also pack some glucose tablets.

- A watch with a second hand with which to time your contractions, especially if you decide to go walk about.

- A camera or camcorder to record the happy event, or at least the result of it! If you intend to film the actual labour you should check with the hospital beforehand that this is permitted and make sure that you do not obstruct midwives or other medical staff in your attempts to capture an Oscar-worthy performance.

- Something to take your mind off the wait, such as magazines, books or a portable music player.

- Some people like to bring along inspirational pictures of friends, family and even cherished pets to help them through the difficult stages of labouring. I blu-tacked a picture of our dog to the wall opposite my bed; it didn't help the pain but it gave me something to swear at!

- A wash bag, with flannel, and travel sizes of shampoo, shower gel, body lotion, etc.

- A bottle of water spray or a hand-held fan to keep you cool.

After the birth

For you

- A going home outfit for you. Unfortunately, you will still have a bit of a baby belly immediately after the birth (and, for some of us mere mortals, for many months afterwards) and you may also be bruised and sore, so choose something loose, comfortable and which can be put on and taken off with ease. The same goes for your choice of footwear. Now is not the time to wear your new kitten heels or multiple lace-ups; if you are going home by car, slip-on sandals or pumps are absolutely fine. If you are going to be staying in hospital more than a couple of days, (for example, if you have had a caesarean), pack more clothes as needed.

- Two or three nursing bras if you intend to breastfeed.

- Breast pads in preparation for when your milk comes in.

- Pre-mixed cartons of formula and bottles if you are bottle-feeding. You may find that the hospital will supply these to you during your stay but do check beforehand.

- A front-opening nightshirt or t-shirt if you are breastfeeding, although the question of modesty will not be uppermost in your mind in the labour ward and after what you have just been through!

- Toiletries, including toothbrush, toothpaste and hairbrush.

- Old knickers and/or disposable knickers. There is quite a lot of blood loss after birth, called Lochia, which goes on for about three weeks so leave your best pants at home.

- Maternity pads.

- Arnica tablets to help with bruising post birth. Alternatively try Feme pads, gel packs that you freeze and then insert into a disposable gauze sleeve to wear inside your pants. They offer great relief to those women who have had stitches and/or an episiotomy although, as they do require the use of a freezer, these are probably best left till you return home.

- Earplugs – labour and post-labour wards are noisy places!

- Your address book and money for calls, or a prepaid hospital phone card. Leave announcement cards and the like for when you get home.

A note about choosing a birth partner

Childbirth is an incredibly intense and personal experience which can last from a few hours to (if you're really unlucky) a couple of days. It can also feel quite isolating and, whilst this may sound contradictory, I certainly experienced periods during labour where I felt completely alone with the pain and exhaustion of it all.

Despite this, I would say without reservation that it helps to have someone other than the medical personnel with you; someone with whom you are comfortable enough not to feel self-conscious or (God forbid) apologetic once the pain starts to kick in. For some women this will be their mums, sisters, best friends or, where applicable, the father of their child-to-be. They, and you, should be prepared for anything and everything, from pooing yourself (which I mercifully avoided), to copious vomiting (which I unfortunately did not).

For this reason, many women prefer a birth partner who has been through the experience themselves and who can therefore sympathise/empathise/not fall asleep (delete as applicable). Only you can decide on the best candidate for the job, although if you do choose to have your male partner along for the ride and he hasn't been a dad before, try and make sure he has a good grasp of what is going to happen. The last thing you need to be focusing on is someone else's distress, nausea or boredom.

As a rider to this last point, I have friends who say that having their partner present at the birth fundamentally changed the nature of their relationship. For some this was a welcome development; for others, less so. For all the above reasons make this decision one of your more considered.

Irrespective of who you decide to bring with you they will need to pack a small bag for themselves which should contain the items listed overleaf.

For your baby

- An infant car seat – some hospitals will not let you leave without one.
- One or two outfits for the trip home. The all-in-one stretchy outfits which fasten through the front with poppers are easiest. Also a baby hat.
- Two/three babygros for when you are in hospital. More if you are anticipating a longer stay.
- A baby blanket.

- A jacket/cardigan or snow suit (if you have a Winter baby).
- Muslin squares or a small towel for little accidents and spillages!
- Disposable nappies. Even if you intend to use reusable nappies, I recommend that you buy some disposables for the first few days, especially if you have had a traumatic and/or long labour. The time for reusables (which I now use) is when you have gotten over the labour stage and are feeling once more like you inhabit Planet Earth.

For your birth partner

- A change of clothes.
- Snacks and drinks – you don't want them flagging on you!
- A mobile phone for use outside the hospital grounds, or plenty of change/a prepaid hospital phone card for use inside.

Once you get home

Congratulations! Getting home from hospital after giving birth will seem like one of the longer journeys of your life. Not only will you be sore and exhausted, you will also be reeling from the realisation that you've got a helpless individual to look after all on your own (and I don't mean your partner). Here are the things you should have bought in preparation:

Clothing for the baby

- Six sleepsuits.
- Six vests/bodysuits.
- Two cardigans.
- Two hats and two pairs of mittens.
- Five pairs of scratch mittens.
- A sun hat.
- One snow suit for Winter babies.

Optional

- A swaddle.
- A shawl.

TIP

NEW babies often receive a surplus of first size clothing as gifts. Ask friends and relatives to buy larger sizes to last you into the later months.

Travel

- A convertible pram, pushchair or travel system.
- An infant carrier car seat (if you don't have a travel system).
- A rain hood.
- A sun canopy/mosquito net.
- Four fitted pram sheets, four top sheets, two pram blankets.
- A window shade for the car.
- A changing bag.

Optional

- A travel cot.

Feeding essentials

Breastfeeding

- Four cotton nursing bras.
- Breast pads.
- Breast cream (for sore/cracked nipples).

If you intend to express milk you will also need:

- Two bottles with teats and caps.
- A steriliser.
- A bottle brush.
- A breast pump.

Optional

- Breast shields.
- Out-and-about kit for expressing at work.
- Steriliser bags for fridge and freezer.

Bottle-feeding

- Powdered baby formula.
- Eight bottles with teats and caps: 4 x 4oz, 4 x 8oz.
- A steriliser.
- A bottle brush.

Optional

- A bottle warmer.
- Disposable bottles for travelling.

Weaning

- Three baby bowls.
- Four plastic spoons.
- Sleeved bibs.

Optional

- Recipe books.
- A baby food processor.
- A jar and bottle warmer.

Bathing and cleaning

- A changing mat or unit.
- Disposable nappies or reusable nappies. For reusable nappies you will also need wraps, a nappy bucket, a sanitiser, non-biological wash, pins, liners.
- A large roll of cotton wool.
- Baby wipes.
- Barrier cream.
- Nappy sacks.
- A bath thermometer.
- Baby shampoo/wash.
- Hooded bathrobes/towels.
- Wash cloths.
- Baby scissors/nail clippers.
- Baby hairbrush/comb.
- Baby moisturiser/barrier cream.

Optional

- A scald ring.
- A baby bath (a washing up bowl will do just as well in the earliest days!)

Bedtime

- A nursery thermometer.
- A cot or cot bed.
- Four fitted cot sheets.
- Four light cellular blankets.
- A baby monitor.
- A mobile.

Optional

- A Moses basket or crib.
- A baby sleeping bag.

Playtime

Optional

- A baby swing.
- A baby bouncer (from 6 months).
- A bouncer chair.
- A selection of age-appropriate toys.
- Cloth/age-appropriate books.
- A baby gym.

Miscellaneous

- Baby care/child care books.

Sources of help, support and advice

Product information and advice

www.babiesrus.co.uk
Baby version of the popular toy retailer, offering buyer's guides, product info and advice for parents and parents-to-be.

www.babyandtoddlergear.co.uk
Online version of the magazine: a great place to see all the latest baby and toddler products tested and reviewed in the.

www.babyworld.co.uk
Leading online magazine and community, with thousands of pages of help and advice for new and expectant parents.

www.boots.com
Pharmaceutical advice and products for everyone.

www.mothercare.com
Online branch of the retail parenting giant with access to products and advice on what to buy.

www.namemybaby.co.uk
Information resource to help you choose a name for your baby.

www.nhsdirect.nhs.uk
Official website of the NHS 24 hour helpline. Also features a searchable database of features and symptoms. Telephone: 0845 4647

Parenting websites / support agencies

www.babydirectory.com
Extensive online directory for mums and mums-to-be, including an encyclopaedia of pregnancy and child care finder.

www.babygoes2.com
Travel guide for parents covering resorts, childcare options, discounts and tailor-made holidays.

www.bbc.co.uk/parenting

Offers practical solutions to the challenges of everyday parenting, including advice from experts and other mums and dads.

www.breastfeeding.co.uk

Articles, discussions, books and videos on breastfeeding along with useful contacts.

www.cry-sis.org.uk

Agency which provides support to parents of excessively crying, sleepless or demanding babies.

www.daycaretrust.org.uk

Info from this National Child Care charity.

FWA Newpin

A unique service that supports parents who are the main carer of a child/children under 5 and who are finding life difficult due to lack of confidence, depression, isolation, insecurity or loss of identity – 020 7738 1004.

www.familiesonline.co.uk

Useful information for parents with children and babies.

www.family2000.org.uk

Advice about family issues, a 150 article archive and access to Jill Curtis, senior psychotherapist and author.

www.fathersdirect.com

Good-humoured online magazine aimed at dads and dads-to-be.

www.fulltimemothers.org

Organisation aiming to promote understanding of the child's need for a full time mother, to enhance the status and self-esteem of mothers at home and to campaign for improvements.

www.homedad.org.uk

The only UK support group dedicated to helping dads who are staying at home to bring up their children.

<u>www.mind.org.uk</u>

The website for the leading mental health charity in England and Wales working to create a better life for everyone who is experiencing or has experienced mental distress.

<u>www.mumsnet.com</u>

Set up in January 2000, this website is written by parents for parents and features product reviews, message boards, advice and media items.

<u>www.parentsnews.co.uk</u>

An extensive information service for parents and families online and in print.

<u>www.raisingkids.co.uk</u>

Offers support, information and friendship to everyone who's raising kids, whatever their circumstances or income.

<u>www.uk-parentingdirectory.co.uk</u>

A selected directory of UK parenting links, including child care and retail resources.

<u>www.workingfamilies.org.uk</u>

A voluntarily-funded organisation supported by Unison, The Public and Commercial Services Union and The Association of London Government which gives help and advice to parents in paid employment. It offers an online guide plus free fact sheets on every aspect of state benefits, including legal advice and support in negotiating family-friendly hours for parents returning to work following the birth of their children. Free telephone advice on 0800 013 0313. Highly recommended.

Extraordinary families

<u>www.cafamily.org.uk</u>

National registered charity, founded in 1979, for families with disabled children that offers systems of support and contact.

<u>www.everychildmatters.gov.uk</u>

A new approach for the wellbeing of children and young people from birth to 19.

www.gingerbread.org.uk
Leading support organisation for lone parent families in England and Wales.

www.nas.org.uk
Online site for the National Autistic Society which aims to champion the rights and interests of all people with autism and ensure that they and their families receive quality of service and information.

www.scope.org.uk
UK disability organisation focusing on people affected by cerebral palsy.

www.tamba.org.uk
Provides information, a confidential helpline and mutual support networks for families of twins, triplets and more.

The Buyer's Guides

Introduction

The Buyer's Guides have been compiled to give you an idea of what products are currently on the market and what features you should consider before you make a purchase. The advice applies whether you are buying new or second hand but if you decide to bid for and buy items on eBay, the guides should also help you ask the right questions of the sellers regarding condition and features.

I strongly recommend that before you buy on eBay you take time to visit some baby shops/showrooms in order to try out the items on your shortlist. This is especially important for higher value items such as pushchairs and cots which need to last a good three or four years and which you will therefore want to ensure are up to your expectations. Try not to be swayed by what is currently in vogue if you don't think that it will match your practical needs, and don't forget to ask other mums and dads why they chose the particular item that they did. Other parents are always the best source of information as they are the ultimate users on a day-to-day basis!

At the end of each Buyer's Guide I have included the contact details and websites of some of the major manufacturers and/or retailers, along with a brief note on their specialisations and emphasis. I have also included an indication of their general price range, denoted by a rating of £ symbols. In this system, a rating of £ or ££ indicates retailers/manufacturers at the lower end of the market, all the way up to £££££ for those moving into aspirational territory! For obvious reasons eBay often comes up trumps for the most expensive items, although bear in mind that you don't always get what you pay for.

I have avoided making specific product recommendations for two main reasons: firstly your priorities may be completely different from my own, and secondly, manufacturers are constantly updating and innovating their products which means that model names and numbers quickly go out of date. In the interests of longevity, therefore, these guides are intended for general information only and should not be taken as an endorsement of any one manufacturer or retailer.

Buyer's Guide to Parenting Books

Parenting is a skill, and like any new (or not so new) discipline it can and does take a lifetime to master – if indeed it can ever be mastered. I guess that this is the reason for the large number of books on parenting and childcare which play both on our hopes that we will be perfect parents and our fears that somehow we will never be good enough.

I want to share three secrets with you that might make your troubled mind a little easier:

- Firstly, no one is born a natural parent.
- Secondly, no one knows everything.
- Thirdly, and most importantly, it is not a crime to ask for someone else's opinion or help.

The last of these is made somewhat less difficult by the fact that as soon as you announce to the world that you are expecting a baby, you will be inundated with people wanting to offer advice: your mother, sister, maiden aunt and the lady who runs the local delicatessen. When all is said and done, however, your children are your responsibility and that means that you will (perhaps instinctively) know what is in their best interests.

Like all the most important decisions in life the best approach is to listen to everything you are told, select the advice that is meaningful to you and ignore the rest. 'Meaningful' in this context may be determined by a whole load of factors, such as your cultural and genetic inheritance, your gender, even your politics and philosophy on life.

Get the latest

The interesting thing about parenting books is that, like all technical manuals, they tend to go out of date. When my sisters and I were born, in the mid sixties to the cusp of the seventies, the advice given to parents was *very* different. Hardly any women, including our mother, breastfed their children, SIDS (Sudden Infant Death Syndrome) was unheard of, and the notion of sleep training hardly ever went beyond putting a nip of brandy in the bottom of the baby bottle.

Even the information that was given to my sisters when they first had their children in the 80s and 90s has largely been updated. Advice on issues such as the best time to start weaning, for example, has changed, and the books they were given, some from the late 70s, now seem to be better guides to the hairstyles and dodgy cardigans of the time than to contemporary childcare. There have been radical shifts in thought since the early days on issues such as sleeping, feeding and child safety, so it is best to buy and refer to the most up-to-date edition of a book that you can get your hands on.

Of course, some things never change, mostly on the emotional front, as parents continue to have the same anxieties and concerns that they have always had. If anything has changed in this regard it's that more men now count themselves amongst the many thousands of parents trying to raise a child single-handedly.

Buy to suit your own style

It is difficult to give advice beyond the very general when talking about parenting books because of the inherent biases that we all have regarding parenting style. As a voracious reader of all types of literature, I have always thought that books are rather like fashion, or other people's shoes: they either suit you or they don't. We all know that instinctive feeling upon reading the first couple of pages of a recommended title. Sometimes it grabs us and sometimes it just seems a little too 'out there', a little dry or even a little too trendy and radical.

"There are certain trends in parenting that come and go."

What I suggest, therefore, is that you go to a largish bookstore, where they have those comfy tub chairs and no one comes up and asks if they can help you, and just have a read through a couple of the parenting books you find there. Browsing through the contents will give you an idea of its slant, and if you take the time to read a couple of pages here and there, you'll know where the writer is coming from philosophically – are they too radical for you? Do you prefer a gentler, more traditional approach, or are you looking to instil a routine into your child's life straightaway?

Not everything you read will appeal to you and that is absolutely fine. One thing I would stress, however, is how important it is that you fundamentally and implicitly agree with the basis of the advice given. As already mentioned, there are certain trends in parenting that come and go, and even in the time it took me to conceive, carry and have my son, there was a shift in attitude away from the 'routine' route towards a more holistic and individual-centred approach to parenting. Do seek advice from these books but don't be afraid to reject it if it is not working for you, or if you decide that you want to go your own way. Your child, after all, is unique and a one-size-fits-all approach is not necessarily the most sensitive or even the most effective way to parent.

So what do you look for in a book? Aside from a sense that the author is not working from an entirely different song sheet from you, you might want to look for a certain lightness of touch, or humour in the pages. I certainly needed this light relief when I was pregnant which is why the Vicky Iovine series of books (see page 42) have a special place in my heart. The fact that I could laugh out loud at my own embarrassing flatulence and my ever-increasing calf size when I was pregnant was testimony to the fact that she is indeed a 'best friend' when it comes to pregnancy, birth and motherhood, and we all need that at some point.

'Technical' parenting books

I also suggest that you get one of the good solid 'technical' manuals that tell you what to expect at certain stages of your baby's life from both an emotional and developmental point of view as these are always kind of reassuring to have in times of paranoia or despair!

Other features you might want to look out for when choosing books are:

- Is it clearly written?
- Does it answer my specific questions?
- Is it sympathetically written by someone who knows and cares about their subject intimately?
- Does it have a comprehensive index?
- What qualifies this person to write this particular book? Is it important that they are a doctor or would I rather they were a parent like me?
- What have other people said about the book?

Check out online reviews

Check out the reviews on www.amazon.co.uk to see what other people are saying about a book. Look for qualitative reviews, not just the "liked it/didn't like it" variety. Amazon also allows people to post up lists of their favourite books based on topic and there are quite a few parenting lists up there to survey and compare. I noted that many of the books that I hadn't read myself seemed to crop up time and again on other people's lists so I have included them here.

Another useful feature on Amazon is the ability to 'search inside' a book, which enables you to look through the contents and read a couple of sample pages of the title in question. Unfortunately, Amazon can only offer this facility if the publisher agrees, and at the moment not many publishers have signed up. Nevertheless, you should be able to find a couple of titles that you can explore in this way. It is an extremely useful tool if you find it difficult to actually visit a bookstore in person.

For the recommended reading on the following pages I have tried to categorise the books according to their main thrust; be it technical, philosophical or what I have termed a 'hybrid' which offers a little of each in a more conversational tone. If you are working to a budget and can only afford one from each of these categories, my list will hopefully assist you when making your purchase.

One final point – **check the country of origin** of the book! It may sound strange but if you are buying a technical type manual, especially, it can be irritating and misleading to constantly read references to the American Health Care system when you are sat in a bedsit in Bradford, or whatever. It's a small point but one worth making. Enjoy!

Recommended reading

Technical Books

Baby Bliss. Your One-Stop Guide For The First Three Months and Beyond, by Harvey Karp

Complete Baby and Childcare, by Dr Miriam Stoppard

Easing Labour Pain: The Complete Guide to a More Comfortable and Rewarding Birth, by Adrienne B. Lieberman

Feeding Your Baby and Toddler, by Annabel Karmel

New Pregnancy and Birth Book, by Dr Miriam Stoppard

Solve Your Child's Sleep Problems, by Dr Richard Ferber

What To Expect, The Toddler Years, by Arlene Eisenberg, Heidi E. Murkoff, Sandie E. Hathaway

What To Expect When You're Expecting, by Arlene Eisenberg, Heidi E. Murkoff, Sandie E. Hathaway

Your Baby and Child, by Penelope Leach

Philosophy/Theory

Does Anybody Else Look Like Me? A Parent's Guide To Raising Multiracial Children, by Donna Jackson Nakazawa

Fatherhood: The Truth, by Marcus Berkmann

How To Talk So Kids Will Listen and Listen So Kids Will Talk, by Adele Faber and Elaine Mazlish

Life After Birth, by Kate Figes

Raising Boys, by Steve Biddulph

Raising Happy Children, by Jan Parker and Jan Stimpson

Sibling Rivalry, Sibling Love, by Jan Parker and Jan Stimpson

The Secret of Happy Children, by Steve Biddulph

What Mothers Do, Especially When It Looks Like Nothing, by Naomi Stadlen

Hybrids

Babies for Beginners, by Roni Jay

Mums on Babies, by Mums.net members, edited by Justine Roberts, Carrie Longton and Rachel Foster

New Toddler Taming, by Dr Christopher Green

The Best Friends Guide to Pregnancy/ The Best Friends Guide to Surviving The First Year of Motherhood/ The Best Friends Guide to Toddlers, all by Vicki Iovine

The Contented Little Baby Book, by Gina Ford

The No Cry Sleep Solution, by Elizabeth Pantley

The Rough Guide to Pregnancy and Birth, by Kaz Cooke

The Secrets of The Baby Whisperer: How to Calm, Connect and Communicate With Your Baby, by Tracy Hogg

Three Shoes, One Sock and No Hairbrush: Everything You Need to Know About Having Your Second Child, by Rebecca Abrams

Buyer's Guide to Pushchairs

Of all the purchases you are likely to make, the one guaranteed to generate the strongest emotional response, from calm determination to complete psychological breakdown is THE PRAM! In my case, it was also the issue, after the weight and sex of my baby, that most people wanted to know the answer to: "What pram did you get in the end?"

This is not particularly surprising given the kind of society that we now live in, where the aspirations of many people begin and end with celebrity and image. Newsagents are awash with magazines showing pictures of pregnant and newly-delivered models and actresses pushing their little wunderkind around in the latest state-of-the-art pushchair, causing sales to skyrocket.

Every day on eBay there are hundreds of new listings for designer prams and accessories, a high percentage of which are accompanied by descriptions like:

"Bought this two weeks ago and used it once before I saw another one that I had to have, hence sale".

If you're looking to buy your pram second hand, their loss, you may, argue, is your gain, but be prepared for some competition as prams at the top end of the market do seem to hold their value rather well and will resell for at least half of their new retail price. That said, if you are determined to bag one of these little beauties, advice on the best way to go about it is to be found in Part 3 of this book.

One thing to bear in mind is that even with a £600 pram you don't always get what you pay for, and the cost of being the trendiest and most envied mum on the high street may well be the sacrifice you make to other more practical considerations such as weight, portability, shopping space, etc.

With this in mind, here are my tips for choosing the right pram for *you*.

Buying considerations

These days most pushchair manufacturers design their products with flexibility in mind, meaning that they can be adapted with a chassis, carrycot or car seat to create the combination you need. Before choosing any system, however, bear in mind the following:

Terrain

Consider the type of terrain where you will mostly be using your pram. Do you live in an urban, rural or coastal resort type area? If most of your journeys are going to be across sand or mud flats then you need a different type of pram to people who live in built-up areas.

Manoeuverability

Do you use public transport frequently or are you more likely to drive with your baby? If you do intend to walk a lot, or indeed want to exercise with your pram, you will need to choose one with good suspension that's also lightweight. If you rely on public transport or live in a block of flats that only has access via a stairwell, look for a pram with a one-handed folding mechanism that is also lightweight. If you are going to be putting it in and out of a car, check the dimensions of the folded pram against the width of your boot.

For easy manoeuvrability and for steering across flat surfaces, look for swivel wheels. Alternatively, wheels which can be locked are better over bumpy, uneven terrain and generally provide better suspension.

Even if you decide to buy second hand, go to a superstore that carries several models and insist on a test drive. Don't restrict yourself to the models on your shortlist as you may be surprised by one which you have not considered. As part of the test drive, practise folding and unfolding the buggy on your own with one hand – in future, there will be many times when you will also be contending with a baby and changing bag. Don't forget that any pram that feels heavy when empty is going to feel even heavier once your little chubster is ensconced.

Room for shopping

If you are likely to use the pram on shopping trips, as many people do, check whether there is a substantial and rigid trolley base, as it is completely unsafe to hang shopping bags from the handles of the buggy.

Compatibility with your car

If you decide to invest in a travel system (more on them and other types of buggies below) ensure that the car seat is compatible with your make of car and that you have advice and a demonstration on fitting it in the car park before you buy. A wrongly-fitted car seat is no better, and can sometimes be *more dangerous*, than no car seat at all. From September 2006 new legislation regarding the use of car seats comes into force. More information on this can be found in the Buyer's Guide to Car Seats starting on page 53.

Bear in mind that sometimes your budget will not extend to all the features that you really want so, instead of breaking the bank, try to compromise on one or two of the less important features by making a list in order of priority.

Different models explained

2-In-One

These models convert from a lie-flat configuration which you use from birth, to an upright pushchair configuration which you use for an older child. They usually come with a fabric hood and apron and provide a nice enclosed ride for a very young or small baby.

2-In-One Plus

These also convert into a pushchair but have the added advantage of a removable enclosed pram seat with handles that can be removed from the chassis and used independently as a carrycot for the early weeks.

3-In-One

These have all the functions of a 2-In-One but, rather than an enclosed pram seat with handles, have a full-sized carrycot which slots onto the chassis and is usually more rigid than that supplied with the 2-In-One Plus. Due to its size, the carrycot may even negate the need for a Moses basket or crib in the early months of your baby's life and is certainly handy for overnight stays if you find yourself away from home.

Some 3-In-Ones are sold as a complete package whilst others give you a choice of components, for example seat units and carrycots, which you can combine to make up your own 3-In-One.

Travel systems

These offer complete mobility and versatility with the minimum disturbance for your baby. Comprising a car seat and chassis, they allow you to move your sleeping baby directly from the car and onto the pushchair in one step. When you get home you can then lift the car seat out again and into the house. The car seat usually clips directly onto the specially designed chassis to form the pushchair shape and can also be used as a baby carrier/rocker.

All terrain pushchairs and 3 wheelers

These are still the pram of choice for many parents as they offer functionality, flexibility and good looks in one package. They may especially suit you if you have an active lifestyle and want to incorporate walking the baby with your own jogging/exercise routine. They tend to have a lightweight but sturdy construction which provides a comfortable ride for your baby and is also exceptionally manoeuvrable across different terrains.

Features to look out for

Adjustable handle height

This is essential if you and your partner, or other regular carer, are very different heights.

Recline positions

If you intend to use your pram from birth, look for a seat that has a number of recline positions, including lie-flat for a newborn.

Reversible seat position

A reversible seat position means that your baby can be both forward and rearward facing. This can be comforting for you in the early days when you want to maintain eye contact, and nice for your baby when, later on, they want to get a different perspective on the world.

One-handed use

A one-handed release and folding mechanism is really, really useful when you are out on your own with the baby and need to fold the buggy – for example, at busy times on public transport.

Shopping basket

A generous shopping basket area will give you somewhere to store the change bag as well as any shopping you may wish to do. Look for a rigid construction as the nets that sometimes come with pushchairs are flimsy and fairly useless when any weight is placed in them.

Safety standards

Check that your pushchair complies with British Safety Standard BS 7409.

Brakes

Make sure that the brakes are easy to reach and that they push down securely.

Extras

Check whether accessories are included in the price or charged as added extras. These are things like footmuffs, cosy-toes, rain hoods, sun shades, etc.

Double buggies

If you have more than one child under four, or are expecting a multiple birth, you will probably want to invest in a double buggy. The main decision to be made is whether to buy a tandem or a twin model.

- With tandem buggies, one child sits in front of the other, and usually one seat will recline fully for a newborn. Tandems are practical for shopping and walking around town as they have a smaller footprint (generally the width of a single buggy) and therefore fit through doorways easier. The disadvantage is mainly felt by the child that sits at the bottom of the tandem as they can get frustrated by the lack of a view!

- With twin buggies, the children are able to sit side by side and usually both seats recline – useful if you are, indeed, expecting twins. You need to ensure that any model you are looking at will easily fit through any doors you are likely to use frequently, as well as into your car boot.

The footprint of tandems and twins when folded is likely to be considerably bigger than that of a single pushchair so bear this in mind when thinking about where you will store it at home. Double buggies are also available as three-wheelers and travel systems, as well as conventional pushchairs.

Features to look out for on double buggies

Handles

Double buggies can have two or three handles, or one long bar across the width of the buggy. You should try out all of these options to see which one you find the most comfortable. Check that they are easy to hold and push and, if you are not choosing the single bar option, that they are set at the right height and distance apart.

Seat positions

Double buggies are generally designed so that the seats can be positioned independently of each other to make them suitable for babies and toddlers of different ages. On twin buggies both seats normally recline fully to accommodate newborn twins whilst on tandems only one seat normally reclines fully, making them suitable for a newborn plus an older baby/toddler. If you want to use the pushchair from birth you will need to check the number of seat positions per seat.

Head-huggers

If you are going to use the pushchair for one or two newborns, look out for those that come with removable head-huggers – supportive padded cushions that hold a newborn's head steady. These ensure that your little bobble-head doesn't go bob-bob-bobbing along too much!

Bumper bars

Bumper bars are protective padded bars across the front of the buggy which usually open out to give you easy access to babies.

Folding mechanism

Double buggies can fold in a myriad of ways, some mind-bogglingly complex, others much more straightforward. Even more important than with a single buggy (for obvious reasons) you should try and find one that has a one-handed or fast-fold mechanism.

Safety rules relating to pushchairs

1. Never leave your baby unattended in its pram.

2. Check that the pushchair you choose has an integral five-point safety harness and that the carrycot, if there is one, has D rings to enable you to attach a harness.

3. Always use the brakes when you come to a stop, even on a flat surface.

4. When in shops or returning home, remove the rain cover from the pram to avoid the baby becoming overheated, and don't use rain covers in bright or direct sunlight as they can act like greenhouse glass.

5. Don't use your pram to carry two children unless it has been specifically designed to do so. You can buy 'buggy-boards' which are like mini skateboards that attach to the main pram with an adaptor and which allow older toddlers to hitch an occasional ride when they get tired.

6. Check that the safety catch that prevents the chassis from suddenly collapsing in on itself is fully functional and not loose in any way.

7. Read and familiarise yourself with all the fitting instructions before even attempting to put your baby in the pram.

8. Do not hang shopping or anything else from the handles of the pram.

Stockist contact details

Babies R Us

Baby-centred subsidiary of the toy retail giant representing many manufacturers and price ranges. Huge inventory means it can often offer great discounts on equipment. ££ – ££££

0800 038 88 89   www.babiesrus.co.uk

Bebecar (UK) Ltd

Designers and manufacturers of high-end prams, car seats and nursery furniture. Pride themselves on being at the cutting edge of both fashion and safety awareness. £££ – ££££

020 8201 050   www.bebecar.co.uk

Bebe Confort

Comfort and fashionable design are the hallmark of this mid/high-end French company. Specialises in baby carriers and prams of every description. £££ – ££££

020 8236 0707   www.bebeconfort.com

Bettacare

Reasonably-priced one-stop shop for prams, changing bags and other baby equipment. Their travel systems are practical, well designed and targeted at the low/mid range-end of the market without compromising on style or features. ££ – £££

01293 851 896   www.bettacare.co.uk

Britax Excelsior

Renowned as the first car seat manufacturers in the UK, Britax have now expanded their repertoire to include 'Vitality', a range of fashionable pushchairs for the 'modern mum'. Low/mid-range price band. ££ – £££

01264 386034   www.britax.co.uk

Bugaboo

Manufacturers of notoriously fashionable pushchairs aimed at the higher end of the market, Bugaboo pride themselves on the quality and flexibility of their designs which are both innovative and functional. ££££ – £££££

020 7385 5338   www.bugaboo.com

Cosatto

Exceptionally well-priced full-spectrum range of pushchairs from an award-winning manufacturer. ££   0870 050 5900   www.cosatto.com

Graco

Mothers' favourite with a very well-priced range of pushchairs and accessories. ££ – £££   0870 9090501   www.graco.co.uk

Maclaren Europe

Well-established and incredibly well-designed pushchairs with comfort and functionality in mind. Mid-price range. £££

01327 841 320   www.maclarenbaby.com

Mamas and Papas

Award-winning and ergonomically-designed collection using the latest paediatric research to provide the best possible support for the growing child. Mid/high price bracket with an emphasis on customer support and information. £££ – ££££   0870 830 7700   www.mamasandpapas.com

Micralite

Manufacturer of mid-price pushchairs and travel systems boasting innovative and user-friendly design. Fantastically portable. £££

01892 615 900   www.micralite.com

Mountain Buggy

Cleverly designed, strong and durable, these buggies are internationally renowned for their quality of build and performance. Available in single and double versions and in a choice of chassis to suit urban or rural lifestyles and pursuits. £££ – ££££   www.onetreehilleurope.com

Phil & Teds

Creators of the excellently innovative e3 buggy which can cleverly adapt in four ways for you and your growing family: suitable from birth to toddler in either a single or double configuration. Fantastic investment and very well reviewed. £££ – ££££   +64 (4) 380 083   www.philandteds.com

Quinny

The choice for trendy urbanites, Quinny has a reputation for being on the pulse of both design and innovation. Mid/high price range. £££

020 8236 0707   www.quinny.com

Safety 1st

Great budget choice with a range of utilitarian but fashionable prams and accessories. Based in the USA and Canada, but available from eBay and in the UK from www.kiddicare.com, 09061 702999 (premium rates apply). ££

www.safety1st.com

Silver Cross

Capitalising on its lengthy heritage as a pram maker extraordinaire, Silver Cross has a vast selection of mid/high-end prams from the traditional to the modern. £££ – £££££

01756 702 412   www.silvercross.co.uk

Stokke

Creators of the extraordinary Xplory pushchair, Stokke pride themselves on their quality of investment in design and engineering. The beauty of their design is matched by the high-end prices! ££££ – £££££

01753 655 873   www.stokke.com

Woolworths

Family favourite with a very well-priced inventory of lightweight and casual strollers suited to those on a budget or to those looking for a disposable option for travel, etc. £ – ££

01706 862789   www.woolworths.co.uk

Buyer's Guide to Car Seats

A baby car seat is one of the most crucial purchases you will make and it is essential that you give proper care and consideration to your purchase. Most hospitals will not allow you to leave after delivery without one and from then until your child is approximately 12 years old you will need to have one, or a booster-type seat, if you intend to drive with your child in the car.

This is also one of the few items which I would urge you to buy new, for two reasons. Firstly, car seat manufacturers are constantly updating their designs to make them safer. You owe it to your baby to get the safest which, other things being equal, means the latest. Secondly, a second hand seat may have been involved in an accident which, however minor, can damage the integrity of the seat and render it unsafe. Even seats offered by well-meaning friends and relatives should be politely declined if they are either loose, show signs of excessive wear or are more than eighteen months old.

There are currently five weight categories for car seats. Some seats will span more than one weight band:

Category	Suitability
Group 0	Suitable from birth to 10kg (Approximately 9 months). These seats should be rearward-facing in the car.
Group 0+	Suitable from birth to 13kg (approximately 12-15 months). These seats should be rearward-facing.
Group 1	Suitable for 9-18kg (approximately 9 months to 4 years). These seats should be forward-facing with an integral harness.
Group 2	Suitable for 15-25 kg (approximately 4-6 years). These should be a forward-facing car seat or booster seat.
Group 3	Suitable for 22-36kg (approximately 6-11 years). These will be a booster seat.

Rearward-facing infant carriers include an integral harness and are held in place by both a lap and diagonal seat belt, whether front or rear seat fitting. When fitted in the front passenger seat they allow the driver to maintain eye contact with the baby although you should never put an infant carrier in a seat fitted with a passenger air bag. It is safer to carry your baby in the rearward-facing position for as long as possible and to look for either the British Standards Kitemark or European Regulations Mark (UN ECE 44.03).

When using a booster seat or cushion, getting the lap strap to go from hip to hip across the upper thigh (rather than across the stomach) is just as important as getting the diagonal strap to fit across the chest properly.

The Motor Industry Consumer Line

The retail motor industry recommends that if anyone else is planning to drive your child in their car, for example a child minder or friend, that you ensure that the seat is suitable for their make and model of vehicle and that they, the driver, know how to fit the seat and monitor its use. For further information and advice, motoring organisations may be able to help. Call the Retail Motor Industry Consumer Motor Line on 08457 585350 or visit www.rmif.co.uk. The RAC also has a useful website where you can obtain information on car safety – www.rac.co.uk

---

Features to look out for

Portability

When trying out car seats look for portability. This is particularly important in the early days when you will probably be transporting the seat from door to door a lot. In addition to portability, you should also look for ease and comfort of carrying as, once your baby is in the seat, he can add to the weight considerably. Some manufacturers, mindful of this fact, design seats with ergonomic handles.

Easy fitting

Ensure that you know how to fit the car seat properly. Many injuries are caused each year by improperly-fitted seats, as well as the absence of a car seat. Ask for a demonstration in the car park of any showroom that you visit and go somewhere else if the shop refuses or does not have a trained fitter in-store. It is vital that you know how to fit the car seat *before* coming out of hospital with your baby for the first time as you are likely to be tired and weak, and struggling with unfamiliar instructions is the last thing you need! Even seats which seem fiddly at first soon become second nature when you are used to them.

Integral base

Look too, for seats that simply click into ready-installed bases, such as those with Isofix fittings. They can save a great deal of time, especially in inclement weather. Be aware, however, that some cars will not be suitable for these bases. Some infant carriers come complete with a special gauge which helps you determine whether you have installed it correctly; others have one-pull adjustable harnesses.

The harness

Always check the fit of the harness around your baby. You should be able to slide two fingers between it and your baby's chest.

Head support

Although most babies will sleep in any car seat it makes sense to look for one which has been designed with comfort in mind. Head support is essential for a newborn so ensure that your model comes with a head-hugger which can be taken out when the baby gets older. Some seats have additional inserts which allow them to recline fully to a lie-flat position, and which can therefore double up as a carrycot or Moses basket. Others offer varying degrees of padding, aprons and padded wings for side impact protection.

Longevity

Although now isn't necessarily the time to skimp on price, be aware that, depending on the size of the first car seat you buy, you could be changing it up to four times between birth and age 11. It is therefore worthwhile comparing features and prices as well as the probable longevity of the seat before deciding to splash out on an all-singing all-dancing model which may only last a few months. An alternative is to look for a seat which can adapt – for example, change from rearward-facing to forward-facing and 'grow' with your child. These make sense from an economic point of view but should be weighed up against other features such as comfort and portability.

Versatility

Look for versatility. Car seats which can double as a carrier, low chair or rocker can be great for soothing a fractious baby and useful when feeding both at home and when out whilst the baby is too small to sit in a highchair. Some car seats also come as part of a travel system, allowing them to go straight from the vehicle and onto a pram chassis. This can be advantageous if you use the car a lot for shopping etc, and want a way to easily transport a sleeping baby from the car to the pushchair without undue disturbance.

Washable covers

Although ultimately a convenience, washable covers are a useful feature. If the covers are not actually removable do ensure that they can at least be sponged down in the event of a spill.

The New Seatbelt Laws: What You Need To Know

Occupant	Front seat	Rear seat	Responsibility
Driver	Seat belt must be worn if available.		Driver
Child up to 3	Correct child restraint must be used.	Correct child restraint must be used if available. If not available in a taxi, the child may travel unrestrained in rear.	Driver
Child from 3rd birthday up to either 1.35m height or 12 years	Correct child restraint must be used.	Where seat belts are fitted, correct child restraint must be used. Must use adult belt if the correct child restraint is not available in these scenarios: • In a licensed taxi or private hire vehicle • for a short distance for reasons of unexpected necessity • when two occupied child restraints prevent fitting of a third In addition, a child of 3 and over may travel unrestrained in the rear seat of a vehicle if seat belts are not available.	Driver
Child over 1.35m or 12 to 13 years	Seat belt must be worn if available.	Seat belt must be worn if available.	Driver
Adult passengers (i.e. 14+ years)	Seat belt must be worn if available.	Seat belt must be worn if available.	Passenger

For more detailed information visit www.dft.gov.uk. More advice on choosing the correct child restraint for your child can be found at www.thinkroadsafety.gov.uk/advice/childcarseats01.htm

Stockist contact details

Aprica

Manufacturers of the Aprica Euroturn Group 0+/1 car seat, a unique and revolutionary concept in car-seat safety. Suitable from birth to approx 4 years, the Euroturn swivels on its base through 360 degrees and reclines to 170 degrees. Wow design matched by pocket-stinging price tag. £££££

00 39 02 7602 5806   www.aprica-montenapo.com

Britax

Hailed as the first car seat manufacturers in the UK, Britax pride themselves on mid-priced solutions for child comfort and safety. £££

01264 386034   www.britaxchildcare.com

Graco

Mothers' favourite with a very well-priced range of car seats and accessories. ££ – £££

0870 909 0501   www.graco.co.uk

Hauck

Designs solution with both the family and reality in mind. Mid range. £££

www.hauckuk.com

Mamas and Papas

Award-winning and ergonomically-designed collection using the latest paediatric research to provide the best possible support for the growing child. Mid/high price bracket with an emphasis on customer support and information. £££ – ££££

0870 830 7700   www.mamasandpapas.co.uk

Mothercare

The UK's number one parenting website offers a huge range of car travel solutions representing a wide spectrum of manufacturers and price brackets. ££ – £££

0845 330 4030   www.mothercare.com

Recaro

Specialising in safe seating solutions for both domestic and industrial clients, this company also have a range of car seats aimed at children with special needs. Mid/high price range but justified by their specialisation. £££ – ££££

0116 266 4112   www.capitalseating.co.uk

Buyer's Guide to Baby Carriers and Slings

Many parents choose to have a carrier or sling as well as a pushchair. They can be especially useful in the early days as they keep your baby safe, happy and close to your body, which has, after all, been their default position for the last nine months.

Using a sling also frees up your hands for shopping or housework and, if this is your second baby, makes it easier to go out and about with an older child. Slings can also be a great way to settle a fractious baby as the movement lulls them to sleep or into a sense of calm reassured by the sound of your heartbeat.

Different models explained

There are several types of baby carrier on the market, from those suitable for occasional use to heavy duty backpacks designed for travelling across difficult terrains. In addition, the wide choice of fabrics available means you can choose a carrier to match the season or climate in which it will be most used. The following list should give you some idea of the choices open to you.

Ring slings

These are made from a single piece of fabric threaded through two rings, to form a loop. The sling is worn like a sash over the shoulder and is adjusted via the rings which can then be locked into place. Some rings are padded at the shoulder and at the edges, which allows them to be worn more comfortably for longer periods of time, although this does add bulk.

Pros

- Quick and easy to get in and out of unassisted.

- Suitable from birth to approximately two years, making them good value for money.

- Easy to lay down a sleeping baby without disturbing them.

- Can be worn in a variety of positions.

- Distributes weight of the baby evenly between the shoulders and the pelvis.

Cons

- The one-shoulder design can sometimes lead to back pain.
- One size may not fit all, especially if the parents have vastly different body types.

Pouch slings

These are made from a single piece of fabric sewn together at the ends, to form a loop. The sling is worn over the shoulder like a sash and then folded in on itself lengthways, to form a pocket or pouch for the baby. Many are not adjustable although some do come with poppers or zips. Some form a double pouch that you wear on both shoulders.

Pros

- Quick and easy to get in and out of unassisted.
- The non-adjustable varieties are a good option for those on a tight budget.
- If you are handy with a sewing machine they are easy to make yourself.

Cons

- The non-adjustable varieties are a very specific fit and so may not be suitable for both parents.
- It can be more difficult to get a good position for the baby as they are less adjustable than a ring sling.

Wrap-around slings

These consist of a single piece of fabric wrapped and tied around the body in such a way that the baby is held securely against your body. There are two main types: those made of woven fabric and those made of a lightweight t-shirt type fabric, which are very stretchy. They come in a variety of lengths which you adjust according to the size of the wearer and the carrying position you wish to adopt. Of all the carriers I tried this was the type of sling I liked best and, although it was extremely intimidating to begin with, the accompanying DVD with its step-by-step instructions was very informative. If your baby is quite large, as mine was, you may find it difficult to insert him into the sling to start with, especially in the forward-facing position, but this comes with practice!

Pros

- Distributes the baby's weight excellently so they are very comfortable to wear over long periods, even when carrying a toddler.

- Suitable from birth to approximately age two, so good value for money if you intend using it long term.

- Offers a variety of carrying positions including one for discreet breastfeeding.

Cons

- They can be overwhelming when you get them out of the packet and are faced with a huge length of fabric! You may find them tricky to get the hang of.

- They are not that quick to put on unassisted although this does improve with practice.

- Because of the tight fitting wrap shape around the body, some people find them a little hot in the Summer and in warmer climates.

Soft carriers

This is a fairly large category, encompassing many features and designs. Broadly speaking, soft carriers tend to be more structured than both slings and wraps, incorporating shoulder straps with which to secure the carrier and often a waist strap too. The baby's weight is supported either by their crotch or across their bottom. Some, but not all, are suitable from birth and for carrying on the hip or back as well as the front. Soft carriers are generally fastened via clips or feature a wrap and tie facility. Both sorts are usually very adjustable.

Pros

- Good for older/heavier children.

- Good adjustability for multiple wearers.

- Generally carry a baby in the optimal position for comfort.

Cons

- Can be fiddly to get on and off unassisted, especially when worn on the back.

Backpacks

Mention backpacks and most people immediately conjure up images of ruddy-faced outdoor types ascending the Himalayas with baby and donkey in tow. In reality, they can be a very versatile and convenient option for the averagely intrepid, especially on long journeys and across difficult and uneven terrains.

Backpacks are great for all types of environment, be it the beach, woodland, cross-country or even down crowded shopping streets. Being hands and pram-free means that you can carry bags and even luggage if you are holidaying. Most older babies and toddlers also love the piggyback position for the increased field of vision it gives them and they are a great alternative to a double buggy before upgrading to a buggy board.

Most backpacks are suitable from around 6 months or whenever your baby can support the weight of its own head, all the way up to about 20kg if you're brave and strong enough! Some models offer inserts in order to take very young babies. The good thing about these carriers is that they offer a great deal of adjustability and padding although you are advised to try them out before you buy in order to find the model that is most suitable and comfortable for you.

Pros

- Good lumbar support.
- Versatile across a wide age and weight range.
- Can generally be worn in comfort over longer periods.
- Gives your baby a good 'adult' perspective on the world.
- Leaves your hands free.

Cons

- Can be cumbersome to get on and off unassisted.
- Are generally heavier to wear empty so may get very hot in warm weather.

Features to look for

Comfort

Comfort for you and your baby should be given priority over looks and price, especially if you intend to use the carrier more than occasionally. Look for a carrier that holds a baby high up and tight against your body. By the time a child is big enough to sit in a carrier, 70% of its body weight should be taken on your hips and the remaining 30% on your shoulders.

Carriers which are designed only to hang from the shoulders can be very uncomfortable to wear, even after short periods. Choose a carrier with broad shoulder straps which can help distribute the weight of the baby across the back and torso. Also look for easily adjustable straps.

Research suggests that upright baby carriers which spread the baby's legs wide help the pelvis to develop in the optimum position. For a newborn, the carrier should support the baby's entire spine. Many carriers allow for the baby to be positioned in a fully reclined position.

Adjustability

Look for carriers where the height of the seat can be adjusted – some offer bolster cushions as an added extra. If you intend to use your carrier for trekking cross-country ensure that it has additional restraints which add security for your baby. Don't forget to match the fabric of your carrier with the climate that you will be visiting to avoid overheating. Look for fabrics such as Cordura which help wick away moisture.

Think about how you will use your carrier. For example, if you want to breastfeed whilst wearing it, look for one that allows this. If you are only going to use the sling occasionally you may not want to spend as much as you would if you were using it everyday, around the house, etc.

Adaptability

Think too, about the age of your child. If you have a newborn do you want a carrier that can adapt as your child gets older or will you upgrade to a hip-type seat once your child reaches toddlerhood? Don't forget that some basic models can cost up to £60, so upgrading several times may be less economically savvy than a larger initial investment.

If you are going to be using the carrier unassisted, ensure that you feel confident getting it on and off, with your baby in and out, on your own.

Added extras

Look out for added extras which come with some models and can be very useful, such as bottle pockets and dribble bibs which may negate the need for an additional bag on short trips to the shops. Weatherproofing is another important feature which may not be included in the ticket price.

Stockist contact details

Baby Bjorn

Excellent range of carriers aimed at simplifying parents' lives whilst not compromising on comfort and safety. £££ – ££££

0870 1200543

www.babybjorn.com

Baby Hut

UK specialist in cotton slings. Sell a wide range and offer excellent customer advice. £££ – ££££

0845 601201

www.babyhut.net

Free Range Kids

Emphasis on organically-sourced and manufactured products. Excellent advice service for a full range of slings and baby carriers. ££ – ££££

01253 896290

www.freerangekids.co.uk

Hippychick

Manufacturers of the innovative hip seat which makes carrying larger babies and toddlers much easier! £££

01278 434440

www.hippychick.com

Hug-A-Bub

Natural, innovative and versatile carrier that comes with its own DVD support (you'll need it!) and excellent aftercare service. Pricey but worth it! ££££

+61 26685 5589

www.hugabub.com

Little Life

Ergonomically-designed back carriers built to last and with safety and comfort as standard. ££££

0118 981 1433

www.littlelife.co.uk

Natural Child

Stocks a wide range of baby carriers with advice on hand to aid your selection. Wide price range from the basic to the luxurious. ££ – ££££

01242 620988

www.naturalchild.co.uk

SlingEasy

Wearable and versatile 100% cotton carriers in a choice of fabrics. Prices range from mid to high. £££ – ££££

01189 404942

www.slingeasy.co.uk

Tomy

Brand leader with over 80 years experience. Sell a vast range of soft carriers popular with parents. ££ – ££££

02380 662600

www.tomy.co.uk

Wilkinet

Adaptable and wearable carriers available in a wide choice of fabrics and colours. Reasonably priced for their longevity. £££

01239 841844

www.wilkinet.co.uk

Buyer's Guide to Beds

Whether your baby sleeps like an angel from the off or is a committed insomniac, one of the essentials on your shopping list should be a bed. Much like prams, your ideal baby bed will be determined by many different factors including your decor, available space and budget.

Even for parents who decide that co-sleeping is their preferred option, it makes sense for your baby to have a bed of his own. The space will encourage independence and allow you and/or your partner, especially if you are returning to work, to get some undisturbed shut-eye.

For safety reasons, health professionals now recommend that your baby should sleep in his own bed in your room for the first six months. Adult bedding is unsuitable for babies and may cause them to overheat or get trapped beneath duvet covers, etc. Babies should not have a pillow or duvet cover in their bed until well after twelve months.

Other safety considerations include never sleeping with your baby if you or your partner have been drinking or are on medication, both of which lessen your awareness and reaction times. If you or your partner smoke it is also unwise to co-sleep, irrespective of whether you smoke in bed or not.

Different models explained

Because your baby grows and develops so quickly in the first few months and years, his sleeping needs also change very quickly. What follows is a comprehensive guide to the choices you may face when choosing different types of beds and the features you should look for in each.

Moses basket

Moses baskets are the more aesthetic and comfortable alternative to the linen drawer which parents of my mother's generation sometimes used. They are designed to keep newborns and very young or small babies snug at night, and as a means of carrying them around from room to room in your own house or when visiting.

Due to their design as a short-term sleeping arrangement, however, you shouldn't put too much store in the construction of these baskets, especially the handles, and should ensure that you support the base whenever you are carrying it. The British Safety Standard for Moses baskets, by the way, is BS EN 1466. You should never use a Moses basket as a makeshift carrycot by placing it on a pram chassis, table, or other unsuitable base. They can easily slip off.

Moses baskets vary in size and come in a range of natural fibres. Less substantial materials such as palm leaves or similar bring the cost down considerably but also mean they will last for a much shorter time; wicker is a hardier, albeit pricier, alternative. Either way, they are generally designed with lightness and portability in mind and many come with a lining, sometimes padded, that stretches over the body of the basket and is easily removed for washing. Almost all models come with a collapsible sun hood.

Most baskets are supplied with a round-end mattress – either the ventilated type with a breathable cover, or those wrapped in a PVC coating. Although the latter are extremely easy to clean they can lead to some babies becoming overheated and sweaty as they sleep, a problem that tends to be exacerbated in centrally-heated homes. If you inherit a Moses basket from a friend or relative, I recommend that you replace the mattress as they can be a breeding ground for germs.

> "Never use a Moses basket as a makeshift carrycot by placing it on a pram chassis. They can easily slip off."

It is essential to dress the basket with the correct bedding for the temperature and the season, and you should invest in blankets and sheets specifically designed for the smaller dimensions of these beds. Some baskets come with a thin quilt-type cover but again, do be guided by the temperature of your house and guard against blankets with trimmings which babies can become tangled in or accidentally swallow. Similarly, if you decide to use cellular-type blankets, ensure that the weave is not so loose as to allow small fingers to become trapped.

Moses baskets can be placed either on the floor or on a (usually) optional stand which can save your back and avoid tripping accidents. As baskets are generally manufactured to a standard size you may find that you can mix and match stands with baskets, but do check the fit of the stand and don't use it if it seems at all unstable. Some stands have the facility to double as a rocker.

An alternative to the Moses basket is the carrycot which serves a similar purpose but tends to be of a more rigid construction. If you have bought a travel system which includes a carrycot you may find that this is all you need in the early days, although your baby may protest if you try to make it a long-term sleeping solution!

When your baby grows to around 9kg, or when he starts to become more mobile, it's time to graduate to a proper cot. The 'open' environment of the cot may come as an unwelcome surprise to your baby so one option is to gradually wean him onto the idea by using a Moses basket with the hood off for a few days before making the move proper.

Cribs

Cribs are a more substantial but less portable alternative to a Moses basket. They are also much more expensive and take up more space – though they do score points on aesthetics, particularly if you are after a traditional nursery-type look.

Most cribs come with a rocking facility, and this can be useful if you have a particularly fractious baby or if he suffers from colic, as he may be soothed by the motion. Most come with a stop pin which can be used to lock the crib into a static position.

The British Safety Standard for cribs is BS EN 1130-1.

Cots

Cots are suitable from birth to approximately two and a half years, or until your toddler is able to climb out on his own, at which point you need to upgrade to a junior bed.

Comfort and safety are the primary considerations when deciding on a cot and it is, of course, essential that it conforms to British Safety Standards. Many parents have cots passed down to them through several generations of their family and whilst these can be beautiful, they may not be suitable if they have old paint finishes, many of which may contain lead or lead residues.

Ensure that the model you choose fits into the space you have set aside for it, and don't forget to allow for a drop-side mechanism or drawers if the cot has them.

There are many variations on the cot theme, including cot beds which are generally larger than the average cot (usually 10cm wider and 20cm longer) and can be adapted as the child grows to become a first or junior bed. Others convert to a child-friendly sofa or chairs. If you have the space, these often make excellent economic sense as, although the initial outlay is much greater, they can often see your child through to around the age of 5 or even beyond.

Bedside cots are a further variation. These have either a removable or drop side which allows them to be pushed up against the side of your bed and varied in height to give a perfect match to the top of your mattress. They can be an excellent choice for breastfeeding mothers who do not necessarily want to co-sleep with their babies but want to be able to do the night feeds with minimum disturbance. They also allow your baby to sleep under his own covers, alleviating the danger of overheating.

Bedside cots can convert to normal cot status once your baby is sleeping through the night or for longer periods.

The British Safety Standard for cots is BS EN 716.

Travel cots

Travel cots deserve a special mention as, by and large, they will be used much less often than either a conventional cot or a Moses basket. However, for some parents they are an essential purchase, especially if you plan to visit relatives or otherwise travel on a frequent basis.

Theoretically at least, travel cots have the advantage of being highly portable, and may enable your baby to sleep better when in unfamiliar surroundings or where there are inadequate baby proofing options such as when you are on holiday.

The reality, however, is that many travel cots aren't really *that* well suited to travelling, apart from being put in the boot of a car and unpacked at your final destination. Anyone who has struggled at the airport with a baby, buggy, suitcases et al. will appreciate that another bulky contraption is the last thing you need.

Before splashing out on a travel cot for a one-off occasion, check whether you can borrow one from friends or relatives. You may also find that some holiday destinations, especially self-catered ones, offer the facility of either borrowing or hiring a travel cot for your stay. Alternatively, if the travel cot is being bought solely for use at a grandparent's house, ask whether you can leave it there to save you the trouble of transporting and storing it.

There are several styles of travel cot to choose from, the latest of which is a pop-up variety that folds away to a small pouch. The advantage of this type is that they are fabulously light and can be

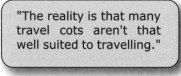

"The reality is that many travel cots aren't that well suited to travelling."

stored in a drawer due to their compact size. Unfortunately, this is also their biggest downside as their structure means that they will not last more than a few months and will probably not sustain much punishment.

The traditional style of travel cot collapses to fit into its own, not insubstantial carry bag. They are suitable from a young age and some come complete with bassinets for newborns. They generally last well into toddlerhood and many can double as a playpen. However, they are far from truly portable and not particularly comfortable. When my son used one recently at a friend's house he was not only overwhelmed by the height of the sides but seemed terribly uncomfortable to boot!

Features to look for

Drop-side mechanism

A drop-side mechanism makes it much easier to lift your baby in and out of the cot, which is essential if you or your partner suffer from back pain, or if you are sore after birth following surgery. They are also very handy, as already mentioned, for mothers who wish to breastfeed during the night as the side can be lowered and the cot pushed up against the parent's bed. On some cots you even have the option of lowering both sides.

You should ensure that any drop-side mechanism is easy to operate, preferably with one hand, as you will often have your baby in your arms when you want to use it. Some models have the added convenience of a drop side that folds completely under the body of the cot which allows you to position it at your bedside.

Mattress height

A vertically-adjustable mattress height will lengthen the life span of your cot and you should look for the one with the most positions available in your price range. The mattress should be lowered in stages to take into account your baby's growth and his ability to climb out of the cot. As cot sizes do vary, make sure that you get the correctly-sized mattress for your model by checking the gap between the mattress and the side of the cot. A gap of more than 4cm means that your baby could easily trap an arm or a leg in the spars of the cot.

When setting your budget for a cot, remember that mattresses are not generally included in the price. As already mentioned, always buy a new mattress, ensuring that it conforms to the current British Safety Standard BS 1877, part 10:1997.

If longevity is a priority, invest in a sprung mattress which offers the best support for a developing baby's bones and spine. Foam is absolutely fine, however, for younger babies and, if allergies are a concern in your family, look out for odour-free, mildew-resistant, non-allergenic and/or anti-microbial fabrics and materials. Other alternatives are natural fillings such as coconut coir or wool.

Castors

Castors on a cot make it easier to move around your house – important if you eventually want to move it from your bedroom to the nursery, etc. Do ensure that the castors are lockable, and keep them in the locked position when your baby is in the cot.

Teething rails

Teething rails are soft plastic guards fitted onto the top sides of the cot. They can be handy when your baby is a little older and starting to teeth, allowing your baby to gnaw at the rails (something you cannot really stop or constantly monitor!) without causing damage to either his mouth, teeth or, indeed, the cot!

Baby amusements

Some models feature beads or rollers at one end of the cot for the baby to amuse himself with as he wakes or goes to sleep. These may allow you an extra ten minutes in the morning but do weigh up their novelty factor against the extra cost.

Storage

Drawers built into the underside of the cot are advantageous if space is at a premium to you, but bear in mind that constantly bending down to retrieve stuff you have put in them can take its toll on your back. A cheaper alternative is to put a box on castors underneath which can be moved more easily when needed and will reduce the overall cost.

And for travel cots

Castors

Some travel cots can weigh up to 18kg (i.e. more than a pram!) Buying one with wheels attached makes them slightly more manoeuvrable.

At the other end of the scale, there are some models weighing less than 10kg. As mentioned previously, the pop-up variety is a much lighter alternative and if you think that it will be used on an occasional basis only, makes a good choice overall.

Footprint

Check the footprint of the cot when folded as if it is only to be used on an 'as needed' basis you will need to make room for it to be stored in your house. Similarly, if you are going to use yours as a playpen make sure that there is adequate room for it to be assembled without causing a dangerous obstruction or tripping liability to others, especially other children.

Padded mattress

If you are likely to use a travel cot a lot, you may like to look at models that come with an additional padded mattress. There will be an extra cost, but it may be worth it. Some companies, such as BabyDan even manufacture a larger model which may be worth considering if you have a taller than average child.

Pockets

Pockets in the body of the cot or on the carrier may override the need to carry extraneous bags and are handy for storing a favourite toy.

Assembly of cots

Check the assembly instructions on any cot you are interested in and, ideally, have a go at putting one together in store. Some models are fiendishly complicated to set up, especially on your own, and this is hardly the thing to first discover when you arrive at your destination, tired and with a screaming baby to contend with.

My advice, as a victim of one of these notoriously difficult contraptions, is to take note of the online reviews from other parents before you buy anything, and, when you have bought, to practise putting the cot together well in advance of your trip.

Bedding

You will need at least four sheets, top and bottom, which should be washed on a regular basis, and four blankets. Cotton cellular blankets are a good choice as they allow the air to circulate. **You should never use duvets for babies under 12 months.**

Baby sleeping bags are a great way to keep your baby warm at night whilst preventing them becoming dangerously tangled in loose bedding. You should always match the tog rating to the environment in which the baby will be sleeping, and be guided by the manufacturer's instructions as to the amount of clothing that should be worn inside the sleeping bag.

Note that not all sleeping bags are suitable from birth as newborns are unable to regulate their own temperatures.

TIP

NEWBORNS cannot differentiate between night and day. Encourage good sleeping habits right from the start by investing in heavy curtains or a blackout blind to help them nod off during daytime naps or in the longer evenings of Summer.

Stockist contact details

BabyDan
Innovative and well-designed travel solutions for your baby. £££
01704 537843
www.babydan.com

Baby Travel
Specialises in Samsonite travel cots and accessories. £££
01746 769676
www.baby-travel.com

Clair de Lune
Luxurious baskets, cribs and accessories. Beautifully designed. £££ – ££££
0161 491 9809
www.clair-de-lune.co.uk

Cosatto
Traditional and modern design solutions for travel and nursery. Beautiful quality and finish. £££ – ££££
0870 050 5900
www.cosatto.com

Graco
Manufacturers of top-quality travel cots that have everything and the kitchen sink. Not particularly portable but your baby will probably love it! £££
0870 909 0501
www.graco.co.uk

Izziwotnot
Luxurious design solutions for your baby featuring an excellent delivery and assembly service as standard. A wide range of finishes including metamorphic cots and cot-beds. £££ – ££££
0161 830 1919
www.izziwotnot.co.uk

Natural Mat

Designers and retailers of innovative high quality mattresses and nursery furniture in a variety of materials. Glowing testimonials. £££ – £££££

020 79850474

www.naturalmat.com

Nature's Nest

Based on the principles of the hammock, the Nature's Nest is designed to ease the transition from womb to outside world. Invented by an Australian to appease his newborn's colic, anecdotal evidence also suggests it may aid other more serious conditions such as cerebral palsy. ££££

01689 860 932

www.naturesnest.co.uk

Purflo (for mattresses)

Safe and hygienic mattresses and covers designed to provide the optimum sleep environment for your baby. £££ – ££££

01788 891890

www.purflo.com

Stokke

Beautifully designed and wonderful to look at, this range also has an almost infinite life span due to its clever metamorphic properties. Accordingly pricey. ££££ – £££££

01753 655 873

www.stokke.com

The Kids' Window

Pricey but delightful selection of beds obviously designed with kids at heart. Funky and colourful. ££££ – £££££

0800 542 5093

www.thekidswindow.co.uk

Buyer's Guide to Baby Monitors

There is now a vast array of monitors on the market, playing up to parents' fears for their younger children or, indeed, their need or desire to keep a more permanent eye on the older ones. Because of this, monitors are one item of nursery equipment which potentially have a longer life span than most.

The frequency with which you use your monitor will probably dictate the features you want and the amount you are willing to pay. Some parents find, especially in the earliest days, that they cannot sleep without the monitor on. As your child gets older, however, you will feel more confident about occasionally turning it off once you know they are sleeping safely. Just go with the level of security that you feel most comfortable with. Unless you are lucky enough to live in a stately home, however, it is likely that you will always be awakened by the sound of your crying baby!

Different models explained

Mains vs. Battery-Powered

Most monitors have the ability to be both mains and battery-powered. Battery power is handy if you intend to use it outdoors, say in the garden when you have friends over, etc.

Some manufacturers, including Philips, sell monitors with rechargeable batteries. These make economic sense if you plan to use them a lot both in the early days and when your kids are a bit older. Be prepared to pay more for this versatility, though.

Digital vs. Analogue

Another choice you will have to make is whether to go for digital or analogue. Be aware that some monitors boast a digital *display* but not a digital *signal*. The signal is the more important of the two since a digital signal reduces interference and improves sound clarity. The newer, more expensive models all tend to use a digital signal but again, you may only be able to justify the cost if you intend to use your monitor frequently.

Pressure-sensitive monitors

A relatively new development in monitors is the introduction of a sensor mat or regular listening device. These models come with a pad which you place under your baby's mattress. The sensor within the pad is programmed to activate an alarm if it detects no movement from your baby within a specific time frame (usually 20 seconds).

If you have a premature or otherwise special needs baby, these may provide the extra reassurance you need; for others they may just increase levels of paranoia tenfold as you wonder whether the sensor is working correctly, etc. In addition, as they are still quite new to the market, there are other potential flaws which need to be addressed, such as their tendency to give a false alarm signal when the baby accidentally rolls off the sensor pad.

Features to look for

Channels

All monitors should have two or more channels for good sound reception, and to avoid confusion if someone else in your neighbourhood is using their monitor on the same frequency. If you live in a densely populated area such as a high rise, you may like to choose one with more channels to avoid interference.

Lights

Most monitors have a series of lights that illuminate progressively as the baby's cry becomes louder and more urgent. You can turn this feature down as appropriate, especially if you are near to the baby's room and can hear as soon as any crying begins. Others have an indicator light which tells you when the battery is low/needs recharging.

An inbuilt light on the baby's unit is handy for night feeds or when you don't want to disturb your baby unduly by turning on a separate light. The glow they give off is generally low but adequate for a quick check.

Temperature

Some of the newer models also transmit and display the ambient room temperature which is an excellent idea if you are in any doubt about how much bedding the baby should have – in theory. Personally, I found this feature less reliable than actually feeling my baby's skin and checking his temperature that way.

Portability

If you want the freedom to roam around a larger house whilst still keeping an ear on your baby, look out for a portable mains/battery powered parent unit which you can clip onto your belt or clothing. If you plan to use the unit outdoors, however, do ensure that the range of the monitor is adequate.

Intercom

Quite a few models, including those made by BT and Tomy, have an intercom facility which allows you to communicate with your baby or with another adult in the room. One obvious caveat to this feature is that there is a risk of you being overheard when you don't want to be, so watch what you say when the monitors are switched on! I recall at least one advertising campaign and several soap opera plot lines which took advantage of this flaw to humorous and dramatic effect!

Some of the most expensive monitors now feature a facility which allows you to either tune the monitor in to a channel on your TV or to watch on the portable screen exactly what your baby is doing. Whilst this may be of more use for older children that you want to keep an eye on don't forget that kids also need their own personal space and privacy.

Stockist contact details

Baby Monitors Direct

Great range of manufacturers, prices and devices from this dedicated outlet. Specialists in video monitors. £££ – £££££

08000 191929   www.babymonitorsdirect.co.uk

Fisher Price

Trusted branding and reasonable prices from this child-centred manufacturer. ££ – £££

01628 500303   www.fisher-price.com/uk

Lindam

Well-designed, budget-priced range of baby monitors. Fully-featured and parent-friendly. ££ – £££

08701 118118   www.lindam.com

Philips

Impressive range of monitors with an emphasis on cutting edge technology. Prices to suit most budgets. £££ – ££££

0208 781 8699   www.philips.com/babycare

Tommee Tippee

Very well priced range from the very basic to the new sensor pad technology. Good customer support. ££ – £££

0500 979 899   www.tommeetippee.co.uk

Tomy

Impressive range from this family favourite. One model even boasts 120 channels to guarantee interference-free reception. Priced according to features but pleasantly reasonable. ££ – ££££

02380 662600   www.tomy.co.uk

Travelling with Children

Sells an innovative range of monitors that work in conjunction with your mobile phone. Aimed at the aspirational end of the market. ££££ – £££££

0845 2600 892   www.travellingwithchildren.co.uk

Buyer's Guide to Highchairs

Of all the childrens' furniture that you buy in the early years, the highchair is the one that is likely to become a semi-permanent fixture – despite your best intentions to put it away after every mealtime! It therefore makes sense to think carefully about its design and features. Like much child-oriented equipment, there is a wide array of styles, designs, and price tags to choose from.

Different models explained

Cube

These models work on the principle of metamorphic furniture, starting off as a highchair, then as your child grows, separating and adapting into a child's table and chair arrangement.

Many are made from wood and, as such, may be more aesthetically suited to your decor than the plastic variety. As with all wooden furniture, however, you need to ensure that there are no jagged, splintery edges that a child could catch themselves on, especially if you buy or are given one of these chairs second hand. The advantage of plastic, of course, is that it is easier to keep clean than wood and does not absorb stains in the same way.

Highchairs without trays

These, too, are often made of wood. Some can be adjusted for height, so that you can position them up to the edge of your dining table, which allows your baby to be included in the social aspect of mealtimes. Some even convert into chairs suitable for older children.

They can make sound economic sense, but do think about how long you will want to use them as they tend to be on the pricier side. If you like the look of these models but aren't that bothered about the longevity issue, there are some good budget versions around.

On the downside, these chairs tend *not* to come with inclusive padding, and they can therefore be uncomfortable for babies and young children, for whom mealtimes can already be a trial.

Also, the lack of a tray may prove inhibiting if you don't have, or always use, a formal table for eating at, or if you want a safe place for your child to do some quiet play.

On a more safety-conscious note, highchairs without trays will often need extra harnesses as they do not have the additional security that a tray offers.

Freestanding highchair with tray

For most parents, this traditional form of highchair will be the model they are most familiar with. What makes them useful is the ability to sit in front of your child and assist with feeding. Their self-contained structure also makes them easy to clean and allows the child the freedom to experiment with feeding themselves.

There are lots of examples of this model that come with good padding, making them as comfortable for a small baby as for a more sturdy toddler. However, be cautious about paying for extra functions that you may not use after the first few weeks, such as a recline feature.

Portable highchairs and boosters

A portable highchair or booster generally straps onto an existing dining chair and can even bypass the need to make space for a proper highchair. It can also be useful at restaurants or whilst travelling.

The compromise that you generally make with these seats is in their lack of adaptability and comfort, although some do have a recline function. The benefits over conventional highchairs, of course, lie in their relative compactness, their portability and their price.

Features to look for

Think about what you yourself would look for in a chair and apply it to your choices. There should be some element of padding, no sharp edges and perhaps a foot rest which allows plenty of room for growth. I personally think this latter feature is essential if you intend to use the chair for more than just feeding as it quickly becomes tiring for a baby to have their legs dangling in mid-air!

Recline feature

Look for a recline feature if this is important to you, but recognise that most babies will not use it after the first few weeks.

Tray adjustability

If a chair has a removable tray, check its adjustability and whether it gives easy access to a stroppy toddler who refuses to bend his legs!

Adjustable seat height

Different seat heights can also be useful if you and your partner are vastly different sizes but both want to take turns to feed the baby or, indeed, if you want to pull the chair up to the family dining table.

Ease of cleaning

Ease of cleaning is not simply a wood versus plastic issue. Look out for hidden crevices where food can become trapped and become a breeding ground for germs. Does the tray come out easily for washing? Is the seat cover removable for washing, or at least capable of being sponged over?

Portability

Many parents end up using their highchair as a temporary restraint for their baby whilst they get on with housework etc. so you may want to consider the ease with which you are able to move the chair around the house. Some models come with lockable wheels which should always be engaged once your child is seated in the chair.

Storage burden

The storage demands of a chair are important if you don't have the space to store an assembled chair permanently. Check that the stored highchair will fit into the designated cupboard or alcove without becoming a tripping liability for others. Also check that it will fit into the boot of your car if you plan taking it away on trips.

If space is at a premium, look for models which are highly adjustable, portable, and easy to fold away. There will simply be no incentive to pack away a chair if it takes the strength of an ox and the dexterity of a gymnast! Be aware that some models have quite a significant footprint both when assembled and folded, so check this out when trying models in store.

Safety features

From a safety point of view, look for a wide, sturdy base to the chair and a proper harness, or at least the possibility of adding one.

Your child should be secured firmly across the hips and between the legs to ensure that they cannot slip out from under the tray or indeed, stand up. Check the straps of the harness for adjustability as they will need to accommodate your growing child.

If there are wheels to the base make sure that they can be locked to prevent your child rolling away or rocking in the seat.

Aesthetics

Although the look of a chair may not feature high on your list of priorities, and should certainly not come before safety, do bear in mind that you will have to live with your choice for a good few years. Plain wood designs may appeal more to those who tend towards the minimalist in their decor, although a multicoloured plastic monstrosity will probably eventually blend in with the rest of the detritus you accumulate in your new role as parents!

Safety considerations

Once your baby is in a highchair he will be able to socialise with other diners and see the world from a more adult perspective, and whilst this is wonderful, there are certain safety precautions to bear in mind. The highchair you use and the way that you use it can make the difference between a safe dining experience and an accident waiting to happen.

Generally speaking, your baby is ready to graduate to a highchair as soon as he can sit unassisted. This may occur around six months but be guided by your own child's development and don't rush into it.

Many injuries have been recorded where seats have separated from frames or where adjustable seats have fallen from the highest to the lowest position. Often these injuries are not attributable to the manufacture or design so much as the parents' failure to assemble or adjust the chair correctly.

The harness

Children can be injured so easily if they are not fastened correctly into the seat via a harness. It can be tempting to rely on a single strap when you are in a hurry or distracted by other commitments, but it only takes a second for a baby that has not been harnessed correctly to slip and injure their head or neck, sometimes severely. Look for both a crotch strap and a central pole which fits between the child's legs and prevents slipping. Five-point harnesses, such as those found in pushchairs, are always the safest option.

The British Safety Standard to look for when buying a highchair is DDENV 1178 (sometimes displayed as DDENV 1178-1) and BS 5799.

The base

A wide base will be more stable and make it less likely that the chair will topple should the child push against something like a table or 'bounce' the chair on a slippery kitchen floor. If lack of space prevents the use of a wider-based chair, position the chair where it cannot fall.

Other dangers

Sharp objects

Keep sharp objects away from nearby tables and worktops and move tablecloths and placemats out of reach of hands that could pull them and danger towards them. Never leave a baby unattended in a highchair.

Trapped fingers

Many minor injuries are caused by fingers becoming trapped in safety straps or trays so take your time over feeding and don't rush when getting a child in and out of their chair.

Germs

"Bacteria thrive in the nooks and crannies of a highchair."

As babies get older they love to explore food with their hands, and that includes throwing anything they may come into contact with! For safety and peace of mind, install a splash mat around the highchair and make sure you clean up any spillages as soon as you can, especially on tiled surfaces that could become slippery. Bacteria thrive in the nooks and crannies of a highchair so make sure you wash it down thoroughly after every meal with hot soapy water or a diluted cleanser such as Milton.

Loose fittings

Check your highchair regularly for loose fittings or sharp edges and general degradation of materials.

Your safety!

Last, but not least, take care of your own posture and back when using a highchair, especially when lifting a child in and out, or when picking up dropped items.

Stockist contact details

Babies R US

Massive range of styles and prices from this retail superstore. ££- ££££

0800 038 8889

www.babiesrus.co.uk

Bebe Confort

Luxuriously specced highchairs with an emphasis on comfort and practicality. Pricey! £££ – £££££

020 8236 0707

www.bebeconfort.com

Bibs and Stuff

Retailer of the wonderful Svan highchair, beautifully crafted in a choice of woods for the aesthetically discerning parent. Pricey but worth the investment as the chair grows with your child to finally become an adult seat. ££££   01293 774924

www.bibsandstuff.com

Cheeky Rascals

Sells the Handysitt portable highchair: an award-winning design recommended by endless parent-centred periodicals. ££££

0870 8732 600

www.cheekyrascals.co.uk

Chicco

Wonderfully versatile highchairs with longevity of use in mind. Choice of fabrics to blend in with your decor. £££

01623 750870

www.chicco.co.uk

Cosatto

Great range of chairs including portable, easy-to-fold models aimed at homes where space is at a premium. Some models include deluxe versions with extra features allowing you to spend according to your budget. £££ – ££££

0870 050 5900

www.cosatto.com

Kuster

Creating products with passion, innovation, style and functionality. The futuristic Kuster highchair may be a little too modern for some tastes but is certainly striking and reasonably priced for its quality of build. £££

0845 0204277

www.kuster.co.uk

Mozzee

Home of the über-trendy Nest Highchair; again, not to everyone's taste but a thoughtful and clever design makes this the celebs' favourite. ££££

020 7060 3636

www.mozzee.co.uk

Stokke

Makers of the best-selling Tripp Trapp highchair, a metamorphic model that grows with your child. Available in a range of colours and finishes. A good investment you won't be embarrassed to have in the front room. ££££

01753 655873

www.stokke.com

Buyer's Guide to Children's Books

Encouraging your baby to have an enjoyable and lifelong relationship with books is one of the most valuable contributions you can make to his future development, paving the way for the accumulation of vital social, emotional and verbal skills.

In the modern world, with its emphasis on technology, electronic gadgetry and on-demand television, reading can seem like a rather old-fashioned pursuit and one which many parents don't participate in with their children. Whether this is due to time constraints, a sense of inadequacy or self-consciousness is unclear; what *is* clear, and frighteningly so, is that more and more children are now entering secondary education with reduced aptitudes for both numeracy and literacy.

An innate sense of the value of books is not something that comes naturally to most children. Rather, it needs an enthusiastic and motivated mediator to guide them, which is where your input is so important. Even if this sense of value was missing from your own childhood, there is much you can do to ensure your child doesn't lose out; you may even find your own interest in books re-invigorated.

The value of early reading

It is never too early to start reading or exploring books with your baby. Even before they are born, reading aloud can elicit a strong physical response from the womb as your child becomes familiar with the sound and rhythms of your voice.

For babies and toddlers, books are a way to explore the world through both words and pictures. Studies suggest that

> "Putting a baby in front of the TV may over-stimulate them to the point at which they effectively tune out."

simply putting a baby in front of the TV does not do as good a job and may even over-stimulate them to the point at which they effectively tune out. The intimacy achieved by quiet time spent with a book is far better. As well as creating a bond between parent and baby, reading encourages specific skills of communication and comprehension, and whets a child's appetite for imaginative role play later on. It also aids visual literacy, enabling children to become adept at interpreting non-verbal cues such as signs and facial expressions. The ability to read these cues has obvious implications for their future social development whether that be at nursery, school or later in the workplace.

Learning what books to buy

Given the vast choice available it can be overwhelming for first-time parents to know which books to choose for their babies and toddlers. Experts now believe that due to inherent brain differences between male and female children, they like different kinds of book, boys preferring more literal informative styles. Despite these differences, however, there are some kinds which babies of either gender seem to enjoy in the early stages. These include:

- Storybooks with rhyming or narrative text.

- Information books, for example ABC or look-and-point.

- Song books.

- Novelty interactive books such as touch-and-feel, or books that produce sound effects when a button is pressed.

Perhaps the most appealing books to very young babies are those with bold photographs or brightly-coloured illustrations, and although there are some excellent published examples you can also create your own versions by compiling photo albums of all the significant people in your baby's life and narrating their stories on a regular basis.

In the early days it is pictures that make a book memorable; as your baby gets older you will find them more and more attracted to the actual narrative of a story, remembering the rhythms and 'punchlines' where applicable.

Another alternative which costs nothing is to sit with your baby in front of a mirror and to sing rhymes or make up stories with physical actions.

Don't forget, too, the value of story and song tapes; listening is a crucial part of learning both language and reading. When using resources of this type ensure that there are no outside distractions such as the television or radio.

Wherever you go to choose your books, whether a bookshop or library, be guided by what your child finds interesting or attractive even if their choices are not particularly to your taste!

Hints and tips to make reading enjoyable for you and your baby

Make reading together a special activity that has its own time and space in the day. Don't try and 'fit it in' whenever you can.

Similarly, show your child that books are valuable, and should be treated with respect. Allocate a place in your home where books will be kept, ensuring that they are easily accessible by your child so that they can be both taken out and returned after use.

A baby and toddler's comprehension is always evolving and can be enhanced by talking 'around the book' as well as sticking to the literal story inside it. There are many ways to read a book; you may want to try some of the following:

- Reading the actual story/text.

- Paraphrasing the main parts of the story.

- Talking about the story, for example, what people did, where they went, what they wore, how they felt, etc.

- Relating elements of the story to baby's own life, for example, creating a relationship between a dog or cat in the story and your own pets.

Each time a book is re-read a child's understanding of it increases, and some books may become firm favourites to be revisited time after time. Indeed, once your baby starts to acquire language, you may find that one of their most frequently used words is 'Again!' It may seem tedious to you to read the same story night after night, but such familiarity fosters a sense of permanence in a child's world which in turn makes them feel secure. In addition, revisiting books helps forge neural connections, builds confidence through memory and perception, and enables children to relate and extrapolate the events in a story to their own experiences.

Once an interest in books has been established you may find that your child starts to develop a personal relationship with their favourites. If this happens allow them the peace and quiet to browse on their own – it really is wonderful to watch from a distance as they babble away to themselves, attempt to turn the pages and try to emulate the rhythms they have heard. Children have their own way of 'seeing' so don't try and impose your own method onto them. Give them time to scan the pages before turning them, allowing them to take in the pictures, colours and text patterns.

Reading is supposed to be pleasurable so be aware of a baby or toddler who seems over-stimulated or tired when reading, and put the book away for another time. On several occasions I have been reading what I thought was a particularly exciting story to my son only to spot signs of him tuning out. In this situation you simply have to close the book and wait for next time, even if it means sneakily catching up on the ending yourself!!!

The wonderful thing about books is that they are portable, so make sure that you have one or two with you whenever you are going somewhere where you may be delayed or have to wait, such as the doctor's surgery.

Never worry that you are not doing a good enough job reading to your baby. The intimate bond created by the activity in itself is highly valuable, even if your range of animal noises leaves something to be desired...! In any case you'd be surprised how quickly your repertoire improves especially under the guidance of an appreciative audience.

Look out for initiatives in your area designed to foster a lifelong relationship with books. BookStart is a National Programme, founded in 1992 which aims to promote just this kind of relationship. Its admirable philosophy is that every child, whatever their background, should have access to a wide range of books from as early an age as possible. To this end BookStart distributes learning packs, the first of which should be delivered to families of babies aged between 7 and 9 months, usually through their Health Visitor.

Early reading – some suggestions

The following books all come highly recommended by both myself and other mothers of babies aged between birth and 3. The recommendations are followed by a list of useful agencies for further information.

Books for babies

Where's Woolly? by Heather Amer, illustrations by Stephen Cartwright
A soft plastic bath book with a simple clear story. Babies are encouraged to find Woolly the Sheep and his friend the duck on every page.

Mirror Me! by Julie Aigner Clark, illustrations by Nadeem Zaida
Written as part of the famous Baby Einstein range, this is a board book which introduces babies to language, poetry, music, science and art.

Goodnight Poppy Cat, written and illustrated by Lara Jones
Sweet book which encourages understanding about the routines involved at bedtime.

Baby Says Hooray! by Opal Dunn, illustrations by Angie Sage
Colourful action flap book encouraging children to communicate and use actions. One of a series of recommended books by this author.

Pets, by Fiona Watt, illustrations by Rachel Wells
Four pages of textured jigsaw pieces for babies to touch and feel. Objects named on one page are matched by full colour illustrations on the other.

Fuzzy Bee and Friends, published by Priddy Books
Rhyming text, bold illustrations, lots to touch and washable too!

Frog, by Fiona Watt, illustrations by Rachel Wells
Follow the jumping trail and feel the squeaky lily pad.

Hey Diddle Diddle, by Paula Knight
A first rhymes board book which includes sparkly textures and sounds to copy.

Dad Mine/Mum Mine, by Jane Kemp/Clare Walters, illustrations by Dawn Apperley
Small colourful board book with very simple text. Relate you and your baby to the pictures.

That's Not My Bear, by Fiona Watt, illustrations by Rachel Wells
Touch-and-feel book. Big clear pictures of bears with different textures to explore.

Baby Boo! by Templar and Emma Dodd
One of the Amazing Baby range of board books featuring photos of babies' expressions with a mirror on the last page. Simple text encourages imitation and expressive language.

Books for toddlers

I Kissed The Baby, by Mary Murphy
A hardback picture book. Graphic black and white art trimmed with colours and featuring lots of repetition for children to emulate.

Ten In A Bed, by Jan Omerod
Variation of the song encouraging the skill of counting from 1 – 10 and back down to 1.

Catch! by Trish Cooke, illustrations by Ken Wilson-Max
Tells the story about the bond between a young girl and her mum. Beautiful for toddlers to relate to.

The Best Party of Them All, by Hiawyn Oram, illustrations by Lucy Su
Telling the story of twins in search of a birthday party.

Smile Crocodile, Smile by An Vrombaut
Story about Clarabella Crocodile and her search for assistants to help clean her many teeth!

Little Bear Finds A Friend, by Maurice Jones, illustrations by Anna Currey
A warm story about friendship, great for bedtime reading.

Bunny and Bee's Playful Day, by Sam Williams
Heartwarming story with easy words to say and remember.

The Very Hungry Caterpillar, by Eric Carle
Gorgeously illustrated story following the evolution of a caterpillar into a butterfly.

Brown Bear, Brown Bear, What Do You See? by Bill Martin
Gentle repetition and gorgeous tissue paper collage illustrations make this a real winner with parents and children alike.

Elmer: The Story of a Patchwork Elephant, by David McKee
Delightful and world-famous story celebrating an elephant's right to be different!

Useful organisations

The National Literacy Trust

A charity founded in 1993 to work in partnership with others to enhance literacy standards in the UK.

www.literacytrust.org.uk

Book Trust

Independent charity promoting books and reading through its work in education. Also commissions reports on schools' spending on books.

www.booktrust.org.uk

Talk To Your Baby

A campaign run by the National Literacy Trust to encourage reading and a lifelong relationship with books.

www.literacytrist.co.uk/talktoyourbaby

BookStart
www.bookstart.co.uk

Buyer's Guide to Toys

You'll really know you've had a baby when half the stock of the local toy store arrives on your doorstep in the form of presents from friends and relatives. You'll also know which of these people have children of their own, as they are the only ones likely to understand that, at birth, babies can barely see beyond their own nose and have the manual dexterity of a hammer!

In this section we will look at a baby's development and its relation to the sorts of toys that are appropriate from birth to age 1 and beyond. We will also examine what to look for when choosing toys, including safety marks and labelling, upkeep and storage, and considerations to be made when giving, receiving and buying toys on eBay.

Choosing toys

If you visit any toy store or, indeed, watch any of the TV advertisements for toys around the key seasons of Christmas, Easter and the Summer holidays, you will probably be overwhelmed by the choice.

Ideally, a good toy should combine *entertainment, stimulation* and *education*. Of these three, entertainment is the most important, as without your child's interest the other two factors are unlikely to follow. In the earliest months, 'education' is defined merely as the ability to encourage new skills such as holding, pulling, pushing, and the recognition of different shapes and colours.

Don't forget that for the first couple of months, the most entertaining things in your baby's life are the people around him, and that means YOU! At this stage he can only see clearly for a distance of around 25cm and has little or no manual dexterity, so most of the toys that you receive and may indeed have bought will simply be beyond him.

Also, whilst it is true that developing babies and toddlers need lots of things to touch, discover and play with, expense is not necessarily the key. We all know of the baby who, faced with an array of (on the face of it) exciting and expensive Christmas gifts, spends the rest of the day preoccupied only with the colourful packaging. Indeed, carefully selected objects from around the home are just as exciting to a young baby's eyes as the most elaborate of shop-bought gifts. Don't forget that everything at this stage is new to your baby and they do not take the world for granted in the way that we jaded adults do! Even objects like a saucepan and wooden spoon banged together will teach your baby important physical concepts such as cause and effect.

> "If your child has an all-time favourite, a toy that he would be mortified to lose, it's worth buying a back-up in case one gets lost or is in the wash."

One way to avoid buying toys which your baby has no interest in is to make use of toy libraries. These give you the opportunity to try different toys with your baby, without commitment, to see which ones he likes most. If you cannot find a local toy library why not set up a toy swap facility within your local mother and baby group? It's a wonderful way of introducing your baby to social skills whilst saving you money into the bargain.

If you have already splashed out on the latest gizmo for your baby, don't be disappointed if they show little or no interest initially. Every toy will have its moment and some may, in time, graduate to the status of firm favourite. Which reminds me of an essential tip: if your child has an all-time favourite, a toy that he would be mortified to lose, it's worth buying a back-up in case one gets lost or is in the wash!

One of the key considerations when looking at a toy is its age-appropriateness to the recipient. What follows is a basic run-down of what you can expect developmentally from a baby at each stage of its early life, and what toys may interest them accordingly.

Which toys to buy?

For the earliest months, toys that incorporate texture, noise and movement will be of most interest and, in addition, will help your baby develop an understanding of important concepts such as colour and shape recognition, the principle of cause and effect, and hand-eye co-ordination.

Look for cot mobiles that rotate and play a nice tune. The tune is important as you are likely to be hearing it for some time to come! Some mobiles are multi-coloured and some are designed with strong graphic monochrome shapes. There is evidence to suggest that very young babies can see in mono better than in colour, so the latter may be more appealing initially.

An alternative to a mobile is a light show that projects colours and shapes onto the ceiling above the baby's cot, or an activity centre that clips onto the cot side. These are particularly good for a child once he has learned to sit unaided and may help keep him amused when he wakes up in the morning, perhaps giving you an extra few minutes in bed!

Soft activity toys that are bright and colourful have lots of play value too, but if you do decide to buy a plush toy, look for those that have different textures or sounds built into them. Cuddly toys are often given to babies but are much better suited to older children. Be wary too, of hairy toys or those that have ribbons and other trimmings, as they are a potential choking hazard for young babies.

"Cuddly toys are often given to babies but are much better suited to older children."

Other appropriate toys for this age group are rattles, squeakers and teething toys, as babies love having a good shake and chew. You can often buy this type of toy as an attachment for the bumper bar of a pram or highchair and they are great for soothing fractious babies.

For the later months, toys that a baby can control will continue to develop the skills he has already learnt. They will also help balance and mobility, imaginative play and manipulative skills. You can look for things like shape sorters which a toddler will find both challenging and satisfying; pull and push-along toys which will encourage crawling and walking; musical toys which help develop a sense of rhythm; stacking toys and building blocks which assist hand-eye co-ordination and manual dexterity, and sit-on-and-ride toys which give a sense of adventure and independence, as well as expending some of the seemingly endless energy a toddler possesses!

Don't forget to think out of the box and use other activities with your baby to incorporate an element of play. For example, if your baby is a reluctant bather, you may find that foam letters and squirty toys put the fun back in bathtime.

As your baby reaches 15-24 months, he will start to enjoy role-playing toys such as telephones and play kitchens. These are excellent at encouraging emulation and imaginative skills.

Electronic toys

Whilst the majority of toys are still made with traditional play concepts in mind there has been a big explosion in electronic type toys in the last decade or so. If you are considering buying this type of toy, weigh up the relative potential they will have for your child against the additional costs of batteries. Remember, too, that many of the speaking varieties come complete with an American accent!

All battery-powered toys for children of this age group should have toddler-proof battery casements, and you should always be vigilant that your child cannot gain access to the batteries.

Important tips regarding toys

Age range

Check the recommended age range on the toy. Most packaging will state this but do not regard the information as set in stone. Relate it to your own child's maturity and whether they are physically ready for the toy, especially as regards any small pieces which it may include. Toys which fire projectiles are generally unsuitable for children under the age of four and sometimes older.

Choking hazards

Look at the size of a toy and if it is smaller than mouth size, or contains parts that are, do not buy it or use it for a baby: it is a potential choking hazard. Similarly, consider whether a toy is too big and heavy for your child and whether it would pose a danger if it fell on them. Will a baby be able to hold it or will they simply drop it?

Sharp edges

It goes without saying that toys should not have any sharp or rough edges, spikes, dangerous protrusions, or splinters. Beware of collector's toys which are aimed at adults but which are often appealing to a child. Similarly, family heirlooms, such as tin toys or automata, are not suitable for children and may contain residues of lead paint.

Other dangers

Look at the quality of manufacturing of any toy, checking for loose hairs and/or poorly attached features such as eyes or noses. For very young babies, stick to embroidered as opposed to beaded or plastic features. Check that the seams on cuddly toys are intact and that there is a label stating the fabric composition of any filling. Check toys, also, for any moving parts that could trap little fingers, such as springs, doors or slots. You should not use toys that have strings or cords attached as these can pose a strangulation or tangling risk for young babies. This includes cords or ribbons which form part of an outfit or costume.

Imitation food

Imitation food can be quite confusing to a child. If you think that yours are not yet old enough to know the difference between real and imitation, do not buy the fake toy variety. This also goes for real sweets and chocolate that are sometimes packaged with toys and which may not be suitable for younger children.

Ride-on toys

If you intend to buy a ride-on toy for your child, be guided by their size and not necessarily their age. Beware of fingers becoming trapped in rockers or moving parts and make sure that they have adequate supervision at all times.

Safety standards

If you buy or receive a new toy that you suspect is unsafe, report it to your nearest Trading Standards Office. Check that new toys comply with all the relevant safety standards; the CE mark and the Lion Mark are the key ones to look out for.

Cleanliness

All toys should be kept clean, especially those which come into contact with food or which have been outside. Young babies love to mouth anything they come into contact with. Dust mites from soft toys can be killed by placing them in the freezer for at least six hours prior to being washed. You can also vacuum them to remove mite faeces.

Storage

Whilst it is difficult to always keep toys tidily in cupboards, do try and keep them confined to a particular corner of the room to avoid creating a tripping hazard.

Toys should be stored in a place that is not too high for your child to reach. If you keep some toys in drawers or cupboards use safety catches to ensure that little fingers don't get trapped.

Inventory

Carry out an occasional inventory of your child's toys and check the seams and any fixtures or fittings for signs of degradation. If toys are broken, resist the temptation to keep them in the hope that you will repair them. Even if you do get around to it, the repairs are likely to make them a hazard to your child, so it is easier and safer to throw them away.

When they have to go . . .

Never give away or sell toys without first checking that they are in sound working order. Apply the same stringent checks that you would to a new toy. If you have lost the original packaging, do try and indicate the appropriate age range for them. Similarly, if you are given second hand toys, check them over and if in doubt, discard.

If you don't wish to resell, consider giving good quality toys which your child has simply outgrown to your local nursery or similar project so their enjoyment can be shared by others.

Safety marks and what they mean

Each year, manufacturers, importers and Trading Standards Offices spend millions of pounds making sure that new products are safe. Accordingly, there are certain signs you should look for which verify that the necessary standards have been met.

British and European Standards

These are drawn up by manufacturers, safety experts and others to establish minimum quality standards. By law, goods must have passed the relevant safety standards before they are allowed on to the market. The numbers and letters appear on the packaging of the toy/product and sometimes on the toy itself. At the time of writing here is what you should be looking for:

Child Safety Seats	ECE R44.03
Children's Toys	EN71
Cots	EN 716
Fireguards	BS 6539
Highchairs	BS 5799
Pushchairs and Prams	BS 7409
Safety Gates	EN1930
Smoke Alarms	BS 5446

The Kite Mark

The Kite Mark is a symbol that most of us are familiar with, and which we recognise as a sign of safety and reliability. Whenever you see a toy or product bearing the Kite Mark, it indicates that the British Standards Institution has independently tested it and it has been found to conform to the relevant British Standard. The manufacturer is then granted a BSI licence to use the Kite Mark. This service is paid for by the manufacturer and any products carrying the mark are tested and reassessed at regular intervals.

Manufacturers are not legally required at the present time to display a Kite Mark on their product, but many products with a BS reference such as those listed above will also have a Kite Mark displayed.

$C\epsilon$ The CE Mark

The CE mark, together with the name and address of the first supplier is required by law to appear on all toys placed on the EU market on or after January 1990. Its purpose is to indicate to authorities that the toys bearing it are intended for sale in the European Community, that they meet the essential safety requirements of the European Toy Safety Directive, and are entitled to access European Community markets.

There may be warnings printed alongside the mark and these should be heeded, as a toy regarded as safe for a five year old may by implication be dangerous for a younger child. Anything that looks like a toy but does not have a CE mark should not be given to a child. The CE mark is now appearing on many other products including cycle helmets and protective safety pads.

 The Lion Mark

The Lion Mark was developed in 1988 by the British Toy and Hobby Association (BTHA) as a symbol of toy safety and quality for the consumer. While the mark is only used by BTHA members, its membership includes many major international and European companies. In all, BTHA members supply around 95% of all toys sold in the UK.

For a toy to display the Lion Mark the supplier must have signed a strict code of practice which, in addition to covering toy safety matters, demands the highest standards of ethics in advertising.

The Lion Mark for Retailers

The British Association of Toy Retailers (BATR) joined with the BTHA to develop the Lion Mark for use by retailers. By displaying this sign the retailer is letting you know that all products in their shop and/or catalogues meet a certain standard of safety. It indicates that the retailer has agreed to the code of practice and, as such, is prepared to make strenuous efforts not only to offer safe toys for sale but to ensure management and staff employed by the retailer are briefed on any safety-related issues.

Second hand toys

Whilst all new products should meet minimum safety standards, second hand toys may have been built to an old standard or there may not have been a standard in place at all when they were made. In addition, wear and tear may have made them unsafe, so you need to check them carefully before selling, buying or using them.

If you buy toys on eBay, check whether the seller has retained the original packaging and/or instructions which can offer important information. If this is not available you can often cross-reference model numbers printed on the toy itself against those on a manufacturer's website to check for any product recalls or updates.

TIP

If your child loses a treasured toy whilst out and about, help is now at hand from the founders of childrenswear company, Mini Marvellous. 'Toys Reunited' is an online service which aims to pair up lost toys with their distraught owners via a bulletin-board system. To read more about the website or to avail yourself of its services visit:

www.toys-reunited.co.uk

Stockist contact details

Baby BeeGee

Makers of the world-famous Sophie the Giraffe; a tactile, sensory toy suitable from birth. Also sell a selection of comforters. ££ – £££

020 8944 8674

www.babybeegee.com

Fisher Price

Advocating child development through play, this company has a wealth of experience and advice to offer on its wonderful website. Manufacturing toys for every budget and every age range from 0-5, they are highly recommended. ££ – ££££

01628 500303

www.fisher-price.com/uk

Galt

Specialising in old-fashioned interactive games and puzzles. Wonderful for encouraging learning with parents and thereby increasing social skills and enjoyment. Reasonably priced. ££ – £££

0161 428 9111

www.galt.co.uk

Holz Toys

Beautifully crafted old–fashioned toys for parents with an ecological conscience. All are crafted in an environmentally-friendly and natural way.

Astounding selection of role playing toys. ££ – £££££

0845 130 8697

www.holz-toys.co.uk

KS Kids

Wonderful range of interactive and original toys, games, playmats, etc. from this award-winning retailer. Features an easy reference guide to your child's development and the toys which may be appropriate. ££ – ££££

01582 503503

www.kskids.co.uk

Lamaze

Range of educational toys based on the famous American Lamaze philosophy and its trademarked Infant Development System. Uses colour-coded toys to guide you to make the most appropriate choices. Quite pricey. £££ – ££££

01392 281900

www.lamaze-rc2.com

Leap Frog

Best known for their electronic interactive books, this company also has a wide range of physically-engaging toys and activities suitable from birth upwards. £££ – £££££

01895 201521

www.leapfroguk.com

Mulberry Bush

Traditional toys, gifts and games with an emphasis on nostalgia and creating memories from a parent's own childhood. Huge range of prices to suit everyone. £ – ££££

0870 7776 776

www.mulberrybush.co.uk

Oh Baby London

Small but gorgeous selection of vintage-inspired comfort blankets and retro styled toys/activities for toddlers sit alongside an impressive range of unique clothing. Perfect for sourcing new baby gifts. ££ – £££

020 7247 4949

www.ohbabylondon.com

Soft Play Zone

Specialists in play mats with educational and stimulatory value suitable from birth. Very reasonably priced and excellent quality. You can buy direct from their website and also from their eBay shop. ££ – £££

0113 269 8181

www.softplayzone.co.uk

Taggies

The original and best. Sensory security blankets which babies and children of all ages love. Incredible range of designs and products. ££ – ££££

01749 672 437

www.taggies.com

The Early Learning Centre

Aimed at babies and children from birth to 6, the ELC has a proven track record in providing toys and games to help children grow in confidence and ability. Lovely range and great customer service. £ – ££££

08705 352352

www.elc.co.uk

Tomy

Established brand of over 80 years standing. Manufacturers of toys and games for children of all ages. Great range, widely available and trusted by parents for quality and value. ££ – ££££

02380 662 600

www.tomy.co.uk

Buyer's Guide to Bouncers, Rockers and Swings

From an early age, babies love the sensation of movement, be it up and down or backwards and forwards. It's likely that this affection is fostered in the womb where they are constantly on the rollercoaster ride provided by your day-to-day movements.

Bouncers, rockers and swings are all useful additions to your nursery arsenal, as they not only give your baby the exercise he needs to strengthen and develop important muscles, but also give you the chance to have a few minutes to yourself. So what are the essential differences between these particular items?

Different models explained

Rockers

Rockers are small chairs which gently move backwards and forwards. They are generally suitable from birth and are roomy and comfortable. Their movement can calm a fractious baby, even to the point of sleep, or they can simply be used to keep a baby happy for short periods of time. Some rockers include removable toy bars to make them more stimulating.

Rocker chairs can generally be set to a rocking or a static position, whereas bouncers have only one mode. Some models of rocker can also be positioned in a multitude of ways, from totally reclined to more upright, depending on your baby's mood and the effect you want to achieve.

My son loved his rocking chair so much he used to eat, sleep and play in it till the day it finally surrendered to metal fatigue. From a practicality point of view, therefore, you should try and look for a model with removable or spongeable covers.

Bouncers

Bouncers work on the principle that the baby sits in a fabric seat or saddle which supports their body. The seat is then suspended from an elasticated strap, via a spring-loaded clip.

The most common type of baby bouncer attaches to the top of a door frame, although you can also buy freestanding models.

Bouncers are only suitable for babies who have learned to support the weight of their own heads, usually sometime between three and five months. You should also check the maximum weight allowance of the bouncer which varies between manufacturers but is, on average, around 12kg. Babies who exceed this maximum, or who are showing signs of a desire to walk, (whichever is soonest), should not be placed in a bouncer.

When using a bouncer, a baby should be positioned so that his feet just touch the floor. They are not designed to be used for long periods at a time so make sure you don't exceed fifteen to twenty minutes per session.

Some bouncers have plastic or fabric rings to cushion a baby and stop them bumping into other objects. Whatever model you choose, make sure that it complies with the current British Safety Standards BS EN 14036:2003 or BS EN 14039:2006

Again, from a practicality point of view, look for a saddle or seat that is easily washable.

Swings

Swings are a more versatile alternative to a bouncer although you will pay considerably more for them.

Most models come with a variable speed option to take account of the fact that babies enjoy different rhythms according to their mood. You can also look for a choice of musical tunes but as these all tend to lose their novelty eventually (for you, if not your baby!) you may also want to choose a swing where the movement can be set to work independently of the music!

Younger babies who have not yet mastered the art of holding up their head will automatically slump forward if placed in an upright position. For this reason, ensure that the swing you choose has at least two recline positions and if you intend to use them from birth make sure they are designed for this purpose. The recline feature will also prove useful for older babies who tend to fall asleep in the swing. The different positions should operate smoothly, however, in order to avoid jarring the baby whilst they are asleep.

If the swing has a fold-out tray or toy bar, it is important that this can be flipped open so that a sleeping child can be extricated easily and without injury.

Important safety considerations

- With door bouncers always ensure that there is sufficient adjustment in the seat to fit snugly around the baby and support his back.

- Ensure swings have a wide base and will not tip over if the baby leans to one side.

- Check that the swing, rocker or bouncer has a safety belt system. As with car seats and highchairs, a five-point harness is the safest option. Shoulder and hip straps reduce the chance of a baby sliding out of the equipment and/or successfully learn to climb out.

- Never leave your baby unattended when using this type of equipment.

Stockist contact details

Argos

Huge range of styles and prices make this an essential stop for parents and parents-to-be. Home delivery service. ££ – £££

0870 600 8784

www.argos.co.uk

Fisher Price

Lovely wide range of swings, bouncers and rockers from the basic to the luxurious. ££ – ££££

01628 500303

www.fisher-price.com/uk

Lindam

Great range of baby bouncers. Well reviewed. ££ – £££

08701 118118

www.lindam.com

Mothercare

Dependably large range and excellent advice make Mothercare a continual favourite amongst parents. Wide price range so something for nearly everyone. ££ – £££££

www.mothercare.com

Woolworths

Family favourite with a very well priced inventory suited to those on a budget. £ – ££

01706 862789

www.woolworths.co.uk

Buyer's Guide to Changing Tables

A changing table is one of those items which you will either definitely want or not. With neither the space nor the inclination to use one, I have found that a changing mat on the bed works just as well. However, with their optional shelves and baskets, there's no doubt they can be a useful and attractive piece of nursery furniture.

Generally, you can choose between three types: wooden ones with guard rails, fold-up models, and the less common hinged chest adaptors. The last is not generally recommended, as dressers with these adaptors have been known to topple over when a baby's weight was placed close to the edge.

Some of the more expensive models are based on a chest of drawers or 'tallboy' but simpler units are basically trolleys. You can also buy cot-top changers which consist of a tray with a padded mat that sits across the body of the cot.

Features to look for

Height

If possible, try out a model on the shop floor before purchase to see whether it meets your needs and requirements and is at a good height for whoever will be using it most.

Weight

Always check the age/weight range that the table is designed for. The more weight it is certified as being suitable for, the more durable and sturdy it is likely to be.

Guardrails

Look for substantially-constructed, wooden changing tables with guardrails at the side. These are least likely to sway or tip over should a baby pull himself up on them. Guardrails should be at least 5cm (2 inches) high. Don't forget to use the safety straps each time you place your baby on the table. These should be easy to fasten in order to resist the temptation not to use them at every change.

Sturdiness of fold-ups

Although they tend to score better for convenience and portability, fold-up tables are generally more flimsy and more likely to topple. If you're thinking of buying one, check it for sturdiness. Apply some weight to it to ensure that it won't collapse.

Width of base

Tables with a wide base are much harder for a baby to pull over onto itself from the floor.

Storage

Look for shelves or compartments for storing everything you'll need at change time. As this can be quite a large piece of furniture these additional features will help it earn its keep. Storage facilities in the body of the table will also make it less likely that you will take your eyes off the baby as you search for things. If there is no storage facility do question your purchase and ensure that you always store change time essentials close by.

Pads

Choose pads that are easy to keep clean and make sure that you wash them down frequently.

Suitability to your cot

If choosing a cot-top model, make sure that it is suitable for your particular cot. These are usually highlighted as an optional extra at the time of purchase. It goes without saying that it is an absolute safety no-no to have a changer that slides around on the top of the cot.

Baby bath

Some models feature an optional baby bath. Although these may seem like a good idea, don't forget that the bath will have to be filled and emptied on every occasion which means transporting the whole unit to a basin or a bath and draining the baby bath through a hose. Some of these wholly-integrated units are made from a lighter type of material in order to increase their portability, but you may compromise on looks for this added benefit. If you're set on a wooden model, look for those which offer a hinged lid into which a plastic bath can sit and be easily fitted or removed.

Durability

Wooden tables tend to have a longer life span than their intended 2-3 years, as they look more like 'real' furniture and can be redeployed. Some of my friends' tables have tables which have been resurrected as a miniature desk and even a hi-fi stand!

Safety considerations

- Ensure that whichever changing table you buy conforms to British Safety Standard BS EN 12221-1.

- Follow all the manufacturer's instructions as regards assembly of the table and ensure that all fixings are fastened tightly and checked periodically for loosening etc.

- If at all possible, place the table against a wall, away from windows, patio doors, balconies etc.

- A padded mat beneath the table can be a good idea in case the unthinkable occurs and your baby rolls off.

- As the baby grows and gains weight be aware of any additional strain on the table. This may be indicated by rocking, wobbly joints, cracked surfaces or loose screws or bolts. Watch out for product recalls by manufacturers and know the product number. Store the instruction booklet for the table along with every other baby-related equipment manual in a safe place.

TIP

BUY a lever arch file or folder and keep all receipts, guarantees and instruction manuals for baby-related items together for ease of reference or if you need to return an item. It's a point of fact that the one piece of information you will need will be the one that you cannot find unless you keep everything organised!

Stockist contact details

Argos

Extremely competitively priced range of nursery furniture. Good choice from well-known brands. ££ – £££

0870 600 8784

www.argos.co.uk

Hippins

Extremely pricey but beautifully crafted wooden nursery tables in a range of finishes and designs. Definitely aimed at the aspirational end of the market. £££££

01531 650843

www.hippins.co.uk

Jack-Horner

Small, traditional company specialising in traditional finishes at an affordable price. Limited range of roomsets but beautifully finished. £££ – ££££

01788 891890

www.jack-horner.co.uk

Mamas and Papas

Lovely range of versatile wooden pieces that look wonderfully inconspicuous from normal furniture! Mid–high prices though. £££ – ££££

0870 830 770

www.mamasandpapas.com

Mothercare

Dependably large range and excellent advice make Mothercare a continual favourite amongst parents. Wide price range so something for nearly everyone. ££ – £££££

www.mothercare.com

Stokke

Attractive and versatile changing unit blends in with the now famous sleepicot. Streamlined and wonderfully made but pricey. ££££

01753 655 873

www.stokke.com

Buyer's Guide to Breast Pumps

Breast vs. Bottle

As a new mother you will not have escaped the 'Breast is Best' literature from health experts and government advisors which asserts that breastfeeding gives your baby the best start in life. The debate over breastfeeding versus bottle-feeding is an emotive one and beyond the scope of this book.

On a personal level, I would always defend a mother's right to choose, recognising that there are many factors in play when it comes to making the decision. I also think that for mothers who, for whatever reason, decide *not* to breastfeed their babies, there are countless ways to support their child's development and not feel as though they have shirked their duty. Ultimately, the philosophy of this book is based on the principles of choice. To this end, I have included a dedicated section on bottle-feeding, beginning on page 123. For now, however, we turn our attention to breastfeeding, and more specifically, to the equipment you will need if you choose this option.

Why express with a breast pump?

Investing in a breast pump will be one of those vital purchases you will not regret, as expressing your milk can be of benefit in a variety of ways.

Firstly, expressing helps with the painful problem of engorgement, releasing the excess milk from your breasts which you may find you produce later on in your baby's feeding career. Few women find this a problem in the early days when their milk is just coming in, and generally speaking, your breasts will only continue to make milk in order to keep up with the demands of your baby. However, some women do find that their supply exceeds demand and there are programmes now being trialed in certain hospitals where women who produce more milk than they need can supply their excess to maternity departments to be used by other mothers whose own supply is low.

Expressing can also be the perfect way to continue breastfeeding your baby if you decide to return to work fairly soon after the birth.

Finally, it can be a great option if you would like your partner to participate in the feeding/bonding of the baby or simply if you would occasionally like a break from feeling like a giant milking machine!

Different models explained

The three most important criteria when choosing a breast pump are:

- Can it do the job effectively?
- Can it keep up with my milk supplying needs?
- Is it comfortable to use?

There are basically two choices: *manual* or *electric.*

Manual pumps

A manual pump, as the name suggests, is operated by hand, usually with a lever mechanism. They tend to be quieter than electric pumps, give you more control over suction, and are kinder to sore breasts! On the minus side, they can be fiddly to assemble and clean.

Manual pumps are comparatively cheap, and are a good choice if you think you may only want to express now and again.

Electric pumps

An electric or battery-powered pump can be single or dual action (the latter allowing you to express from both breasts at the same time) and is a more efficient, albeit more expensive method than manual pumping.

If you think that you may be expressing on a regular basis, or, indeed, if you are returning to work fairly soon, electric pumps are well worth the investment. Do ensure, however, that a mains adaptor is included with the battery versions as they tend to deplete battery life very quickly.

A common criticism of the electric pump is the relative lack of control you have over the suction, although some models do offer the choice of two or more levels of power. They can also be noisy and not the ideal choice if you are suffering from sore or cracked nipples.

> **NOTE**
>
> If you intend to express directly into bottles, you need to make sure that your bottles match/fit your pump.
>
> If your baby has been exclusively breastfed before you start to express, you may need to experiment with a variety of bottle shapes/teats to find one which your baby accepts easily. It is generally agreed that it is much easier to introduce a bottle, even on a very occasional basis, fairly early on to avoid rejection later. Manufacturers have recognised the fact that some women want to combine breast with bottle-feeding and have invented innovative breast-shaped bottles which some babies instinctively prefer.

Factors to consider

Number of cycles

A pump's ability to mimic a baby's suckling action is determined by the number of cycles it performs a minute. These currently range from 30 to 60. An electric pump is obviously more efficient at this, but some women find that they can get a realistic rhythm established with a manual pump.

One or two breasts

Think about whether you intend to express from both breasts at once (which can be more time efficient and/or good for multiple babies) or are happy doing one at a time. Again, the electric models are more efficient at working both breasts simultaneously – though they can be very pricey.

Durability

When deciding how much to spend, ask yourself why you are getting a pump. For some women it will be to maintain their milk supply, for example if they have had a premature birth or are likely to be away from their baby for extended periods of time. For others it will be to increase their milk production either because it is naturally low or because they have had a multiple birth. Rental pumps of the kind generally used in hospital maternity wards are excellent at addressing all these concerns. They also tend to have more durable motors to cope with the demands placed on them by more frequent expressing. For less demanding use, an ordinary electric or manual pump should be perfectly adequate.

Portability

Think about how mobile you need to be. Portability is becoming a feature high on many women's wish lists, especially with more of them choosing to return to work soon after their babies are born. Manufacturers have answered the call by making models that are lighter and less bulky and which can therefore be taken to work in their own discreet carry bags. If this option appeals to you and you have somewhere at work where you can express in, for example, your lunch hour, check whether your kit includes cold storage compartments which will keep your milk chilled for several hours until you return home.

> "You can get some amazing discounts on the more expensive hospital grade models, especially by buying on eBay."

One-handed use

Can the pump be used one-handed? Some women find that their let down reflex is at its strongest when they feed with one breast and express from the other. Others just want the freedom to hold a book/magazine or cup of tea whilst they express!

Noisiness

How noisy a particular model is may be of consideration to you, especially if you intend to express whilst at work and feel self-conscious about the sound or simply if you want to be able to watch TV or listen to the radio whilst expressing.

Ease of assembly and disassembly

Most pumps are now fairly easy to assemble and clean but do examine the various models first hand if you can, and see whether they suit you in terms of how they fit together. This can be especially important in the early days when you can be cross-eyed with tiredness!

Don't forget that the component parts of a pump will need to be sterilised along with any bottles which you use. Because of their ability to be thoroughly sterilised between uses and users, I have no qualms about buying a second hand breast pump and you can get some amazing discounts on the more expensive hospital grade models especially, by buying on eBay.

Cost

Cost should not be the determining factor when you buy a pump, but it would be foolish to pretend that it isn't a consideration at all. Bear in mind that you want a pump that is going to be comfortable and efficient at its job and if this means compromising slightly on cost this may be a prudent decision.

Other essentials

Storage bottles and bags

In addition to a pump you will need to make a small outlay for storage provisions – either bottles and/or milk storage bags which can be kept in the fridge or freezer.

Breast pads

If you are going to breastfeed you should also prepare yourself by investing in some decidedly unglamorous but nevertheless important accessories. These include breast pads, which come in both disposable and washable varieties and which help to prevent leakage through your clothes. You should try out both types for comfort and convenience.

Cream

Other accessories include breast shields and a good cream such as Lansinoh which does not affect the taste of your milk for your baby but is vital if you suffer from sore or cracked nipples. Finally, you will need to buy a good nursing bra and perhaps some nursing tops, both of which allow you to breastfeed discreetly, especially useful in public places.

Underwear

I have written a dedicated guide to maternity wear, including nursing bras, beginning on page 137. Don't forget, too, to have a peruse of the next section on bottle-feeding, as some of the equipment discussed there is also relevant to nursing mothers, including bottle and teat types.

Stockist contact details

Ameda
Breast pumps for sale and hire featuring unique piston technology. Over 50 years experience. Reasonably priced. £££

01823 336362

www.ambermed.co.uk

Avent
Great selection of budget and deluxe models. Good advice and aftercare and a wide range of accessories make this an obvious choice for many mums. ££ – ££££

0800 542 8368

www.avent.com

Boots
Good range of own-brand and well-known models at competitive high street prices. ££ – £££

0845 070 8090

www.boots.com

Medela
Hospital grade breastpumps for hire on next-day delivery. Reasonable rates allow you to try before commitment. £££

0870 950 5994

www.medela.co.uk

Mothercare
Dependably large range and excellent advice make Mothercare a continual favourite amongst parents. Wide price range so something for nearly everyone. ££ – £££££

0845 330 4030

www.mothercare.com

Whisper Wear
World's first hands-free breast pump. Currently only available in the US – check on eBay for imported items.

0770 984 0905

www.whisperwear.com

Buyer's Guide to Bottle-Feeding

If you have decided to bottle-feed your baby, either through personal choice or for medical reasons, be reassured by the fact that commercially-prepared milk formulas are now closer than ever to breast milk. Thanks to decades of research by scientists and medical experts, they now deliver a high-quality and nutritious source of first food.

Unlike mothers who have chosen to breastfeed, you will not need equipment such as breast pumps, nipple shields or pads, but you will need to invest in bottles, teats and various bottle-feeding accessories, the variety of which can be quite bewildering for the first time parent. There is also a selection of baby formula milks to choose from, a guide to which is presented below.

Along with your chosen formula you will probably need at least six bottles with teats and collars, sterilising equipment, and a bottle and teat brush.

Choosing the right formula milk for your baby

Deciding which formula to use means considering a number of factors such as your baby's age, health and dietary needs, as well as the cost of each type of formula and how much time you wish to spend in preparation. If you begin bottle-feeding immediately after giving birth your midwife may recommend a specific type or brand which you should not change except in accordance with their advice. Whichever formula you choose, you will be given a choice of two basic types: milk-based or soya-based.

1. Milk-based formula

Most infant formulas are based on cow's milk which is then modified to more closely resemble a mother's natural milk. To make the milk suitable for human babies, manufacturers adjust the levels of fat, protein and carbohydrate and then fortify them with minerals and vitamins. There are also specific formulas aimed at premature babies.

Although science has yet to come up with a direct replica of human milk (hence the claim 'Breast is Best') there have been enormous strides made, especially in the last decade, in the development of formula milk which means that your baby will not be deprived of a nutritious first food.

Some manufacturers produce two types of formula: first-stage and second-stage, the latter of which is aimed at 'hungrier' babies. In both cases, the protein in milk is broken down into curds (also called casein) and whey.

- **First-stage formulas** are whey-dominant, as is breast milk, with a casein:whey ratio of 40:60. These are suitable from birth and are generally easier for your baby to digest.

- **Second-stage formulas**, also called 'follow-on' milks, adjust this ratio to become casein-dominant (about 80:20). These take longer to digest which is why they keep hungrier babies fuller for longer. As first-stage milks are meant to last until a child is up to a year old, however, do not switch to a second-stage formula unless your health visitor agrees that it is okay to do so. Switching too soon can lead to constipation in your baby. You should also seek advice before switching between different brands or types of formula.

"One of the great benefits of breast milk, is that it is free."

If your baby is over six months old you may be tempted to switch to a follow-on milk in order to meet his increased nutritional needs. Some experts maintain, however, that it is better to continue with standard formula and 'top up' by including solids in their diet which are high in calcium and iron. I think this is sound advice as it also encourages your baby to make the gradual shift from an all-liquid diet to one which incorporates solid food.

Unmodified cow's milk is not suitable for babies under six months, as they are not developed enough to digest the protein and salt that it contains. It is also low in iron and vitamin C so is not really recommended as a regular drink until a child is over the age of 1. It is generally okay to give a baby who is six months or older a little cow's milk in cooking or in cereal.

2. Soya-based formula

This, as the name suggests, is made from soya beans which, like the milk-based formulas, is then modified and enriched with vitamins, minerals and nutrients. Babies should only be given this type of formula on the express advice of a health professional.

If you are concerned that your child has an allergy to cow's milk and its derivatives, you may be tempted to switch to soya-based milk. Be aware, though, that there is no guarantee that your child will tolerate soya-based milks either, and you are strongly advised to seek professional advice before switching over. There are some cow's milk-based formulas available which have been specially modified for babies with an allergy or intolerance. Similarly, there is no evidence, except anecdotally, that a soya-based formula can soothe a baby who is sleeping poorly or suffers from colic.

The cost of formula

One of the great benefits of breast milk, over and above its nutritional value, is the fact that it is free. Unless you are entitled to milk tokens from the State (available for low-income families) you will find the cost of formula does add up over the course of a year. Exactly how much it adds up, however, depends on the format you choose to buy.

The cheapest option is to buy formula in dry powdered form in a tin. Bottles are prepared by adding scoops of the dried milk powder to cooled, boiled water (generally one scoop per fluid ounce). Some brands also make individual sachets of milk which are enough for a 6 or 8 ounce feed and these can be useful – for instance, when travelling. You can also buy ready-to-drink formula in cartons which can simply be poured into a sterilised bottle. Although convenient you will pay much more per ounce this way so it probably isn't practical to use on a regular basis.

The price of formula milk varies across different brands and amongst different retailers but you will probably pay a similar price for both milk and soya-based products.

Bottles

Nursing bottles come in three basic sizes: 4oz, 8oz and 9oz. The smallest is typically used for newborns and is also an ideal size for storing expressed milk. As your baby gets older it also makes an excellent travel-sized bottle for water or juice.

As far as *types* of bottle are concerned, there are two basic categories:

Standard bottles

These have straight necks and bodies and are designed to be reusable. They generally have markings on the side for precise portion control. Although you can buy some standard bottles with fun prints or even coloured bodies I prefer the clear ones as these make it easy to see exactly how much your baby has drunk. Along with the more common plastic variety you can also buy standard-sized bottles in glass and in an anti-colic form.

Plastic

Pros

- Widely available and relatively inexpensive (with the exception of special anti-colic bottles).

- Designed to be used in conventional warmers, sterilisers and carriers.

- Come complete with teats and collars.

- Can be bought with wide or standard necks.

Cons

- Some babies swallow a lot of air with these bottles, which can lead to wind, reflux or colic. You should always ensure when bottle-feeding your baby that the teat is filled with milk to minimise the amount of air being taken in.

Glass

Pros

- Environmentally friendly and free of chemicals.

Cons

- Possible danger related to babies swallowing fragments of glass.

- Not widely available and therefore comparatively expensive.

- May not be covered by European Safety Standards.

Disposable bottles

These are made of a hard outer shell, sometimes called the nurser, into which you insert the disposable bags. The bags come pre-sterilised for one-time use with either formula or expressed milk and are handy if you are travelling and want to limit the number of bottles you take with you or if you won't have access to a means of sterilising standard bottles when you get to your destination.

This system comes with its own teat and screw-on collar designed to hold the bag in place. One distinct advantage of these bottles is that the disposable bags contract to prevent babies from sucking in air as they drink, which can cause wind and reflux. Plus they are sold ready-to-use and require no cleaning. As with any bottle system, however, you need to ensure that the teats are thoroughly cleaned after each use.

Pros

- Handy, especially for travel.

Cons

- Only suitable from three months onwards.

- Not an ecologically friendly choice.

- Expensive if used on a regular basis.

Teats

As with bottles, teats come in a variety of shapes and materials, and with a differing number of holes in the top. The flow of milk is determined by the number and size of these holes.

When bottle-feeding make sure that the teat hole is the right size. If your baby appears to be sucking too hard you may need a faster teat so you should upgrade to the next size. An overly-resistant teat could collapse under the baby's sucking motion which is why it is important to match the teat to your baby's ability. Conversely, a teat whose flow is too fast for your baby may make him gag and splutter when drinking. For a newborn, you know the size of teat is correct if the milk comes out in a spray for a couple of seconds when the bottle is inverted but then slows to a drip.

Bell-shaped teats

Bell-shaped teats are the type you will probably be most familiar with, and come with a range of hole sizes, from small for newborns to large for toddlers or thicker juice drinks. Some brands have just one hole in their teat while others have 2 or 3 to ensure an even flow. It is better not to mix and match teats and collars from different manufacturers, in case they don't fit together properly and create leaks.

Latex teats

Latex teats are elongated to imitate the suckling motion of breastfeeding babies, and cause the milk to be delivered to the back of the tongue as opposed to simply into the mouth. They are therefore a good choice for parents who want to mix and match breastfeeding with bottle-feeding. Latex deteriorates faster than other materials, however, and the teats should be checked regularly for cracks or clogging.

Silicone teats

Silicone teats are made of a clear, heat-resistant material that can sustain being cleaned in the hot environment of a dishwasher. Less porous than latex, they are generally felt to be more hygienic and also typically last three to four times longer. You should also, however, periodically check these for faults.

And the rest

Other types of teat you may want to consider are anti-colic teats which purport to reduce the amount of air your baby swallows, and orthodontic teats which minimise harm to developing teeth. Babies should not be allowed to fall asleep with bottles in their mouth, due to the risk of choking as well as the risk to their unformed teeth. There are also teats shaped like a nipple for babies who are mixed feeding or being weaned from the breast.

TIP Once prepared and refrigerated, bottles of formula will stay fresh for up to 24 hours. You could therefore try and prepare enough for the day ahead in one sitting. Choose a quiet time of the day, perhaps during your baby's morning nap, so that you can concentrate on the task and ensure that all measurements are correct.

* The Government advises feeds should be made up freshly each time. Refer to preparation instructions on packaging.

Bottle-feeding accessories

In addition to the bottles themselves, there are several accessories which you will need as part of a bottle-feeding regime. Some of these are essentials, others a nice indulgence. The choice of which to buy is, again, very much an individual one.

Brushes

Whatever else you purchase, bottle brushes are a must to ensure that your bottles are thoroughly cleaned. The best brushes have narrow flexible bristles and an optional teat cleaner. Don't forget to keep them separate from your normal washing-up brush which will harbour bacteria from pots, pans, etc.

Coolers/warmers

Day or night cooler/warmers are designed to reduce some of the stress of night feeds in that they enable you to keep bottles cool for up to two hours, and then warm them on a heated electrical element in a matter of minutes, all without having to traipse downstairs in the middle of the night. Their relatively small footprint means that they will fit onto most bedside tables and are therefore ideal if your baby sleeps in the same room as you. Check whether they have a night light feature which further reduces the disruption to your baby (and your sleeping partner!).

Insulator bags

A hot/cold insulator bag is a useful accessory if you make frequent long car journeys or take extended outings with your baby as it will enable you to keep milk and snacks fresher for longer. Some manufacturers produce a variation on this theme which hangs over the back of a standard car seat – a great idea.

Steriliser

Whether bottle-feeding or breastfeeding with the use of bottles, a steriliser is essential in the early months to keep equipment bacteria-free. Even when your baby has progressed to weaning you may want to use the steriliser to clean spoons, bowls, etc. A detailed guide to sterilisers begins on page 133.

Storage basket

If you are going to use your dishwasher to clean baby bottles and equipment you may want to invest in a small basket in order to keep things separate and organised. Even if you don't have a dishwasher, some type of storage system is always useful so that you aren't constantly looking for little things like collars and teats.

Feeding pillows

Feeding pillows can help position your baby, whatever method you use. If you bought one of these for use in pregnancy you will find it continues to earn its keep after your baby is born and is one of the reasons why I think they are such a great investment. Later on, they can also be used to support your baby whilst he learns to sit unaided. They give your arms and back a rest during long feeds and can also be a godsend if you have experienced post-natal trauma such as stitches or a c-section.

Handy tips to remember when bottle-feeding

1. Abide by the sell-by date shown on the packaging.

2. Follow the manufacturer's guidelines for making up formula, both in method and hygiene.

3. Ensure that all bottle-feeding equipment is sterilised and maintain the cleanliness of your steriliser by descaling and cleaning on a regular basis; once a month is the recommended guideline.

4. If using ready-to-use formula ensure that any opened cartons are kept refrigerated and used within 48 hours.

5. Don't store bottled milk in the door compartment of the refrigerator as it does not reach a cool enough temperature to kill bacteria. Use the main body of the fridge only.

6. If your baby fails to finish a bottle discard any formula that has been left as germs from your baby's saliva can quickly breed in the warm environment.

7. Don't retain prepared but unused formula for more than 24 hours even if refrigerated.

8. Don't use a microwave to heat formula as its temperature may be uneven, leading to hot-spots and possible scalds to your baby's mouth. It is far safer to stand the bottle in a bowl of warm water for a few moments. Don't forget to test the temperature before offering the milk to your baby.

9. Don't put cereal or other solids into a bottle as it creates a choking hazard. For the same reason you should never prop up your baby's bottle on a cushion or similar.

10. Supervise your baby's feeds at all times.

Stockist contact details

Avent

Teats and accessories designed to be the next best thing to breastfeeding. Wide range of bottles and feeding equipment. Plus helpful advice. ££ -£££

0800 289064

www.avent.com

Boots

Large range of own-brand and more famous name manufacturers under one roof. Well-priced. ££ – £££

0845 070 8090

www.boots.com

Infant Care Direct

Stockists of all the Playtex baby care lines currently available in the UK. Wide range of bottles, teats and soothers including anti-colic ranges. Offers smaller trial packs which are a great idea if you are not sure what will suit you. ££-£££

01954 719899

www.infantcaredirect.co.uk

Mothercare

Dependably large range and excellent advice make Mothercare a continual favourite amongst parents. Wide price range so something for nearly everyone. ££ – £££

0845 330 4030

www.mothercare.com

NUK

Very wide range of teats and bottles from this specialist manufacturer including hard-to-find glass bottles and orthodontic teats. ££ – £££

0845 300 2467

www.nukbaby.com

Tommee Tippee

Originators of the Back To Nature bottles and the award-winning Nuby teat. Pricier than most bottles but well recommended. £££ – ££££

0500 979 899

www.tommeetippee.com

Buyer's Guide to Sterilisers

Sterilisation basics

For the first year of their lives, babies are at their most vulnerable to viruses, bacteria and parasitic infections. These can lead to anything from a mild attack of thrush, to the more serious gastroenteritis with its symptoms of vomiting, diarrhoea and subsequent dehydration.

Before sterilisation became the norm in this country, it is thought that this serious illness was the cause of many infant deaths. Whilst it is not practical or even desirable to prevent all germs from coming into contact with your baby, sterilisation will ensure that the risks are minimised during the first tender months.

Unlike your own utensils and dishes, it is not enough to simply wash your bottles and other feeding equipment in hot soapy water, although this should certainly be done prior to sterilisation. You should be especially vigilant as regards the cleaning of teats where milk can easily collect. Don't forget to pass water through each teat to ensure that all traces of both milk and detergent have been removed and to ensure that the hole has not become clogged. Use this time to periodically check that there has been no degradation to either teats or bottles in the form of splits or cracks which can hold bacteria and compromise the safety of equipment. If you spot any signs of fatigue, throw the item away.

> "It is not enough to simply wash your bottles and other feeding equipment in hot soapy water."

Whilst dishwashers are a mainstay of the modern household, adequate sterilisation can only occur when the temperature exceeds 80 degrees centigrade. If this is your choice of sterilisation, bottles should be filled immediately with formula and then refrigerated to prevent recontamination.

Don't forget to sterilise associated items such as measuring spoons and bottle caps. If you are breastfeeding you should also sterilise the component, non-electrical parts of breast pumps, in addition to any bottle equipment, nipple shields, etc, used in the course of expressing.

How long should I sterilise for?

You should continue to sterilise all your baby's feeding equipment up until his first birthday, including all weaning equipment and accessories.

Even though babies eventually start to put everything and anything in their mouths, their immune system remains very immature and they can be susceptible to infection between 6-12 months. The bugs that stick to milk curds can be especially unpleasant. By the time a baby reaches the age of 1 he will start to produce his own antibodies and be more resistant to harmful bacteria. However, you should not pack away the steriliser just yet, as it is a good idea to continue sterilising bottles, dummies, teats and other equipment until he either outgrows them or stops using them.

Different models explained

Steam

Electric steam sterilising is the method used in most hospitals and is a quick and efficient method, taking between 8 and 12 minutes per cycle, plus cooling time. You should ensure that your equipment is able to take this method of sterilising as some small parts, from breast pumps, for example cannot be cleaned in this way. Bottles, teats and caps should be inverted inside the steriliser to ensure they are properly cleaned.

You can also buy microwave sterilisers that work on the steam principle, although you must of course ensure that nothing metal or metal-based is placed inside the microwave. These take slightly less time than the electric steam method, typically 5 to 8 minutes, plus cooling time, but you should be extra careful when removing the lid from these sterilisers as the insides become extremely hot.

The main advantage to using the steam method, either electric or microwave, is that there is no associated smell or taste and, as long as the lid is not removed, the contents can remain sterile for up to three hours. Some models are also quite portable making them a good choice when you are travelling.

Recent additions to the steam sterilising method include bottles which can be placed on their own in the microwave and which take about a minute and a half per item to complete the process. You have to remember to leave the bottles unsealed, however, to avoid the build up of pressure.

Another innovation is the microwave steriliser bag into which you can place up to three bottles and teats. You then add a small quantity of water to the bags and place them in the microwave for about two minutes. I have used these myself when I have been away from home and found them to be very efficient, although I think the manufacturers have been a tad optimistic in their estimates of just how much you can fit into one of these bags and still be able to seal it! The other benefit is that they can be used up to 20 times each without losing efficacy, making them an excellent choice for holidaying – as long as you have access to a microwave, of course!

Boiling

Both boiling and cold water sterilisation techniques are worth knowing about in case you are caught without access to your normal steriliser or, indeed, a microwave.

With the boiling method, you need to boil most equipment for about ten minutes and whilst this may be a cost-effective method in the short term, in the long term it does tend to lead to the faster degeneration of more fragile items such as teats.

Cold water sterilising

This method uses a non-toxic solution, such as Milton, which can be bought in either bottle or tablet form. The solution is highly effective against bacteria, is safe to use, and can even be ingested without causing harmful side effects. Although you can buy special containers for cold water sterilising, a clean bucket or a container with a lid is perfectly adequate.

You will also need some kind of weight to keep the bottles submerged beneath the solution, and to ensure that there are no air bubbles, in order for the process to be completely effective. This method takes about thirty minutes and the equipment can then be left in the solution for a further 24 hours. You need to refresh the solution daily and you should observe proper personal hygiene before handling clean equipment. Bottles can then be rinsed with cold water, if desired, but then must be filled with formula immediately.

Avoid leaving empty sterilised bottles on kitchen counters as their sterility quickly becomes compromised. If your steriliser has built-in storage you can use bottles as and when they are needed.

Stockist contact details

Avent

Electric and microwave models available. Reasonably priced. Well made and easy to use. ££ – £££

0800 289064

www.avent.com

Lindam

Electric plus microwave and cold water sterilisers in addition to the innovative microwave steriliser bags for parents on the move. Well priced and thoughtfully made. ££ – £££

08701 118118

www.lindam.com

Retailers

Babies R Us

Good range from this retail superstore. ££ – £££

08457 869778

www.babiesrus.co.uk

Boots the Chemist

Good range; good advice. ££ – £££

0845 070 8090

www.boots.com

Mothercare

Dependably large range and excellent advice make Mothercare a continual favourite amongst parents. Wide price range so something for nearly everyone. ££ – £££

08453 304030

www.mothercare.com

Buyer's Guide to Maternity Wear

A walk through the annals of social and fashion history reveals a litany of frightening crimes against the female form in the name of maternity wear. Indeed, seeing the photos of tent-like shapes and other shrouds that were the norm in previous decades leads me to ponder the real reason why pregnancy was once termed 'confinement'...

Thankfully, designers have at last cottoned onto the fact that women want to celebrate their pregnant form and that, in their second trimester especially, many actually look their most beautiful. The increased surge in hormone levels makes your skin glow and your hair shine – which is just as well as the rest of your body starts to play tricks on you that you never thought possible.

More and more specialist shops have sprung up to tap into the demand for fashionable, wearable clothes for pregnancy and beyond. Even high street retailers such as Top Shop, Dorothy Perkins, and H&M have launched their own capsule maternity ranges which means you can look perfectly 'normal' whether you are after everyday wear, formal work wear or something for a special occasion such as a wedding or party. The prices in the high street are also reassuringly inexpensive and, because these clothes tend to have a relatively short life span, there are tons of bargains to be had on eBay and other websites such as The Maternity Exchange which offers the chance to swap clothes with other mothers-to-be.

Of course, like every other area of fashion, there are high-end designer stores if you are so inclined, but be prepared to pay accordingly. Spawned by our preoccupation with celebrity mums and mums–to–be, there are even maternity lingerie ranges now created by supermodels, although they *don't* promise that you'll spring back to their sylph-like pre-pregnancy shape once your time is up.

There are many areas to consider when looking at maternity wear, one of the most important being that of foundation garments, including pants and both maternity and nursing bras. These will all be discussed in this section, but first let me share with you some tips for dressing for success when pregnant, garnered from both my own experience and that of other mums:

10

COMMANDMENTS

of Maternity Wear

I. Thou shalt not simply wear bigger versions of your normal pre-pregnancy clothes

Maternity wear is designed to give you extra room only where you need it, principally the bust and stomach area, and not your legs or arms. This applies especially to items such as trousers, unless you want to look like you are wearing the Mersey Tunnel.

II. Thou shalt choose natural fabrics as far as possible, such as cotton, wool, silk and linen.

You have noticed that you feel hotter during pregnancy, especially if you are largest through the summer months. This is due to increase in both your blood volume and your metabolic rate which causes your blood vessels to dilate, if you wear nylon and polyester you will sweat. It is also quite common for pregnant women to develop a sudden sensitivity to man-made fabrics resulting in a red itchy rash. Clothes made from natural fibres will allow the air to circulate around your body and keep you cooler and more comfortable.

III. Thou shalt not buy maternity clothes until you need them.

Many women find, especially with their first pregnancy, that their normal clothes don't become tight until the fourth or fifth month. Until they do, hang fire on spending loads of money on maternity wear.

There are devices you can buy called belly belts which basically extend the life of your normal trousers and jeans (where you will notice the bulge first) by extending the waistline a couple of inches. If you buy maternity wear now, you will probably find that they are much too big. You may then end up buying a smaller size only to have to reinvest once your pregnancy advances.

I used to take a small cushion with me when I went shopping so I could see what the clothes would look and feel like when I reached my eighth or ninth month. Many maternity clothes are designed with this very fact in mind and come with adjustable straps, stretchy panels, drawstrings, etc. These take up the extra fabric which you will certainly need come the later months and will also accommodate you if you put on a bit of extra non-baby weight too!

IV. Thou shalt buy basic items in stretch fabrics.

Cotton jersey is a wonderful fabric and with the addition of lycra it adds extra 'give' and shape-retaining properties.

V. Thou shalt plan your wardrobe carefully so you can mix and match.

This really will extend the wearability of your chosen items. In addition, if you have a friend of a similar body shape who is also pregnant, consider sharing your pieces for even more variety at less cost.

VI. Thou shalt allow yourself to splurge on a couple of special items that make you feel really great.

This was a great morale booster to me, especially in my later months when I began to resemble a stranded oil tanker. Treat yourself to a fantastically flattering pair of jeans or a lovely dress for special occasions such as a wedding or Christmas party.

VII. Thou shalt allow yourself time to get back into shape after pregnancy.

Remember that labour does not immediately leave you looking like you did before you got pregnant – it may be a good few months before you even resemble your pre-pregnancy shape. Don't beat yourself up about it, but do choose maternity clothes that you will be happy to wear after the happy event. If you're planning to breastfeed try to build a couple of suitable tops into your wardrobe budget such as those with concealed panels or which are easy to undo or pull open.

VIII. Thou shalt be kind to your feet!

Did you realise that your feet sometimes get bigger in the third trimester? By the end of my pregnancy I was wearing shoes that now look like you could go sailing in them! Even if you don't actually go up a size do yourself a favour and invest in some comfy shoes such as clogs or slip-ons. If you have been an exclusive heel-wearer before getting pregnant think about taking a rest from them in the later months when your posture dramatically changes, putting extra stress on your spine and legs. Be careful, too, about buying shoes that require you to bend down to fasten them as by the time you near your due date you will hardly be able to see your feet let alone get near them!

IX. Thou shalt ensure you get the right support for your growing bust.

Get fitted regularly for bras to ensure you've got the best and most comfortable support going for your new cleavage. Also see the section on Maternity Underwear.

X. Thou shalt enjoy your new shape

It will be over too soon!

What should I buy?

Below is a list of items that form the basis of a maternity wardrobe. In addition, I have added some pointers on what to look for within each category.

Trousers and skirts

Choose trousers with good quality spandex or lycra content and with adjustable waist fastenings. Plain or neutral colours that go with most tops will stand you in good stead. Fastenings that allow the trousers to grow with you will ensure that they look good at various stages and give you some support when your bump starts to grow heavy.

> "Seeing the photos of tent-like shapes and other shrouds that were the norm in previous decades leads me to ponder the real reason why pregnancy was once termed *confinement.*"

Despite being super comfy, be aware that if you buy trousers or jeans with sewn in stretchy panels you will always need to wear a top that covers them as they can look a little 'obvious' without this coverage. Alternatives to consider are drawstrings, side panels and elasticated waistbands that are fully adjustable.

As for leg shape, I personally find a wider cut to be more flattering, especially as you near your due date. Tapered, or drainpipe leg shapes simply make most women with an obvious bump look like a toffee apple. For skirts, a gentle A-line is a great shape for balancing out your torso.

Maternity tops, jumpers and cardigans

Your standard clothes will last much longer into your pregnancy if they contain lycra. However, in your sixth month you may start to find that, even with the benefit of lycra, tops start to feel a bit snug or, indeed, start to ride up around your tummy.

Choose tops with drawstrings or toggles that can be let out as you grow. If you have to dress formally for work you may find that a more tailored style looks smarter, even though you will have to buy two or more of these as you get larger. As for necklines, I personally found that a lower shaped V was very flattering to my growing bust and drew attention away from my squirrel cheeks! Lower necklines also mean that you can accessorise with a nice piece of jewellery.

Don't forget to factor in a couple of versatile wraps or shawls which can look equally good dressed up or down and are less restricting than jackets and coats when the weather permits.

Maternity bras

Buying supportive, well-fitting underwear is a minefield at the best of times, but as one of the most important purchases in your maternity wardrobe it's well worth shopping around and taking the time to get right.

As there are no actual muscles in your breasts they need support to prevent sagging both during and post pregnancy. What's more, the right bra can help to alleviate backache and may even minimise stretch marks (look, we'll try anything...).

You shouldn't wait until late into your pregnancy to buy a pre-natal bra; go and get a fitting as soon as your own bras start to become uncomfortable. Be aware that many women will go up at least two bra sizes during pregnancy but be guided by your own shape.

All you may need in the early stages is a good soft-cupped bra which will be comfy and supportive for your growing breasts. Although you may have depended on the support of an underwire before you were pregnant these are not recommended for pregnant women as they can restrict your developing milk ducts and possibly cause the very painful condition Mastitis in your later stages and after birth.

As your pregnancy progresses you will eventually notice your rib cage starting to expand and your cup size changing accordingly. This is the time to go and visit an experienced bra fitter who can measure you and advise on a size and shape to suit you. Many maternity bras now come with nursing clips or poppers so that they can be used after the birth if you are planning to breastfeed. These are good from an economic point of view as, in effect, they do double duty.

When trying on a pre-natal bra ensure that it is fitted on the tightest hook to ensure that there is room for growth. There should be no bulges under your arms and avoid the push-up variety of bra which can squeeze your breasts into unnatural shapes, again impeding the development of your milk ducts.

For nursing purposes you will probably want to have another fitting at around 37 weeks; this bra will be slightly larger (about one cup size) to allow for when your milk comes in and your partner, if you have one, discovers the real benefit of the pregnant shape!!! The extra sizing will also allow you to fit in nursing pads and breast shields if you use them. About 6-10 weeks after the birth when things settle down in the breast department you will be able to use your maternity bras again.

Unlike when you shopped for a pre-natal bra, nursing bras should initially be fastened on the loosest hook to allow you to tighten the strap as you regain your pre-pregnancy shape.

Choose a style that allows easy access to both breasts; drop-cups are ideal for this. Avoid small restrictive openings as they can inhibit your milk production and flow and cause infections. You should also invest in a soft sleep bra which enables you to wear breast pads at night and prevent leakage onto the bedclothes. Sleep bras are also soft and comfy and great for wearing at home during the day.

Features to look for

Sleep bras

- Strap adjustments.
- Quick-release nursing clips.
- Built-up back for comfort and support; 'racer' type backs are especially good.
- Cotton/lycra mix fabric for comfort.
- Soft wide elastic on the strap.

Nursing bras

- Broad, non-slip shoulder straps.
- Quick-release nursing clip.
- Enclosed inner cup seams for added comfort and protection.

- Cotton sides/back for comfort and support.
- A cotton lined undercup for extra support and comfort.

Maternity pants

As for things in the pants department, lingerie companies are starting to realise that not all pregnant women want to wear knickers the size of a small country and if you wore a thong before you may find that this style will still be the most suitable for you. Other women prefer the more 'secure' feel of an over-the-bump style or those with a foldable waistband which give you the benefit of both over and under styles.

Features to look for

- Soft fronts designed to fit over and under a bump.
- A wide gusset and extra-soft elastic at the waist and around the legs.
- A percentage of lycra and 100% cotton aids stretching and hygiene.

Maternity swimwear

Swimming is one of the most beneficial forms of exercise you can take when pregnant but even if you just want to lie on a beach during your last holiday as a single person you still want to fit in with other holidaymakers.

Maternity swimwear ranges from plain bathing suits made with extra stretchy materials or pleated panels to maternity tankinis. These consist of two pieces; a lower bikini bottom and an upper vest or skirted vest which can be worn high over the tummy or pulled down over it. Tankinis can be particularly flattering to a big bump.

Other maternity wear

Other items you may be interested in include support belts which can help ease an aching back, belly-belts which can extend your normal jeans waistband, special maternity hosiery, bra expanders, and breast pads for nursing.

Don't forget, too, the power of accessories such as jewellery and hair ornaments which can transform or revitalise an outfit.

Stockist contact details

General maternity wear

Abound

Reasonably-priced wear for everyday. Plain shapes make for a good mix and match wardrobe of basics. ££

0870 413 8000

www.abound.co.uk

Blooming Marvellous

Wearable range of everyday and special occasion wear. Good price range. ££ – £££

0845 458 7408

www.bloomingmarvellous.co.uk

Crave Maternity

Lovely range, especially strong for work wear. Well-tailored pieces at the more pricey end of the spectrum. £££ – ££££

0870 240 5476

www.cravematernity.co.uk

Fun Mum

Great casual range, with good interpretations of the current high street trends cut for the pregnant figure. Well priced. ££

www.funmum.com

Great Universal

Good for swimwear and basic pieces. Largish range, shop from home catalogue so need to buy before you try. ££

0870 1515 700

www.greatuniversal.com

H&M

Great maternity range. Shame it's not universally available in all branches. Reasonably priced and fashion conscious. ££

020 7323 2211

www.hm.com

Isabella Oliver

Classically beautiful clothes with emphasis on creating the perfect capsule wardrobe. Basic pieces you will want to live in forever. Pricey! £££ – ££££

0870 240 7612

www.isabellaoliver.com

Jojo Maman Bebe

Great for basics and stronger occasion pieces such as dresses. Well priced and well made. £££

www.jojmamanbebe.com

Maternity Wear Exchange

Quality new and nearly-new maternity wear at discount prices. Great service with a 10-day no-quibbles return service. Well reviewed. ££ -£££

www.maternityexchange.co.uk

Seraphine

Makers of the maternity *jean du jour!* Also sells fabulous basic range of tops, trousers and skirts and special occasion dresses. £££ – ££££

020 7937 3156

www.seraphine.com

TopShop

Great-on-trend maternity range from this high street giant. Well priced and suited to younger fashion-conscious mums-to-be. ££ – ££££

0870 606 9666

www.topshop.com

Vertbaudet

In addition to great kids' clothes this company also stocks a good range of maternity wear including lingerie and swimwear. ££ – £££

0845 270 1880

www.vertbaudet.co.uk

Underwear and hosiery

Figleaves Maternity Underwear

Huge range of styles and colours to choose from with good range of prices from budget to spoil yourself! ££ – ££££   www.figleaves.com

Maternity Tights

Well-reviewed, albeit pricey, tights. Still, probably worth it in the later months! £££   01353 624 624   www.pebbleuk.com

MotherNature

Great range for all budgets. Offers sizing assistance and a swimwear section, too. ££ – £££   01782 824242   www.mothernaturebras.co.uk

Royce Lingerie

Emphasising a new mum's desire to look elegant and feel sexy this site has a great range of attractive as well as practical bras. Very reasonable prices, too. £££   01295 265557   www.royce-lingerie.co.uk

Bridal wear

Tiffany Rose

Beautiful gowns and special occasion wear. Not the cheapest but not intended for everyday either! £££ – ££££   0870 420 8144
www.tiffanyrosematernity.com

Brides 'N' Bumps

A huge range of bridal dresses and accessories available in sizes 6 -24. It even stocks dresses for pregnant bridesmaids! Prices on a par with conventional high end bridal wear. £££-££££   01252 377725   www.bridesnbumps.com

Fleur Uno

Smallish range but everything at the time of writing was under £100 so fantastic for those on a budget. Classic designs, too. ££   0115 913 0665
www.fleuruno.co.uk

Swellegant Maternity Hire

As the name suggests, this online boutique offers all manner of maternity outfits, including bridal gowns on a per hire basis. Quite pricey per wear but worth it for your special day. £££ – ££££   01279 810814
www.swellegant.co.uk

Buyer's Guide to Reusable Nappies

My own journey

One of the realities of having a new baby is the endless rounds of nappy changing that you have to contend with. Straight after the birth, most parents cannot countenance anything other than disposables – certainly not until they have settled themselves into a daily routine.

Eventually, however, you may start to wonder what exactly happens to the millions of nappies parents use everyday, and to consider the natural and sociological strain their disposal causes. For some people, this realisation is the first step in switching to reusable nappies.

Before I got pregnant I was well aware of ecological issues and did my best to follow initiatives such as recycling, using energy saving light bulbs, etc. I must confess that this was not pure altruism, as I quickly found that living ecologically also benefited me financially.

When I became pregnant I was forced to look at the issue of the type of nappy I wanted to use for my baby. I did, and still do, live in a tiny flat with no garden and absolutely no interior drying space. I did not even have a tumble drier, yet I still could not bring myself to contribute to the 8 million disposable nappies which are used everyday in the UK alone. The more I looked into the disposable issue the more shocked I became, which eventually gave me the push I needed to make the move to reusables.

Lest I give the impression of being holier-than-thou, I confess that for the first three weeks following birth I *did* use disposables. I was reeling from the ordeal of a complicated 28 hour labour and the idea of folding, wrapping and laundering cloth nappies did not appeal in the slightest. I also still occasionally use disposables when going on extended trips with my son and at night, as for convenience and absorbency they generally can't be beaten.

Once they get the hang of reusables, however, most parents don't look back. On average they take about a minute more than disposables to put on your baby, and though there *is* the issue of laundering them, to be honest with all the additional washing that a baby creates, an extra load every 2-3 days doesn't make much difference. The one concession I did make was to invest in a tumble drier which increased the ecological and financial cost but in my small flat is essential.

In recent years, the cost of disposables to the environment has become such a concern that some councils now offer parents incentives to switch to reusables. These vary from a free starter pack to heavily-subsidised laundry services. I have even heard of one council which provides free ironing! The waste management department of your council will let you know if they participate in such a scheme.

If you are looking at, or even just considering the idea of reusable nappies, I hope that this section will provide food for thought. The nappy issue is a big one, and all parents should have access to the facts before making an informed decision about which nappy to use.

Different types of reusable nappy explained

Flat nappies

These types of nappy bear the closest resemblance to the ones that previous generations used, but nowadays come in a variety of different sizes to fit across the age ranges. They can also be folded to offer more absorbancy down the central core where it's needed.

Generally, all nappies in this category are folded and fastened with either pins or special clips called Nippas and/or covered with a waterproof wrap. The wraps are generally made of modern, breathable fabrics or even wool which has a natural moisture-repellent property. The wraps are generally fastened with Velcro, poppers or an elastic waistband.

Shaped nappies

These can be made of cotton flannel or terry towelling and are shaped and elasticated at the waist and leg to give a more snug fit. Unlike flat nappies, they do not need to be folded prior to use and are secured either with Velcro or poppers before being covered with a separate waterproof cover.

Shaped nappies are more expensive, costing between £4 and £10 each. As your baby grows you will generally need to buy a bigger size although some manufacturers now make shaped nappies to last throughout the pre-toilet years which you simply adjust with the aid of poppers or ties.

The cost of disposables, and the virtue of reusables

- A child in disposables for an average of two and a half years will probably use around 6,000 nappies. This compares to 25-50 nappies for the same child using reusables.

- It is still not known how long disposables take to biodegrade, although it is probable that the very first to be manufactured are still in existence today and will continue to be for hundreds of years. 50% of all the rubbish in a typical one-baby family is composed of disposable nappies.

- Compared to reusable nappies, disposables use 90 times the amount of renewable resources and 8 times the amount of non-regenerable resources. For example, each disposable uses one cup of crude oil to manufacture.

- At least four and a half trees are destroyed for each child using disposables until they are toilet trained.

- Every council tax payer pays 10p to dispose of every £1 worth of disposables. This amounts to £40 million each year in taxes.

- The cost of disposables is more than ecological: to take a baby from birth to toilet training will cost from around £700 (the cheapest brand) to £1,200 (the most expensive). By contrast, a reusable birth-to-potty pack costs around £400. This includes the cost of the nappies, accessories, washing agents, energy and allowing for £150 wear and tear on a washing machine. Of course, this cost goes down considerably if you buy second hand or on the internet. I bought my birth-to-potty pack, brand new and with extras, for £60 on eBay.

- Reusables can often last for more than one baby and do not contain any potentially irritant super-absorbent gels, deodorants or chemicals. Also, because they are made from the same fibres that we use in normal clothing, the risk of an allergic reaction to reusables is much lower. Despite initial fears to the contrary, research has also shown that there is no evidence of a higher incidence of nappy rash amongst babies in reusable nappies.

- Unlike the nappies our mothers' generation struggled with, today's reusable nappies are much simpler to use. Some use 100% biodegradeable liners which contain solid material and can be disposed of like toilet paper. Nappies are then placed in a lidded bucket and put into the wash every two to three days on a 60 degree cycle. The wraps can be rinsed or washed at 40 degrees and left to air dry. A tumble drier does of course make the whole cycle quicker and easier although if you have the space, line drying is just as effective. If you really can't bear the thought of laundering the nappies yourself visit the National Association of Nappy Services website at www.changeanappy.co.uk, or call 0121 693 4949 to see what's available to you locally.

- There is such a variety of reusables to choose from now that they can address almost all the problems that disposables tackle, from a newborn's runny poo to a bigger child wetting at night and later on, to hybrid 'pull-up' types of nappy pants.

Source: "Dumping the Diaper: Sustainable Wales' s Reusable Nappy Report" (2nd Edition) Supported by the Women's Environmental Network.

All-in-ones

These are a shaped nappy as above but do not require a separate waterproof wrap as they have an integral waterproof layer built into them.

What will I need if I choose reusables?

Before investing a large sum in a particular manufacturer's nappy, buy trial packs from across the ranges to see which one you prefer. You will also need a washing machine to make this a viable option and preferably, although not essentially, a tumble drier, too. Many terry and shaped nappies are on the thick side and can therefore take a long time to dry naturally. If you don't have a tumble drier this may mean that you have to buy more of the nappies than you otherwise would, just so you have some always ready.

Alternatively you could use a laundering service which basically takes your dirty nappies away to wash and at the same time brings you a fresh clean supply. Contact the National Association of Nappy Services (0121 693 4949) for more information about services in your area.

Once you've made your choice you will need to buy an adequate supply of your chosen brand. Most parents find that they need about 18 nappies and about 6-8 wraps to begin with (the wraps need not be changed with every nappy). This can add up to quite a big initial outlay but do check with your local council for any financial or practical incentives which they may offer.

There is absolutely nothing wrong with buying second hand cloth nappies but if you are worried about cross-infection remember that these are designed to be washed at high temperatures or even microwaved!

If you decide to use flat nappies you will need to learn how to fold them and to have a supply of ready folded ones to hand. Some nappies need to be folded according to whether you have a boy or a girl (with the absorbency prioritised to different places on the nappy). It is worthwhile having a practice before your baby arrives, perhaps on a doll or teddy, as it can be hard getting them to fit snugly on small and newborn babies.

Other items you may want to consider are booster pads (recommended for night-time wear), plastic pants, nappy pins or Nippas, and liners. You will also need a large lidded bucket in which to store dirty nappies before washing.

Advantages of disposable nappies

In the interests of balance it is only fair to state the case for the other side, although with the sales statistics quoted earlier it is obvious that the manufacturers of disposables need no help in their marketing.

What I hope is that you will weigh up the arguments on both sides, before deciding whether the convenience of disposables is worth the financial, chemical and ecological price that they exact.

- Disposables are compact and easy to carry around, meaning less bulk for your bag. There is also no transportation of wet/soiled nappies involved.

- They are very easy to use, meaning that most members of the family, young and old can help with nappy changing.

- They are very widely available, even on garage forecourts and local corner shops, so you will never be caught short.

- They take, on average, less time to assemble and put on your baby than reuseables.

- You don't have to 'handle' poo whereas you may have to scrape the contents of real nappies into the loo. (Did you know, by the way, that wrapping poo in disposables is actually against World Health Organisation guidelines, on health grounds?!)

- You don't have to worry about doing nappy washes or having them hanging round the house to dry.

- When first introduced in the 1950s they played a big part in emancipating women, enabling them to get away from the washtub and allowing their husbands and partners to actively participate in the care of the baby. However, with the huge technological leaps we have made regarding washing machines, etc, this may be slightly less of an issue nowadays.

A compromise? The case for eco-disposable nappies

There is no doubt that disposables are convenient, especially when you are out and about or holidaying with your baby, but concern about their ecological impact is now loud and insistent. In response to this, some firms have latched onto the idea of creating eco-friendly disposables, designed to be both convenient *and* ecologically sound.

If you cut open a conventional disposable nappy you will probably find white granules inside: these are acrylic acid polymer salts which turn to gel on contact with water (urine). These chemical granules are used to increase absorbency but the gel they form can end up on your baby's skin.

In eco-friendly disposables, fewer chemicals are used so harmful waste products are considerably reduced, and they do not generally use bleaching agents which pollute the environment during manufacture and decomposition.

You can also buy completely gel-free disposables which are made of a cotton blend and are also perfume, dye and latex free. This means that they can be up to 70% biodegradable.

Examples of eco-disposable brands include Tushies, available from Green Baby, which are free from chemical absorbants and contain non-chlorine bleached wood pulp. They are also gel, dye, perfume and latex free. Moltex unbleached disposable nappies from The Natural Baby Company are unscented with no unnecessary deodorants or chemical dyes. They are also anatomically shaped to direct moisture into the centre, have Velcro fastenings with variable adjustment, and feature a cloth-like breathable back sheet for improved comfort.

Even mainstream supermarkets such as Waitrose and Sainsburys now stock eco-disposables such as Nature Baby which boast a 70% Biodegradable composition and which have even been featured on the TV series *Friends* – how's that for popularist product placement!

As you might expect, the retail cost of these nappies is considerably higher than normal disposables. Depending on your priorities, you may consider this an acceptable price to pay for a clearer conscience.

The Environment Agency Life Cycle Analysis
on Disposable and Reusable Nappies – May 2005

In 2005, the Environment Agency commissioned a report in an attempt to answer categorically whether there was any real virtue in using a reusable nappy system over a disposable system. Like other commentators before them, the EA concluded that the most significant environmental impacts for the use of nappies were the using up of resources such as fossil fuels for electricity, acid rain and global warming, impacts which happen at different points in a nappy's use.

Perhaps surprisingly, the study concluded that there were no significant benefits to using a reusable nappy system, as the environmental 'savings' made at one end of the spectrum (landfill and use of fossil fuels) were wasted at the other (global warming through laundering of cloth nappies).

Since the report was published other environmental agencies, perhaps most vocally the Women's Environmental Network (WEN), have raised their voices in dissent against the findings of this study. In particular they have criticised the methodology employed, citing poorly-managed and unrepresentative sample sizes and basic contradictions contained within the report itself. Crucially, they believe that the Environment Agency's study seems to ignore the fact that although both systems may use similar amounts of energy, reusables use less materials and therefore have a much smaller impact on landfill. This means that parents who use a reusable system will both save on waste and cause no more global warming than users of disposable nappies.

I doubt this is the end of the debate and, as stressed throughout the course of this book, I am passionately in favour of individual choice in every aspect of life. However, I also believe in our decisions being made on the basis of sound information and, to this end, invite you to read both sides of the story at:

www.environmentagency.gov.uk/yourenv/857406/1072214

and at

www.wen.org.uk/general_pages/Newsitems/ms_LCA19.5.05.htm

Stockist contact details

Bambino Mio

Two-piece cotton nappy system with optional biodegradable liner. Nice range of designs. £££

01604 883 777   www.bambinomio.com

Cotton Bottoms

Two-piece cotton nappy system made by Tommee Tippee. Optional liner. £££

0500 97 98 99   www.cottonbottoms.co.uk

Ellas House

Hemp and fleece nappy system with optional boosters and stuffable inserts. £££

01955 641358   www.ellashouse.co.uk

Fuzzibunz

Nappies made from custom-milled microfleece with a pocket to hold the nappy insert and a waterproof outer layer. £££   www.fuzzibunz.com

Green Baby

Wide range of reuseables and eco-disposables as well as organically sourced baby toiletries. ££ – £££

0870 240 6894   www.greenbaby.co.uk

Minki

Very attractive and fun-looking nappies with the advantage of being able to change the absorbancy levels according to the filling you insert. Three-layer construction. £££ – ££££

0141 550 1514   www.nappiesbyminki.co.uk

The Natural Baby Company

Sells two brands of eco-disposable nappy as well as eco-friendly nappy wipes. ££££

01983 810 925   www.naturalbabycompany.com

Tots Bots

Shaped nappies in a wide range of colours and differently weighted fabrics depending on your personal preference. Trial/multipacks available in addition to great advice and support. £££

0141 550 1514   www.totsbots.com

Buyer's Guide to
Child-Proofing and Safety Around the Home

In the first few weeks after bringing your baby home, life is hectic but at least there's one problem you are temporarily spared: initially, you see, babies don't really *go* anywhere. You can put them down on a bed, sofa, or armchair and there they will stay (happily or otherwise) till you decide to pick them up.

Fast forward a few months and it's a whole different ball game. All of a sudden they have somehow learnt to roll, grab, pull and otherwise move in an erratic fashion when you are least expecting it. If there were prizes for moving backwards my son would win everything going, as he can currently traverse a six and a half foot bed in 4 seconds flat.

This, of course, is all part of normal development, even though it's likely to provoke a nervous breakdown for you! Suddenly, innocuous parts of your home are transformed into the perilous baby equivalent of the Cresta Run.

When this happens you have no choice: **you must baby-proof your home**. Much of this is common sense, so do not be beguiled by some of the so-called experts who offer to pay you a visit and advise you on what you should do. Many people who have done this, out of a genuine concern for their baby's safety, have been conned out of thousands of pounds for baby-proofing equipment that they did not need for at least another five years, if ever. One lady I read about was persuaded to put expensive locks on a set of cupboards that even her fourteen year old had not yet grown tall enough to reach.

Before you think about shelling out for safety equipment, have a good look around your home and think about it from a baby's point of view. You might even try getting down on the floor so that you can really gain a sense of the world from their perspective. What potential dangers can you see? Look beyond the obvious, such as stairways or balconies, to objects that may prove tempting to a baby's inquisitive gaze, such as an open handbag or briefcase. Don't forget too, their tendency to explore everything with their mouths at this stage and act accordingly by moving anything ingestible well out of their reach.

In this section, we'll be taking a tour of the home to see what changes can be made simply and inexpensively, just through common sense.

Kitchen

- Don't keep knives and other dangerous kitchen equipment in drawers or cupboards that a baby or small child can reach. If this is unavoidable, fit locks on all the drawers and doors.

- Drawers containing non-threatening items such as linen or tea towels should be fitted with anti-slam covers to prevent little fingers becoming trapped.

- Ensure that knife blocks, where used, are kept well back from the counter's edge and are not resting on a tea towel or tablecloth that a young child could potentially pull onto themselves. Better still, lock all knives and other sharp objects away completely.

- Lock up ammonia and other household cleaning products. It only takes a minute for a child to open and drink the contents of a bottle. Don't be seduced into a false sense of security by so-called child-proof caps – it is too easy to forget to tighten them properly after use.

- Place foods and drinks, especially hot ones, away from the counter/table edge. Avoid the use of tablecloths that can be pulled from a baby's level.

- Use rear stove burners for cooking and, if you have a narrow galley-style kitchen, consider putting a stairgate across the opening to prevent your child getting under your feet and into the path of danger. If you have to use the front burners of your hob make sure that handles are placed inwards away from the front of the stove.

- If using a highchair in the kitchen area make sure that your child is securely strapped into his harness and clean up any spills immediately to avoid slipping or tripping accidents.

Bathroom

- Store both prescription and non-prescription drugs and medicines in a locked cabinet, preferably at a height that cannot be reached by children.

- Remove and lock up any cleaning materials. Don't forget toilet cleaners and brushes which are often placed next to the lavatory itself.

- Never leave a child unattended in the bath, as they can drown in a few centimeters of water. To prevent burns, set the water heater at a low temperature and test the water before putting the child in the bath. Purchase a plastic disc which changes colour on contact with water that is either too hot or cold, or invest in a bath thermometer. Check that these devices are still working from time to time. You can also buy sleeves to go over bath taps to prevent children burning themselves whilst sitting too close.

> "Never leave a child unattended in a bath, as they can drown in a few centimetres of water."

- To reduce the chance of electrical shocks, make sure that you unplug items such as hair dryers and electric razors when not in use and cover redundant sockets with safety covers. Ensure that items such as razor blades are never left out on the sides of the bath or sink area.

Utility Room

- Lock up bleach and other cleaning supplies.

- Do not leave the iron unattended and ensure that the cord is stowed away up high when not in use.

- If you use a chest freezer make sure that it is fitted with a child lock and that washing machines and tumble driers, which children can easily fit themselves or other objects into, are child-proofed.

Living Room

- Keep fragile or heavy objects and ornaments away from the edges of tables, bookcases, etc. Store any potentially dangerous objects behind cabinet doors or place them high up so as not to be in harm's way.

- Fit locks on the flaps of DVD and video players and store remote controls out of the reach of babies. They can easily open the battery compartments and remove batteries which contain dangerous acids.

- Fit cushioned corners onto the edges of coffee tables to prevent them coming into contact with faces and eyes.

Baby's Room

- Ensure that mobiles are a safe distance above the cot and cannot be pulled down by the baby.

- All toys should be age-appropriate and hold the appropriate safety marks (see pages 103-104 for information on safety marks and what they mean).

- Check that no toys contain parts that are smaller than 1.5 inches thick or 2.5 inches long, as they are a choking risk.

- Don't put stuffed toys into the cot with the baby as they pose a suffocation risk.

- When the baby is old enough to stand, remove anything from the cot sides which could enable them to climb out of the cot.

- Make sure that the gap between the mattress and the cot sides is no more than 4cm so that the baby cannot trap an arm or a leg in it.

- Night lights and other sleep aids should remain cool to the touch when in operation. Make sure that any curtains, bedding and window treatments are never in proximity to naked flames such as candles or night lights.

- When using a changing table ensure that the child is strapped in at all times.

All Rooms

- Pay attention to the location of chairs and other furniture that the child can climb onto or into. Fit soft bumpers onto the edges of all furniture that the baby may come into contact with.

- Install window and door locks especially, but not exclusively, if you have balconies and/or are above the ground floor.

- Check which household agents are toxic when ingested by humans and keep these away from babies and children. If an accident occurs, make sure that you take any packaging with you to the hospital so that immediate medical attention can be given.

- Keep all plastic bags and wrappings away from babies and children.

- Ensure that they do not play unsupervised with ribbons or other cords which could prove a strangulation risk.

- Install and regularly check smoke alarms to ensure the batteries are working.

- Put up safety gates to keep infants away from hazardous areas such as stairs and steps.

Buyer's Guide to Safety Gates

Once your baby starts to crawl, explore or use a walker, it is time to install safety gates around your home wherever there are potential hazards, including at the top and bottom of staircases and at the entrance to rooms such as the kitchen and bathrooms. As well as creating a physical barrier, the presence of safety gates acts as a visual reminder to babies and small children that certain areas are off-limits.

Before purchasing a safety gate you should bear in mind the different types available, their features and the correct and safe way to use them.

Different models explained

Most safety gates are made of metal although there are some models available in a wood finish. Both types have bars which make it easier to see what your baby is getting up to on the other side. Other types of gate are made from an opaque cloth or other flexible material and tend to hide your baby from view. On the plus side, they are portable and therefore ideal for travelling.

There are three basic types of opening used in safety gates:

1. Centre-opening

These have fixed sections on each side and a gate in the middle. This tends to give a narrower opening width which is not adjustable. In addition, centre-opening gates generally have a floor bar at their base which adds to their stability but can sometimes be hazardous for vulnerable people such as grandparents or older children.

2. Side-opening

These gates have no or only one fixed section on the hinged side, so offer a wider opening through which to pass. The downside is that you may need more room for the gate to swing out into, although some models overcome this problem by having a gate which simply rolls open like a blind. Most of these types of gate do not have a floor bar.

3. Fixed barrier

Fixed barrier gates have to be removed each time you go through the opening and refixed afterwards, so from a convenience point of view they are really only suited to doorways that are seldom used. On the plus side they are easily transportable (some come with their own carry bag) so they are a good option to take on holiday where the childproofing facilities may not be adequate for your needs.

Fixing gates

All gates should come with their original fixing instructions. If you are buying second hand, ask the seller whether the instructions are included and if not see whether you are able to obtain a copy direct from the manufacturer or download them from its website. Instructions must be followed to the letter even if the gate appears straightforward, as an improperly-fitted gate is dangerous and liable to fail. All gates should be fitted against sound walls or sturdy banisters.

Gates should be labelled with the minimum and maximum sized openings they can be used in. Some gates are available with extensions although there is a limit to the number you can use, and you should be aware that any extension can compromise the integrity of the gate as a whole. Because of this you should look for a gate that will fit the area in which you intend to use it without having to resort to add-ons.

Gates come with a variety of fixings, as follows:

Pressure-mounted

With this type of fixing, the gate is held in place by the pressure of the fitting. The pressure is managed by turning a small handwheel until the gate is wedged tightly against the walls. The advantage of pressure-mounted gates is that they are quick to install as they require no drilling. This also means that they can be moved/removed easily without leaving holes.

Although convenient, pressure-mounted gates do need a certain amount of strength and dexterity to turn the handwheel which should also be checked regularly and tightened if necessary. Be careful of overtightening, however, especially on banisters as this can warp the wood.

This is the best type of gate to use across a variety of openings or if you do not want the mess associated with drilling holes or sticking pads to your walls. Pressure-mounted gates should not, however, be used at the top of stairways as they cannot withstand as much pressure as wall-mounted gates.

Screw-fixed

Some of these gates have parts that screw directly into the wall, but most now come with up to four cups which are screwed into the wall and into which the corners of the gate slot. Sometimes the cups are only necessary when the walls or banisters are not firm, although do be guided by the instructions.

Self-adhesive

As an alternative to screw fixings, some gates come with cups that have self-adhesive pads attached which simply stick to the wall. These are generally only suitable for smooth, sound walls, however, so beware of sticking them to wallpapered walls or loose plaster.

Features to look out for

One-handed release

Look out for gates with a one-handed release mechanism. As the name implies, these allow you to open and lock a gate with one hand which will be useful for those times when you are carrying the baby.

Opening mechanism

If manual dexterity is an issue for you or for someone else in your home, look for a gate that can be opened and closed with a whole hand action; the easiest and most comfy are those handles which can be squeezed, especially where these are also cushioned. Look also for a generous-sized lever which can be operated with any part of the hand to lift and open the gate.

Opening direction

Some gates are dual or bi-directional (i.e. they can be opened in either direction). These are more useful and practical than gates which open in only one direction. The exception to this is at the bottom of stairs when the gate can only, obviously, open towards you. Some manufacturers, such as Lindam, sell a couple of models that feature adjustable door stops. These can be turned so that the gate can open both ways, one way, or be locked in order to make the gate into a non-opening barrier. These are an excellent idea unless you would find it difficult to bend down and adjust the stop.

Transparency

If it is important for you to keep an eye on your baby *through* the gate choose either a transparent screen or a gate with bars. The opaque mesh variety do tend to make this much more difficult.

Locking confirmation

For peace of mind you can buy gates that make a reassuring click to tell you that they have been locked correctly. Other models feature a coloured disc which shows green when locked and red when open.

Gate width

Ensure that the gate opening is wide enough for you and other users to walk through in comfort; ideally this should be 50cm or more. If there are wheelchair users in your house you will have to take their needs into account, especially if you are considering installing a gate with a floor bar. If floor bars are unavoidable, try finding a model with optional flip-down step plates to facilitate movement through them.

Conformity with safety standards

Ensure that the gate you buy conforms to the European Safety Standard BSEN 1930:2000. This is a European standard for childcare safety barriers that includes safety requirements. Be aware, however, that gates do not *have* to comply with the standard and some that claim to comply do not meet all the requirements. If you come across a gate labeled BS 4125:1991 you should know that this standard is now out of date and has been withdrawn.

Aesthetics

If aesthetics are important to you, gates now come in a variety of materials including wood, plastic, plastic-coated steel, and soft mesh.

Safety considerations

The stairs are the most dangerous part of a house for young children. In 1999, the last year for which figures have been analysed, 35,000 under 4s were admitted to A & E departments in the UK for accidents involving a fall down the stairs. Having a safety gate at the top and at the bottom of the stairs, and ensuring that it is kept closed, will reduce these risks. If you have older children in the house, make sure that they, too, are vigilant in their use of safety gates and understand the risks involved in not using them correctly.

Parents and other adults should also take care around gates, as many injuries are caused each year by adults climbing over the gate instead of walking through it. Babies are most often injured by improperly-closed gates or when they follow their parents through the gate unseen.

Below are some common sense rules for minimising the risk of injury:

- Follow the manufacturer's instructions carefully and anchor the safety gate firmly in the doorway or staircase. When installing a gate with expanding pressure bars, install the bar side away from the baby since pressure bars have been known to be used as toeholds in order to climb over a gate.

- Always close the gate behind you when leaving the room, but only after checking that a toddler or baby is not trying to follow behind you.

- Stop using the gate when your child is 36 inches tall or two years old, whichever is soonest. A safety gate should never be less than three quarters of your child's height since they can climb over a gate which is not high enough.

- At the top of the stairs, do not fit the gate below the level of the first stair. At the bottom, fit the gate on the lowest stair.

- Do not hang toys from a stairgate where they can attract the attention of a baby or toddler.

Useful organisations

Child Accident Prevention Trust
020 7608 3828
www.capt.org.uk

Parentline Plus
0808 800 2222
www.parentlineplus.org.uk

Manufacturers and brands

Centre-opening gates	BabyDan Premier Pressure Gate Beldray Guardian Bettacare Autoclose Gate Lindam EasyFit Premium Lindam Two-Way Safety Gate Mothercare Deluxe Easy Lock
Side-opening gates	BabyDan Multidan Beechwood Bettacare Twist and Lock Opening Gate Brevi Securella Lascal KiddyGuard Safety 1st Pressure Gate
Fixed gates	Bruin Travel Barrier Mothercare Foldaway Travel Barrier Tomy Soft Safety Barrier

Stockist contact details

Babydan

Award-winning manufacturer and member of the Global Safety Corporation. Specialises in designing innovative products to keep children safe. Wide range of products and prices. ££ – ££££

01704 537 843   www.babydan.com

Bettacare

Manufacturers of auto-closing and extending safety gates as well as fireguards. Attractive and unobtrusive. Well priced. ££ – £££

01293 851 896   www.bettacare.co.uk

Clippasafe

Over 45 years' experience in manufacturing child safety equipment. Their innovations include a bump belt for women driving in pregnancy in addition to safety gates, fireguards and various gadgets to safeguard children in and around the home. Wonderful range. Well priced. ££ – £££

0115 921 1899   www.clippasafe.co.uk

Safety 1st

Wide range of gates and smaller care products such as bath thermometers. Quite hard to find but reasonably priced. ££ – £££

01256 356 756   www.safety1st.com

Mothercare

Great choice and advice from this retailing giant. ££ – £££

0845 330 4030   www.mothercare.com

Lindam

A range of metal and wooden gates that are easy to fit and use in addition to being very well priced. Widely available. ££ – £££

08701 118118   www.lindam.com

Cheeky Rascals (for Lascal)

Revolutionary design which works on the same principle as a roller blind which makes it unobtrusive and easy to use. Not the cheapest, but one of the easiest to operate, especially for those with limited dexterity. £££

01428 682488   www.cheekyrascals.co.uk

Having a Baby
on eBay

Why shop at eBay?

In terms of internet traffic, eBay no longer flies under the radar. Indeed, research suggests that one third of active internet users in the UK now visit the UK version of the site each month.

I have long regarded eBay as one of those rites of passage that every computer user eventually undergoes. Like a strange, almost deviant pursuit, everyone talks about it, some people do it in secret, and the rest have at least thought about trying it! I have even seen financial makeover programmes which attempt to 'wean' addicted participants off their daily eBay habit. If, by chance, you have failed to encounter eBay when browsing the internet, you will probably have seen the slick TV advertisements which, using the mantra *"Buy it, Sell it, Love it"*, spearhead its campaign for retail domination.

eBay has, in the space of a few years, made buying second hand goods respectable, and, arguably, threatened the livelihoods of smaller independent shops. Charities like Oxfam, fearing a downturn in their high street sales, have jumped on the internet auction bandwagon, becoming sellers on the site and offering selected vintage pieces from stock. Their philosophy, it seems, has changed from one of David vs. Goliath to 'if you can't beat 'em join 'em'.

The reason that so many consumers have moved from conventional retailers to eBay is the same reason that we all trek to supermarkets these days instead of our friendly local corner shop: **choice**. Never in the real world could we hope to visit a retail outlet with 25 million items in stock at any one time.

The second reason, of course, is the potential to bag a genuine bargain. But do they really exist?

The answer is a definite 'yes', even though with so much inventory there is, of course, a fair amount of dross available, too. The great thing is – you don't having to physically battle your way through the crowds to get to the bargains, something which, if you're pregnant, is the last thing you want to do. Nor do you have to carry your purchases home on the bus. My own personal triumphs from eBay have included:

- a £200 cot for £11.50
- a £400 designer pram for £200

Both brand new, boxed and delivered. Other successes have included:

- baby clothing
- kitchen equipment
- a one-off designer maternity dress for £15 which I proudly wore to give my best friend away at her wedding.

Of course, as I mentioned in the introduction to this book, by the time I found out I was expecting my son I was already something of an eBay veteran, having stumbled onto the site in late 1999. Now, eight years on, much of what I own and value today, from an incredibly beautiful 1940s oak cabinet, to the replacement heads for my electric toothbrush, I bought from the site.

As it has grown, eBay has become much more than the glorified boot sale of its early years, and although the vast majority of its items are still offered by individuals clearing out their attics, there are also thousands of businesses operating on the site selling anything from new cuddly toys to Lear jets.

Apart from the pleasure of snapping up a bargain, many people 'do' eBay for the experience itself, and this has certainly been a factor in my own involvement over the years. There are few other experiences to be had from the comfort of your own armchair which manage to combine desire, predation, excitement and finally, either the ecstasy of triumph or the sickening lurch of defeat. And despite what many people say about the number of hours wasted surfing eBay I have probably *saved* hours by not having to travel to and trawl shops for a relatively limited range of stock.

The purpose of this section is to explain the rudiments of eBay, from registering with the site, to searching for goods, to bidding on items, and finally to paying. Mixed in with this, I provide in-depth advice on how to do all the above efficiently and productively.

There will be lots of tips and tricks, gleaned from personal experience and from that of other seasoned eBayers, as well as sections addressing issues such as security, and what to do if you do have a less than perfect transaction. The aim is to enable you to buy all of what you need both during and after your pregnancy for the lowest possible price and still have some left over for you!

So, let's begin with a brief overview of what eBay is and how it works...

A brief history of eBay

Frequently copied, never bettered, eBay was founded in 1995, and is now firmly established as the dominant force in internet auctions.

Like other breakthrough business concepts, eBay combined an old idea – auction selling – with new technology – the internet. The brains behind the site was Pierre Omidyar, who, like all great entrepreneurs, actually did something about a hunch he had. He knew that auctions had been around forever, dating in one form or another to the ancient civilisations. His genius was to realise that the internet provided a new way for buyers and sellers to participate on a mass scale, and to correctly predict the popularity of a site which synthesised the twin passions of making money and spending it.

eBay, now represented internationally through numerous sister sites, presently has about 120 million users worldwide, almost 10 million of whom are registered in the UK. The items on its 25 million strong inventory range from the mundane to the bizarre and have included Mrs Thatcher's handbag (which went for £15,000) to a Gulfstream Jet which went for nearly three and a half million pounds – the single most expensive sale on the site which netted a pretty hefty commission for eBay!

Whilst lining its own pockets, eBay has also spawned a number of millionaires amongst its members, mainly businesses who have used the site to reach a global marketplace beyond anything they could possibly achieve in a bricks and mortar environment. There have also been individual success stories, most recently of a young student who successfully auctioned advertising space on his website through eBay, charging bidders by the pixel and quickly earning himself the sort of money that could only be dreamt of by his peers.

eBay in a nutshell

Types of sale

There are basically two ways to buy and sell goods on eBay:

1. In an auction

Most second hand items are sold in a conventional auction which lasts between 1 and 10 days and in which, as you might expect, the highest bidder at the end of the auction wins.

2. 'Buy it Now'

The second option is what the site terms, rather prosaically, as 'Buy It Now'. This mainly involves *new* goods sold at a *fixed* price which are available *immediately* to the consumer without any auction taking place at all. It is a method mainly used by businesses because they, more than individuals, have stock of new goods.

Many of the businesses trading on eBay run their own '**eBay Shops**' from which they sell their entire inventory of items. Whilst part of the eBay marketplace, eBay shops have their own unique flavour with customised content and displays. Many of the items available through these shops will be available on a 'Buy It Now' basis. You can tell if a seller runs an eBay shop because they have a red door next to their user ID, like this:

Another place on eBay where you can buy items on a Buy It Now basis is **eBay Express**. This is a fairly new initiative for eBay and only features brand new items sold at a fixed price. In addition, all items bought through eBay Express have the added benefit of being covered by the Consumer Protection (Distance Selling) Regulations 2000 which guarantees you a refund or replacement within seven days should you be unhappy for any reason. As the only items on eBay currently offering this protection as a *requirement of listing* it's a good option for people looking to buy with peace of mind.

Getting started

Although you can browse the site without registering, in order to buy or sell you need to have an eBay account. This can be done from the site's home page and its 'register' link. Although registering is free you need to provide proof of your identity in the form of a valid email address plus credit or debit card details. You also need to choose a unique username and password. As powerful encryption handles this data, registration is at least as secure as any other type of online transaction.

Once your registration has been confirmed you can buy and sell straightaway, but new users would be well advised to spend a few minutes browsing the site and watching the easy-to-use tutorials. These can be accessed through the 'eBay explained' link, also on the home page.

Fees

eBay makes its money by charging sellers a fee when they list an item on the site. As well as this 'insertion' fee, sellers also pay a fee if the item they have listed actually sells (not all items find a buyer). This is called the 'final value fee' and is calculated as a percentage of the selling price. Buyers do not pay fees.

Bidding

Whenever you bid on, win, or are outbid on an item, eBay notifies you instantly by email. If you win an item, you are expected to pay the seller within a reasonable time (on average three to five days after the end of the auction).

Paying for items

Payment methods are specified by the seller in the item description. They can include concealed cash, (now being outlawed by the site but still used by some sellers), cash on delivery, cheque, postal order, banker's draft, or an electronic payment system called PayPal which was once independent but is now owned by eBay. Payments through PayPal are free to buyers, but sellers, depending on the type of account they hold, have to pay a fee based on the value of the transaction.

Of the payment methods outlined above, PayPal is by far the most secure and efficient, especially for relatively high value items such as large electronic goods, as the money is immediately transferred into the seller's account. It is also a quick and simple method of buying from international sellers, and currency conversions are carried out immediately at the current rate.

Feedback

Many beginners on eBay, tempted by an item they see on the site, are (understandably) concerned about what happens if it turns out to be faulty, differs from its advertised description, or simply fails to materialise at all. To put your mind at rest, the vast majority of sales carried out on eBay proceed smoothly, and there is tremendous goodwill between buyers and sellers, supported by eBay's 'feedback' system.

Feedback operates by allowing both buyers and sellers to rate their experience of a transaction by grading the other party's behaviour as positive, negative or neutral. It is not obligatory to leave feedback, but most users do, and it is a very important feature of the site. Reading a buyer or a seller's feedback is your way of seeing both how actively they have traded and how the other parties to those transactions have rated their performance. Legitimate members take pride in their feedback and will usually do their best to resolve a dispute in order to avoid receiving negative comments.

Fraud protection

Sales conducted on eBay are a legally binding contract but only between the buyer and seller. eBay is not a party to the contract and has no legal liability if one side fails to honour its commitment.

It does, however, offer limited protection against fraud, up to a value of £120 (effectively reduced to £105 as there is a processing fee of £15). The amount of protection rises to £500 if payment is made using PayPal. If you paid using your credit card, there may be additional protection from your credit card company.

For really high value sales, such as those for a car, etc, there is also 'escrow', a service where payment is held by a third party and only passed on to the seller once the goods have been sent and received and the buyer is satisfied with the transaction. As you might expect, however, there is a fee for this service.

Before you can begin to buy or sell on eBay, you need to register with the site, so that's where we'll go next.

Registering with eBay for the first time

The link to register with eBay can be found at the top of most of its pages but it's probably easiest to locate it on the home page at www.ebay.co.uk.

Once you click on the *Register* link you will be asked to supply some personal details including your name, address, phone number and date of birth (See Fig. 1). You have to be at least 18 years old to buy or sell on the site, so if you have kids old enough to work the computer in your absence beware of them bidding on your behalf! The safest bet by far is to keep information like your username and password strictly confidential!

Fig. 1 – eBay's registration page

Register: Enter Information

1 **Enter Information**   2. Check Your Email

Register now to bid, buy, or sell on any eBay site worldwide. It's easy and **free**. Already registered? Sign in now.

Your Personal Information - All fields are required

Account Type
Individual Account   Change to Business Account
Business sellers should register with a business account. Learn more about business registration.

First name   Last name

Street address

Town / City

County   Post code   Country or Region
– Select County –   United Kingdom

Primary telephone
(   )
Example: (020) 12345678.
Required if there are questions about your account

Email address

A working email address is required to complete registration. Examples: myname@aol.com or myname@yahoo.com

As part of the registration process you need to supply a current email address. If you use an anonymous web-based email service such as Yahoo or Hotmail you also need to supply details of a valid credit or debit card in order to verify your identity. This is the only purpose these details will be used for and eBay will not make a charge on your card. If you prefer not to do this you will have to obtain another email address from an identifiable service provider.

eBay will then take you to a page where you need to read and agree to its User Agreement and Privacy Policy by ticking the check box.

Your username

After these preliminaries you will be asked to type in a username and password of your choice. The Username (also known as your 'User ID') will be your unique identity throughout your eBay career, and although you are permitted to change it, some sellers and buyers get suspicious of anyone who does this too frequently, as it may suggest some dubious activity such as trying to escape from previous bad feedback.

Your username should be memorable, although with 120 million registered users and rising, don't be surprised if your first choice is already taken. If it is, you will be informed via a pop-up and invited to choose a different ID. Many people simply use their own names or some variation of them, although for privacy reasons you may choose not to do this. You can't, by the way, use your email address as your username.

Choosing a username should be one of the more considered decisions you make, especially as some members will make assumptions – if not buying and selling decisions – based on what you are called. It's probably *not* a good idea, therefore, to choose something like *DoneARunner...*

Your password

Your password should be different from your username and be a word or combination of alpha-numeric keystrokes. When you input your password, eBay will indicate how potentially easy it is for others to guess it by displaying a coloured bar which goes darker the more secure it is. Your password obviously has security implications so you are advised to spend some time making it as impenetrable (whilst memorable by you!) as possible. A combination of letters and numbers is generally regarded as the most secure.

For additional security you will also be asked to provide the answer to a choice of questions – anything from your mother's maiden name to your pet's nickname.

After you have filled out these details, eBay will send you a confirmation email containing a link to a unique registration code. You need to click on this link in order to complete your registration, verifying to eBay that the email address you supplied is indeed your own. Incidentally, if you're sick of third party companies you've never even heard of bombarding you with unsolicited email don't worry. eBay operates a strict privacy policy which, under European law, prevents it from selling your name and details to junk mailers or spammers.

After you have completed this final step you're technically ready to rock and roll. Before you do so, however, you are advised to read a little more about how the site works and, in particular how its bidding system operates.

How eBay auctions work

Isn't eBay just like a normal auction?

Well, yes and no. If you've seen any of the recent glut of auction-based TV programmes you will have a pretty good idea of how a real-life auction works: the auctioneer sets a starting price (which may be lowered if there's no immediate interest) and bidders gradually raise this price by bidding one after the other until only one person remains. That person wins the auction, unless the seller had set a 'reserve' price (the minimum the item can be sold for) and the final bid failed to meet that reserve price.

eBay's online auctions work in much the same way but there are two important differences:

Fixed duration

Firstly, eBay auctions last for a fixed duration, set by the seller, which is anywhere between 1 and 10 days, but usually 7. Unlike a real auction, once this time has passed, the auction ends whether or not there are people still prepared to place a higher bid. Because of this, there are often lots of bids placed in the closing minutes of an auction, and I have personally watched as an item with a relatively modest current bid suddenly leaps by tens of pounds in the dying seconds.

Proxy bidding

The second important difference between eBay auctions and real-life auctions is that with eBay you don't have to keep raising your bid to stay in the auction. eBay operates a system of 'proxy bidding' whereby you nominate the maximum you are prepared to pay for an item, and eBay automatically bids on your behalf at one increment above the current high bid. This continues until you either win the item or your maximum is surpassed by another bidder.

The virtue of proxy bidding is that you can set what you hope will be a high enough maximum and then simply leave the auction to run its course, allowing you to get on with other things. In reality, of course, many people can't resist watching the auction all the way to the finish, sneaking in a higher amount should they be outbid. This tends to be one of the weird psychological symptoms of being an eBayer and at its worst can result in you bidding more than you can either afford or than the item is worth. We'll explore this phenomenon and how to avoid it later on in the book.

Proxy bidding can be a difficult concept for some people to grasp, so let's look at an illustration of how it might work in a hypothetical auction. Let's say you decide to bid on an item whose starting price has been set by the seller at £1.00. 'Starting price' simply means that the very first bid must be at the stated amount or above.

- You decide that a bid of £5 may be enough to win the auction and you enter it as the highest amount you are prepared to pay. What happens now is critical to the whole eBay proxy bidding system.

- eBay notes your highest bid of £5, but it does not display that figure to other buyers. Instead it shows that one person (you) has bid on the item and that the current bid price is £1 (the starting price). So even though you are prepared to pay £5, your first bid goes in at £1, which puts you in the position of leading bidder.

- If the auction ends without anyone else placing a bid, you will win the item at its start price of £1, even though you were prepared to pay £5. Your maximum bid, in other words, is not necessarily the amount you will pay for the item; it is just the maximum you are prepared to pay if the auction develops into a battle between rival bidders.

With good baby items, you will probably face stiff competition from other buyers so that by the time the auction ends there will have been several if not dozens of bids by different people, each bid higher than the previous one by a given 'increment'.

Increments

The 'increment' is the amount by which the price is raised each time a new bid is placed. This in turn depends on the current value of the item. For items selling at up to £1 in price, the increment increases by 5p. As the current bid price of the item rises, the increment increases, as the table overleaf shows:

Current Price	Bid Increment
£0.01 – £1.00	£0.05
£1.01 – £5.00	£0.20
£5.01 – £15.00	£0.50
£15.01 – £60.00	£1.00
£60.01 – £150.00	£2.00
£150.01 – £300.00	£5.00
£300.01 – £600.00	£10.00
£600.01 – £1,500.00	£20.00
£1,500.01 – £3,000.00	£50.00
£3,000.01 and up	£100.00

To see how this works, let's go back to the item which had a starting price of £1. When we last looked, you had placed the first bid with a maximum of £5 and you were the current 'high bidder' at a price of £1. Suppose that Buyer B bids a maximum of £3.50. How does the auction process reflect this?

Although higher than the current high bid of £1, B's bid is lower than your maximum of £5. For a notional split second, B was the high bidder on £3.50, but eBay remembered that you are prepared to pay £5, and therefore instantly restores you as the current high bidder at £3.70.

Why £3.70? Because even though you are prepared to pay £5, **eBay never puts you into the auction at more than you have to pay to be the high bidder.** Since B's bid was £3.50, and since the increment for items in this price band is 20p, the lowest price at which you can be the high bidder is £3.70. That's the price that eBay puts you back in at.

So, the moment Buyer B bids £3.50, the auction shows that there have been two bids (yours and B's), and that the current high bid is £3.70.

Let's say Buyer C comes along with a bid of £6.50, outbidding your maximum of £5. The screen will change to show that 3 bids have been placed and that the current high bid is £5.50 (your max of £5 plus a 50p increment).

In this situation, you would receive an email from eBay saying that you have been outbid, and the same email will invite you to bid again if you still want the item. Because of the increment at this price band (50p) you will have to bid more than £6 if you want to get back in the game.

Let's say you decide to bid £8.01. That's more than C's maximum of £6.50, so you will once again become the high bidder, this time at £7.00. If there are no more bids you will win the auction at £7.00.

Note that there is nothing to stop you bidding for an item, and then bidding again if your maximum is exceeded by another bidder. But repeat bidding of this kind is a dangerous habit to get into.

In the example above, the £7 at which you eventually won the item is not much more than your original maximum (£5), but if you do this on every item you bid on you will soon go over budget. It is better to decide in advance the absolute maximum that you are prepared to pay for an item, to submit that as your bid, and then not to re-enter the race if your are outbid.

Incidentally, bids of the same amount are treated on a 'first come first served' basis. Hence, in the example given above, if you had only raised your final bid to £6.50, Buyer C's earlier bid for the same amount would have been given priority.

Other types of auction on eBay

To make things slightly more complicated, eBay doesn't only operate conventional auctions of the type described above. It also has variations on the theme with slightly different rules. Below is an explanation of the more common ones.

Reserve price auctions

Now and again, you may come across an item on which the seller has placed a 'reserve'. This is the minimum price at which he is prepared to sell, and is set by him at the time he lists the item for sale. Reserves are often used for higher value items or for those which have some sentimental value to the seller.

You may ask why sellers don't simply set the starting price of the auction at the reserve price and have done with it. That would accomplish the same thing, because the starting price is the lowest figure at which the first bid can be made. There are two reasons:

Firstly, it is well established that a low starting price attracts more buyers into an auction and, the more people who get involved, the higher the final bid price is likely to be. The corollary of this is that a *high* starting price deters bidders, and stunts the normal momentum of an auction. So sellers usually avoid high starting prices.

The second reason sellers prefer to set low starting prices for their auctions is that it minimises the fees which they have to pay to eBay. Remember, eBay charges sellers an insertion fee for each item listed and one of the factors in determining the fee is an item's starting price. These are covered in detail on page 329.

The bidding process with reserve auctions is exactly the same as normal except that until the reserve price is met the high bid will be accompanied by a 'reserve not met' notification beneath the current price.

Fig. 2 – Auction in which the reserve has not yet been met

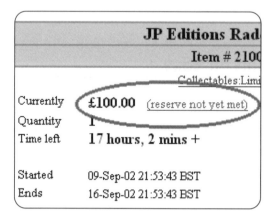

When a buyer bids either at or above the reserve price, the notification is changed to one saying 'reserve met' and that bid starts at the reserve. So if the reserve is £50, and someone bids a maximum of £80, their bid will be shown as a high bid of £50. The price will then rise in the usual increments as further bids come in.

Reserve price auctions incur slightly different charges to normal auctions. The seller pays an additional insertion fee of £1.50 for reserves up to £99.99 and £2.00 for reserves over £100. This additional fee is refunded if the item sells as the seller will then have to pay a percentage of the final price to eBay. Note that only reserves of £50 and above are now permitted on eBay.

If you only intend to use eBay as a buyer then these charges needn't concern you, but if you are thinking of selling at some point, and think you may want to use a reserve, they will be relevant. eBay's fees and other charges are covered in more detail in Part 4 of this book.

'Buy It Now' sales

Although eBay is best known as an auction website, many of the items listed on it are not sold in an auction at all, but on what is known as a Buy It Now (or 'BIN') basis. These listings are more like a normal shop sale, with the price set by the seller, and the buyer given the option to buy or not to buy at that price. There is no bidding, no negotiation, and no auction.

BIN listings can be useful because they allow you to buy an item immediately. Suppose there is a baby item that you've seen repeatedly in auction, but never managed to buy, perhaps because there is always a lot of competition for it. You see another of the same item on eBay, and are determined not to miss it this time. If it is listed on a BIN basis, you can accept the offer price, and it's yours, Immediately.

A BIN listing makes you pay for this privilege however, in that items tend to be priced nearer the full retail price and are therefore higher than they would normally realise if sold by auction.

How do you know if an item is offered on a BIN basis? Easy. Look for the little icon shown below which will appear next to the listing.

'Buy It Now' combined with an auction

This next bit is going to sound complicated, but it isn't really: as well as BIN-only sales, a BIN price can be offered *in conjunction* with a normal auction, so that buyers have a choice of how they buy the product. Such a listing would look like this:

Fig. 3 – Buy It Now combined with an auction

New BNIP Stokke Red Sleepi Cot Bedding Quilt/Duvet

Seller of this item? Sign in for your status

Starting bid	£30.00	Place Bid >
Buy It Now price:	£40.00	Buy It Now >
End time:	07-Jan-07 21:45:31 GMT (1 day 23 hours)	
Postage costs:	£3.50 Seller's Standard Rate Service to United Kingdom (more services)	
Post to:	Worldwide	
Item location:	Copthorne, West Sussex, United Kingdom	
History:	0 bids	
You can also:	Watch this item Email to a friend | Sell one like this	

Listing and payment details: Hide

Starting time:	28-Dec-06 21:45:31 GMT	Payment methods:	**PayPal** (preferred), Personal cheque, Postal Order or Banker's Draft See details
Starting bid:	£30.00		
Duration:	10-day listing		

If you saw this listing and you decided that you absolutely had to have the item, now, you could click on the BIN icon and Buy It Now. You'd pay the £40 price advertised, and the listing would end.

You might, however, decide to take your chances in an auction and enter a bid. The starting price in this case is quite high at £30, so at best you will get it for £10 less than the BIN price. Note that **once a bid has been entered, the BIN option disappears**, and normal auction rules apply.

Some people deliberately bid pre-emptively on these types of auctions in order to sabotage the BIN facility for others – a practice known as 'BIN stomping'. The thinking behind this is that they hope to win the item in the auction at less than the BIN price, and by knocking out the BIN they ensure that the auction takes place. Although this sometimes works, it doesn't always, as there will be occasions when the final auction price actually exceeds the lapsed BIN price.

If you see a lot of identical goods for sale (as can happen with new clothing), you probably shouldn't bother using the BIN option, as there are likely to be ample supplies of the item to satisfy demand. If you are patient enough, you will eventually win an auction below the BIN price.

BIN listings are, useful, however, when you simply can't wait for an auction to finish, or when the item is a one-off that you are unlikely to see again.

'Best Offer' auctions

'Best Offer' is a fairly new innovation to eBay. Used in conjunction with Buy It Now, bidders are invited to either pay the BIN price *or* make an offer to the seller, as Fig. 4 below shows.

Fig. 4 – Buy It Now combined with Best Offer

mothercare travel system base and foof muff + raincover
free postage

You are signed in

⇌Buy It Now price:	£75.00	Buy It Now >
Best Offer		Make Offer >
End time:	15-Jan-07 13:44:44 GMT (2 days 16 hours)	
Postage costs:	Free Other Courier Service to United Kingdom (more services)	
Post to:	Worldwide	
Item location:	halifax, West Yorkshire, United Kingdom	
You can also:	Watch this item Email to a friend | Sell one like this	

View larger picture

Listing and payment details: Hide

Starting time: 05-Jan-07 13:44:44 GMT

Duration: 10-day listing

Payment methods: **PayPal**,
Personal cheque,
Postal Order or Banker's Draft
See details

Making an offer in this way is similar to, but subtly different, from entering a bid on an auction listing:

In an auction, bids are entered in a structured way, and the price rises in pre-determined increments, as we have seen. Once the auction ends, the seller is obliged to accept the highest bid (unless a reserve has not been met), whether or not it meets his expectations.

With a Best Offer, the buyer is literally making an offer to the seller, on a one-to-one basis. It is not public in the way that an auction is and the seller is under no obligation to accept your offer.

If you decide to make a best offer, try and be sensible and offer an amount that bears some resemblance to the BIN price (although the odd cheeky offer sometimes pays off!).

The seller has 48 hours to consider your offer from the time you submit it, after which it will 'expire'. If your offer is declined within this time frame you cannot make a second offer although you can still purchase at the BIN price. If the seller accepts your offer, you are legally obliged to complete the sale. If the offer expires without a response from the seller you are then free to make another offer.

Multiple item listings – a.k.a. Dutch Auctions

A multiple item listing, also known as a Dutch Auction, is where a seller offers multiples of the same item in an auction style format. Unlike a normal auction these can have multiple winners.

When bidding on one of these auctions you specify how many of the items you want and the price you are willing to pay for each of them. eBay does not operate the proxy bidding system in these types of auction as each winning bidder will pay the same amount, equal to the lowest winning bid.

Winning bids are selected in order of bid price per item, so a bid for 3 units at £10 each will outrank a bid for 8 items at £6 each. As with a normal auction, however, if two bidders bid at the same price, the earlier bid takes priority.

If you decide later that you would like more of the item you cannot lower your total bid value to get them for a cheaper price per item.

Example:

- Seller has 12 items for sale and there are 2 bidders.

- Bidder A bids for 9 items at £8 each.

- Bidder B bids for 4 items at £10 each.

The lowest successful bid here is £8. Bidder B bid the higher amount (£10) so he wins all the 4 items which he wanted, and gets them at £8. Bidder A only gets 8 of the 9 items he wanted, also paying £8 for them.

If you are a winning bidder but are only offered part of the quantity you wanted (as in bidder A's case, above), you are not obliged to complete the transaction.

You can see the current bids by clicking on the bidders list links. Bids that are not winning show their bid price but bids that are winning will show the price they would pay if the auction were to end immediately. All winning bids therefore share the same price per item; the lowest winning bid. To be in with a chance of winning at least some units you need to exceed this price.

Now you have some idea of how the different auction types work, how do you begin to find what you're interested in on eBay?

Finding what you need with eBay's search engines

You've registered with eBay, learned how the different auction formats work, and are armed with your shopping list. Now what? You have to locate the items you're interested in buying on eBay. There are two basic search techniques and some more advanced ones which we will come to later. The simplest way to search is to use the search box which appears on all of eBay's listing pages as well as the home page.

Searching using the search box

Under the 'Welcome to eBay' banner, you'll find a blank box where you can enter the name or type of item you're interested in. Let's say you're looking for a cot bumper. In that box, you type in 'cot bumper'.

Immediately to the right is a second box. In there, you can specify whether you want your search to be carried out across all of eBay's inventory or only on specific categories. Using the first option throws up more results, but you may find that many of them are irrelevant. Generally, you get higher quality results if you confine your search to a specific category – in our case *Baby*.

Fig. 5 – eBay's search box

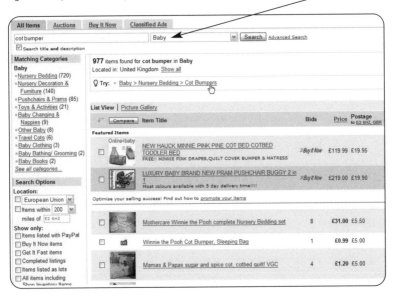

When I did exactly that search – 'cot bumper' in the Baby section – eBay listed 483 items. But underneath the main search box there is the option of searching both item title *and* description; checking this box and searching again reaps a return of 977; more choice but to an exhausting degree!

To help you narrow your search, eBay suggests areas of its site where you might get more specific results: in Fig. 5, below the number '977' it says:

Try Baby > Nursery Bedding > Cot Bumpers

Clicking on 'Cot Bumpers' takes you to a list of items in that subcategory – much better. On the left of Fig. 5 you can see that eBay also lists the many subcategories where the words Cot Bumper appear, such as 'Nursery Decoration & Furniture' and 'Toys and Activities' with the number of items – 140 and 21 respectively – in these subcategories appearing alongside.

Searching by category

The second way to conduct a basic search is by going directly to a specific category. To do this, go to eBay's home page and click on the 'Buy' link. This takes you to a page of categories and subcategories – Click on the 'Baby' one and you get this:

Fig. 6 – eBay's Baby category expanded

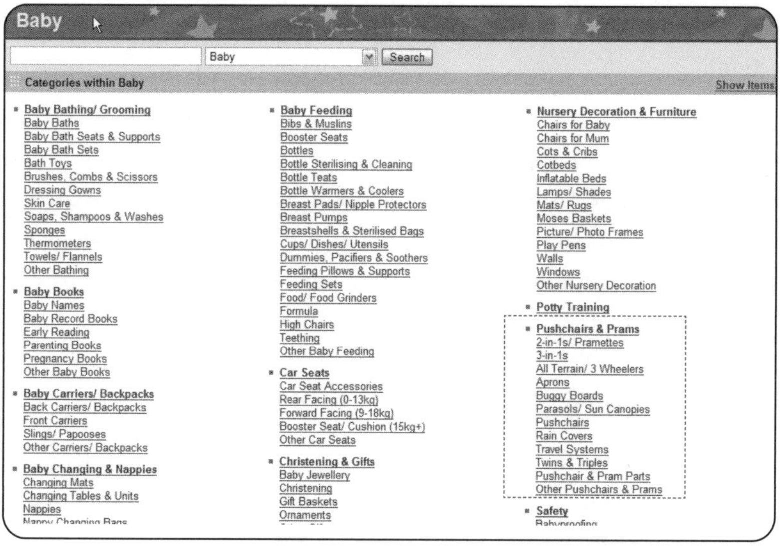

Let's imagine that as well as a cot bumper you want to buy a pram. Under the heading **Pushchairs & Prams** you see the following sub-headings:

2-in-1s/Pramettes
3-in-1s
All Terrain/3 Wheelers
Aprons
Buggy Boards
Parasols/Sun Canopies
Pushchairs
Rain Covers
Travel Systems
Twins & Triples
Pushchair and Pram Parts
Other Pushchairs & Prams

Perhaps you already know from your research that you are looking for a 3-wheeler. If so, you can click straight on the 'All Terrain/3 Wheelers' link. However, this presupposes that the seller of your ideal 3-wheeled pram has listed it in the correct category and, to be honest, you'd be amazed at how many sellers don't.

To be on the safe side, therefore, or if you haven't yet made a final decision, click on the main 'Pushchairs and Prams' heading. At the time of writing there are 7,192 items in this category, spread over 149 pages! That's an awful lot of browsing, especially if you don't have a broadband internet connection!

If you have already decided that you want a particular make of pram you can narrow your search by typing the model or manufacturer's name – for example 'Stokke Xplory' – into the search box. This will restrict the search to items with those words in the title (or in the title *and* description if you chose that option) and although the results may include Xplory accessories as well as the pram itself, that isn't too much of an inconvenience.

The search results page

When you do a search on eBay, you get a page of results showing the items that match your search criteria. If there are lots of items, they will be spread over many pages, with about 20 per page. Each page shows:

- A small photo of the item or an icon of a camera which indicates that there is a viewable photo on the item's full-page listing.
- The title of the item.
- The current number of bids, if any, and a Buy It Now icon if applicable.
- The current high bid.
- The cost of postage and packing costs where specified.
- An icon indicating whether the seller accepts PayPal.
- The time left, in days and hours, before the auction ends.

You can see these items of information in the columns of Fig 7. below.

Fig. 7 – Search result

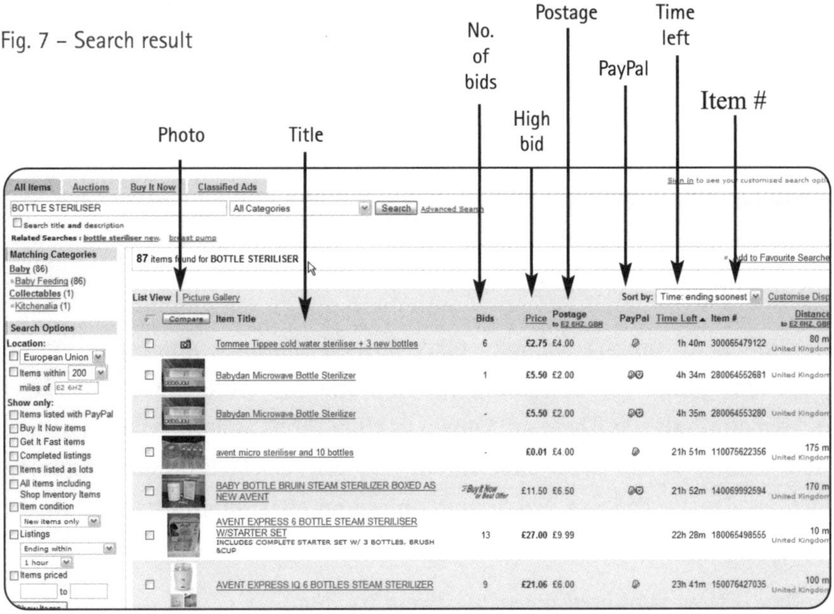

Reproduced with the permission of eBay Inc. COPYRIGHT © EBAY INC. ALL RIGHTS RESERVED

At the bottom of the list there will usually be a selection of additional goods being sold by eBay shops on a Buy It Now basis, just in case you need something immediately.

One other thing to mention is that the items that appear at the top of the list are what are known as 'featured' items. This means that the seller has paid an additional fee to have their item appear in a more prominent position, capitalising on the fact that lots of people simply don't want to trawl through endless pages of goods. However, you shouldn't assume that their high position in the list means that they offer either the best quality or deal.

After the featured items the proper listings begin and, by default, are ordered according to how soon the auctions are due to end, with the soonest appearing first. This will help you decide whether you will need to act quickly or not in placing a bid. As you become more familiar with eBay listings you can change the default so that items are ordered by price and location, (amongst other things), instead of how soon they are going to end.

Another symbol you will see in these listings is 𝒫 which denotes items for which the seller will accept payment via PayPal, eBay's instant electronic payment system. PayPal allows registered users to pay for an item immediately, either with their credit or debit card, or by using funds previously deposited in their account from their bank – but only if the seller of the item accepts PayPal. As you get used to eBay, you will realise how convenient PayPal is, to the extent that if a seller does not accept PayPal you may decide to give their auction a miss. That's where the little 𝒫 icon comes in handy.

'eBay shops'

In addition to running auctions, eBay hosts a countless number of virtual shopfronts which sell everything you can imagine, from nursery goods to architectural salvage. These are known as eBay shops and the retailers behind them tend to be the most experienced and active sellers on eBay, running auctions day-in, day-out. Sales taking place on eBay shops often follow the standard auction format, but there can also be differences. For instance:

- Buy It Now is offered on many inventory items.

- There may be items not available through the conventional auction-style listings.

- Payment can be made directly by credit card.

- Buyers can search and browse a seller's entire eBay inventory.

Perhaps the most significant factor for you, as a potential buyer from an eBay shop, is that you can have confidence and peace of mind that you'll be dealing with a tried and tested eBay seller.

The eBay shops search can be conducted from the home page. You will also find links to shops relevant to your searches on the eBay inventory listings pages. For instance, the screenshot below shows the eBay shops which come up when you do a search on the 'Baby' category.

Fig. 8 – eBay shops asociated with a search on 'Baby' category

eBay Shops in this Category

- Online4baby
- Babzee Baby Goods
- Best 4 BABY
- Cosykid
- Gifts To Remember GTRGIFTS

Other ways of viewing items on eBay

To make it easy to find and browse items on eBay you are given the choice of viewing them in several different ways. Here are some of the most popular and useful:

List view/picture gallery

This gives two alternative methods of looking at items on a search results page. 'List View' is the default setting where items both with and without photos are displayed in a simple vertical list.

'Picture Gallery' enables you to get a larger, clearer view of the accompanying picture as well as featuring all the same basic information shown on the List View. Although there are fewer items per page in Gallery View, the graphics are more detailed so it can take longer to load and browse using this method. However, it is a good option when what you are looking for carries only a limited number of results.

Sort by

eBay gives you the option of changing the order in which results are displayed in your chosen search.

As mentioned above, the default on this is 'Time: ending soonest'. In the screenshot below, you can see in the far right column that the first auction listed had three minutes to run, the second had twenty-seven, while the third and fourth had several hours left.

Listing in Time: ending soonest order suits eBay because it generates excitement and encourages bids, but it is very easy for you to switch to a different order by choosing from the drop-down menu, shown below.

Fig. 9 – Sort options on search results page

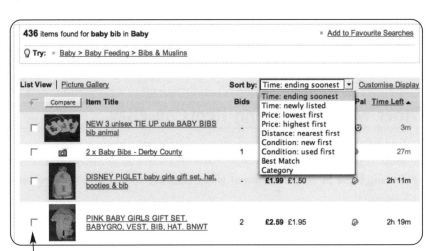

Compare

Check boxes to the left of the item description allow you to compare and contrast different items, similar items, or even the exact same type of item for price, condition, etc.

All you need to do is check (tick) the relevant boxes and click the 'Compare' button at the bottom of the page to see a handy side-by-side view of your chosen items.

The screenshot below shows how the 'Compare' page looks.

Fig. 10 – Comparing items on a single page

Compare Items			
Watch All · Remove All			Sort by: Order Selected: recent first
Remove Item	Remove Item	Remove Item	Remove Item
Stokke Xplory Baby Buggy Pushchair in Sand / Beige	**Stokke Xplory Baby Buggy/Pushchair in Red**	**Stokke Xplory in "Sand"**	**STOKKE XPLORY Beige Luxury 4 wheel pushchair bugaboo**
Bid Now! · Buy It Now	Bid Now!	Bid Now!	Bid Now! · Buy It Now
Watch this Item	Watch this Item	Watch this Item	Watch this Item

Time Left	8 days 21 hours	3 days 23 hours	3 days 22 hours	3 days 11 hours
Bids	0 bids	29 bids	15 bids	0 bids
Seller	(170 ★) 98.9% Positive	(37246 ★) 99.3% Positive me ★ Power Seller	(25 ★) 100% Positive	(181 ★) 100% Positive
Price	£275.00 £425.00 =Buy It Now	£155.00	£132.00	£300.00 £360.00 =Buy It Now
Postage	£30.00 Other Courier	£12.00 Other Courier 📦 Postage discounts available for multiple purchases.	£25.00 Other Courier 📦 Postage discounts available for multiple purchases.	£0.00 Collection in Person
Posts From	United Kingdom	United Kingdom	United Kingdom	United Kingdom

This example compares four products from the same category, but you can also compare items from different pages and even from different categories – just find them, check their boxes, and click the 'Compare' button. They will all appear together on one page.

Customise display

When you search for something on eBay, the results page that you get includes the 'default' columns of information shown in Figure 7. But eBay allows you to change the default options and include different information – the information that *you* want about items, not the information pre-selected by eBay.

To do this, click on the 'Customise Display' link which apppears near the top right of any search results page. (You can see it on Figure 9, just to the right of the drop-down box.) You get a page that looks like this:

Fig. 11 – Customising the search results display

Home > Search > **Customise Your Search**

Customise Your Search

| Customise Search Options | **Customise Display** |

Available Columns

Shop name
Country/Region
Distance
Type of Seller
Item number

Columns to Display

Picture
Title
Bids
Price
Postage cost
PayPal
Time

Title is a required column and cannot be removed.

Column Settings

Display:
☑ Show comparison check boxes
☐ Item title on its own row (see example)
☐ Convert prices to £
☐ Display feedback information

50 ▾ items per page

Show time in:
⊙ Time left format (e.g. 1d 6h 10m)
○ Date format (e.g. 10-Nov 14:02)

Show results in:
○ Picture Gallery
⊙ List view

The 'Columns to Display' panel on the right shows the information that currently appears when you do a search. The 'Available Columns' panel on the left shows what else you can include. To move an item from one panel to the other, you simply click on the arrows in the middle. To move the *position* of an item, highlight the name you want to move and then click on the up/down arrows as appropriate. Easy!

You can also customise a number of other features including currency conversion and how many items are viewable per page. The first would be useful if you were browsing eBay's American site and wanted to see the $ prices in £. The second would be useful if you are running a particularly slow dial-up internet connection.

If all this seems a little advanced for you at the moment don't worry. The default settings (what you see if you make no alterations) are perfectly adequate for basic purposes. As you become more familiar with the interface you can begin to experiment with different options. We will be looking at more advanced search options later in this section of the book. For now, however, let's assume that an item on the inventory has caught your eye.

Navigating an item's full-page listing

When you click on an item in a search results list, it opens up a full-page with much more information than the simple list. Fig. 12 below is an example.

Fig. 12 – Item description screen

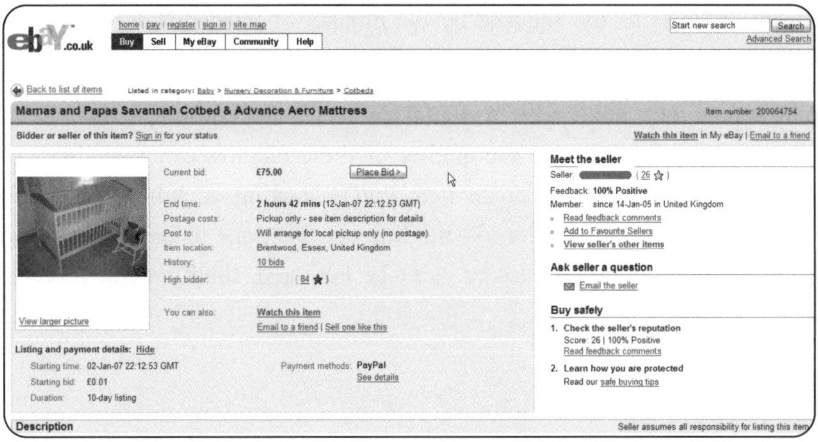

Let's look at the individual components on this page in turn:

Item title

This is the headline that appears in the search results listing. Its purpose is to attract bidders into investigating an item further and for this reason is one of the most important elements of any listing. The title will usually include a brief description of the item along with an indication of its condition. In case you're unfamiliar with some of the shorthand used on eBay and other small ad listings here's a quick tutorial:

BN	Brand New
BNIP/BNIB	Brand New in Pack/ Brand New in Box
BNWT/BNWOT	Brand New With Tags/Brand New Without Tags
VGC	Very Good Condition

Some items will also include a subtitle which elaborates on the above or acts as a further enticement to buy such as 'Free Postage' or 'Cheapest on eBay!'.

Picture

If the seller has included a photo you'll see it here even if there wasn't a viewable one on the search results page. A link beneath the photo will take you to an enlarged image near the bottom of the listing. For some higher value items, or ones where there is a lot of detail, some sellers will include multiple images which you can click on in turn; some even feature a slideshow! Don't be too seduced by the number of images, however, unless they are drawing your attention to an obvious feature or flaw.

Some sellers who don't have a digital camera will photograph their items using a camera phone, and the quality of these pictures can sometimes be poor. If this is the case with an item you're looking at, but you are still interested in it, ask the seller via the link on this page to email you some clearer pictures. If they refuse or can't be bothered, think carefully before bidding on the item.

Summary of item

This will include the current high bid, the date and time when the auction is due to end, postage costs (where applicable), where the seller is willing to post the item (UK only or UK and abroad), where the item is located (handy if it's collection only), the item history (how many bids have been placed so far) and the user ID of the current high bidder.

Beneath this summary you are given the option of either 'watching this item' or 'emailing it to a friend'.

- 'Watching' an item allows you to keep track of an auction without actually committing yourself to a bid. When you watch an item its details are copied over to a section of the site called 'My eBay' which is basically your personalised control panel. There are so many features to My eBay that I have given it its own chapter starting on Page 228.

- Emailing an item's details to a friend allows you to send them to someone else in case they are interested. It's a great feature and, because you can add a personalised note, my sister and I use it a lot when seeking advice from each other before placing a bid.

Meet the seller

This section, on the right of the page, is another very important part of any item listing. I have enlarged it in Fig. 13. below.

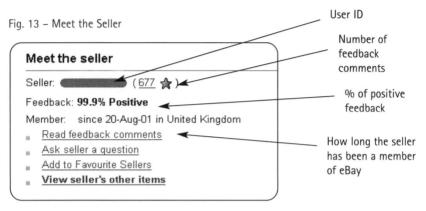

Fig. 13 – Meet the Seller

User ID

Number of feedback comments

% of positive feedback

How long the seller has been a member of eBay

Firstly, it tells you the User ID of the seller and the number of unique feedback comments they have received during their membership of eBay. This is the number in brackets directly after their name. If you click on the number you can access a detailed feedback profile or breakdown of the comments made by other eBayers as a result of their transactions with this seller.

Below that, the feedback received is also expressed as a percentage. 100% is a perfect rating and indicates zero negative feedback from other users.

You can also see how long a member has been registered on the site. Combining this information with their feedback rating and with the number of transactions they have been involved in tells you something about how reliable a particular user is. The higher the positive feedback the more confident you can be that they are trustworthy. Generally speaking, anything above 98% is felt to be safe.

Feedback is one of the principles on which eBay is founded and is behind the 'goodwill' basis that we spoke of earlier. The site depends for both its success and its survival on its members accurately grading their experiences of other users and it is so important that we devote an entire section to the concept of feedback starting on Page 219.

Other things you can do from this section include 'Ask The Seller A Question', which enables you to clarify anything that may not have been covered, or made clear, in the item description. In addition, you can choose to 'Add To Favourite Sellers', a feature which allows you to save the seller's details to a list in My eBay. The list is updated each time the seller adds new items and is handy if they tend to sell a lot of what you fancy and you can't trust yourself to remember their details. Finally, if this particular seller has more than one item for sale at this time you can also 'View Seller's Other Items' from here.

Buy safely

Under this heading you are again directed to check the seller's feedback (I told you it was important!) and can also learn whether you will be financially protected should the transaction go wrong. The most effective way to protect yourself is to pay for the item through PayPal, but eBay also has its own protection policies which we shall examine in detail later.

Fig. 14 – Buy safely

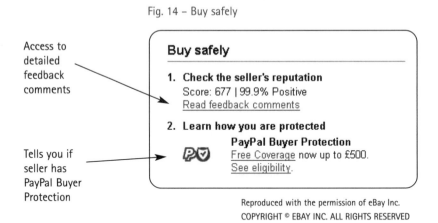

Item description

The screenshot in Fig. 12 on page 199 does not, for privacy reasons, show how the seller chose to describe her cot, but I can tell you that she wrote several paragraphs about it, and included three more photograhs. That is fairly typical of a good seller.

The main body of the description is a seller's biggest opportunity to persuade you to bid and you should therefore read this part very carefully. In addition to describing the item the seller may include specific requirements about the transaction including postage or payment details not included elsewhere. They may also specify buyer requirements such as new members emailing them before bidding to ensure that they are legitimate. If you do not adhere to these requirements you may well find your bid cancelled by the seller.

Beneath the description you will see an enlarged version of the item photo. One thing you should be careful about when looking at pictures is that they are genuine photos of the article being sold and not 'stock' photos taken from the manufacturer's website. Stock photos are often used for cots, prams, and mobile phones, to name a few. Although a seller is allowed to use them to save time when listing, you should ask them to email you a proper picture of the actual item to make sure of its real condition if you are at all suspicious. Again, if they refuse or are rude in any way simply don't bid – another one will always come up!

Beneath most photos you will see a counter looking something like this. This records the number of times an item has been viewed and gives you an idea of how popular it is likely to be.

Questions from other members

If, after reading an item description, there is still something that you want to know, feel free to ask the seller a question using the link.

If the seller thinks your question might be of assistance to other bidders he may choose to display it under this part of the listing. Examples of questions might be those concerning dimensions, weight, age, etc. If your question *does* appear on the listing your username will remain anonymous so that other eBayers are kept unaware of your interest.

Fig. 15 – Ask seller a question

Meet the seller
Seller: ⬛⬛⬛⬛ (26 ☆)
Feedback: **100% Positive**
Member: since 14-Jan-05 in United Kingdom
▪ Read feedback comments
▪ Add to Favourite Sellers
▪ View seller's other items

Ask seller a question
✉ Email the seller

Buy safely
1. **Check the seller's reputation**
   Score: 26 | 100% Positive
   Read feedback comments
2. **Learn how you are protected**
   Read our safe buying tips

Postage, payment and returns policy

Underneath the item description, you will find details of the seller's postage, payment and returns policy. Make sure you read this section carefully as it's here that the seller will specify the postage costs, of the item and the forms of payment they will accept. Some sellers will only accept PayPal and may require immediate payment, so if you can't pay in this way it doesn't make sense to bid. The seller *may* make an exception but it's more likely that you will just create annoyance and possibly even negative feedback for yourself!

Fig. 16 – Indication of which payment methods a seller will accept on an item listing

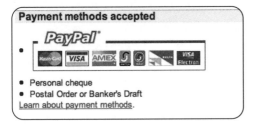

Payment methods accepted

- PayPal
- Personal cheque
- Postal Order or Banker's Draft
  Learn about payment methods.

In the example below, you can see that this seller is only willing to dispatch his item within the UK, and that he will charge £8.99 in postage. You can also see that he posts only after payment has cleared, and on only two days a week.

Fig. 17 – Seller's postage information on an item listing

Postage, payment details and return policy

Dispatches to
United Kingdom

Country: United Kingdom ▾

Postage and packaging	To	Service
£8.99	United Kingdom	Royal Mail 1st Class Standard 1 working day*

*Sellers are not responsible for delivery time. This information is provided by the carrier and excludes weekends and bank holidays. Note that delivery times may vary, particularly during peak periods.

Domestic Handling Time
Will usually dispatch within 2 working days of receiving cleared payment.

Postal insurance
Not offered

Seller's payment instructions
I post Mondays and Thursdays after payment clears, or sooner if agreed.

Postal charges are a sensitive issue and cause a lot of heated debate on eBay forums. This is because some sellers feel it is morally wrong to charge more to post an item than it actually costs whilst others feel it is perfectly okay to add a little extra for handling, packing materials and the time spent queuing at the post office behind the man with 80 bags of coins.

> "Some sellers feel it is morally wrong to charge more to post an item than it actually costs, while others feel it is perfectly okay to add a little extra."

Whilst I tend to agree with the latter group, I have seen some sellers charge more for postage than the actual item itself which should obviously ring alarm bells unless it's something you really can't do without. Beware too, if you decide to buy from international sellers, as you can get severely burned by import taxes and/or customs charges. All of a sudden, your bargain may no longer seem such an attractive purchase.

The postage costs section should also make clear the service used, be it standard first/second class, recorded/special delivery, etc. If you require a postal service not offered you should ask the seller before bidding to see whether they will be willing to oblige and, if so, how much they will charge.

This section should also specify the seller's returns policy (if any) and how soon they expect payment to be made after the end of the auction. Below is an example of one seller's returns policy.

Fig. 18 – Example of a seller's returns policy

Seller's return policy:
Item must be returned within: 7 Days of receipt
Return Policy Details: item may be returned for replacment if defective.always contact seller first. Refunds will only be issued against purchase cost, postage costs will NOT be refunded
Learn about return policies.

Ready to bid

The final section of the listing invites you to place a bid on the item and will tell you the minimum that must be offered taking into account the current bid and the applicable bid increment.

Fig. 19 – 'Ready to bid'

Ready to bid

Used Quinny BUZZ pushchair stroller in Black RRP£330

Item title:	Used Quinny BUZZ pushchair stroller in Black RRP£330
Current bid:	£166.30
Your maximum bid:	£ [＿＿＿＿＿] (Enter £171.30 **or more**)

Place Bid >   You will confirm in the next step.
(PayPal account required)

eBay automatically bids on your behalf **up to** your maximum bid.
Learn about bidding.

It is quite difficult to enter a wrong amount when you bid as eBay asks you to confirm the figure you have input on a separate screen. This means you have the chance to review your bid before finally committing to it, to make sure that you've entered the correct amount.

Now that you've learned a bit about what to look for in an item description we'll examine the bidding process in more detail, namely when to bid and when it's time to stop.

Bidding for an item

The legal stuff

Legally speaking, transactions which take place on eBay are a contract between the buyer and seller only. Although eBay *hosts* the auction, it is not a party to it nor does it accept any liability if things go wrong. It is clearly in its own interests, however, to ensure that transactions pass off smoothly and to this end it does provide some safeguards which we will look at in more detail later. Ultimately, however, it is your decision to proceed with a transaction, so remember the tired but sadly true maxim that applies to all areas of life: "If something looks too good to be true, it probably is".

When to bid

It is essential before you place a bid that you do your **pricing research**. If you've been looking in shops and catalogues you should have a fairly good idea of an item's full retail price. However, the internet generally is an excellent place to cut these prices substantially so it's a good idea to browse some of the price comparison websites such as www.kelkoo.co.uk

For books, you can't go wrong with Amazon at www.amazon.co.uk especially since it launched the facility to shop for items via its private sellers' market.

The reason for doing this research is to stop you buying what are essentially second hand goods at or close to full retail price. Although baby goods, especially, have a relatively short user span and can therefore be found in next to new condition, it just doesn't make sense to pay full price when buying at auction. I have watched items go for way above their true value simply because two stubborn buyers

> "My rule of thumb when bidding on eBay is never to pay more than 50% of the full retail price."

locked horns in the closing minutes of an auction, the desire to 'win' overshadowing the amount of money they should have been willing to pay. The only winners in these cases are the sellers and they won't take too kindly to your complaints after the fact that you paid too much for something.

Another reason why auction prices should be lower than retail prices is that **you have less consumer protection**. If you buy an item at a retail outlet, either on the high street or online, and it turns out to be faulty, you are covered by various consumer laws which entitle you to a refund or an exchange. When you buy from an internet auction site, however, these laws simply do not apply and you are protected only by eBay's own policies or that of your credit card company if you pay via PayPal. If the difference between buying retail and buying on eBay is only a matter of pence, why sacrifice this peace of mind?

My personal rule of thumb when bidding on eBay is never to pay more than 50% of the full retail price for something second hand and no more than 75% for a new item. This also makes sense when you take into account the amount of time invested in researching, browsing and eventually bidding.

I cannot stress enough the need to be disciplined, however tempting it may be to have 'one last bid'. You should also always factor in the cost of postage which can add to the cost of larger items quite considerably. As mentioned earlier, some mainstream retailers will give free postage for items such as prams and highchairs which few sellers on eBay offer.

Another reason not to get into a bidding war, especially over baby items, is that there is nothing so rare that it doesn't eventually come up for sale again. I myself have been disappointed at bowing out of an auction only to win the next time the item came up at a fraction of the cost. eBay is definitely a gamble for sellers in this respect as some items do tend to go in and out of fashion attracting a greater/lesser number of bids accordingly. Don't get caught out!

How to bid

If there is one rule I would urge new(ish) eBayers to hold sacrosanct it is *not to bid too early*. It never fails to amaze me when people bid on an item as soon as it is listed even though the auction still has seven days to run. Bidding too early is bad practice for two reasons: firstly, it announces to everyone that you are interested, which is the equivalent of a poker player showing the entire table his hand. This has the knock-on effect of making other people antsy which leads to the second reason bidding early is a no-

no: it pushes the price up artificially. As more people become interested and see others bidding, they can't resist the temptation to put in a bid themselves and become the 'high bidder'. This results in the initial bidder becoming annoyed at being outbid and bidding again. On and on it goes, with the price going higher and higher.

This need to be 'on top' seems to be a strange quirk of human nature; remember, however, that the only time you need to be on top in an auction is the moment it ENDS. This is why I only ever bid, whenever possible, in the final few minutes (or even seconds) of an auction. To do this successfully, you need a) plenty of nerve and b) a broadband connection which allows you to refresh the page quickly. The first will come with practice, and most of us nowadays have the second.

Bidding in the last few seconds is technically known as 'sniping' and, like gazumping in the property market, isn't much liked by some people. It is, however, perfectly legitimate.

If you want to have a go at sniping but are nervous about it you can try specialist auction sniping software which is widely available on the web. Sniping sites will generally charge a subscription fee but often offer you the chance to have up to three free snipes as an introduction to their service. With these sites you basically tell them what your maximum bid is and they bid on your behalf, generally in the last 3-4 seconds of the listing. If your maximum exceeds the current high bid you will win the auction.

"I have watched items go for way above their true value simply because two stubborn buyers locked horns in the closing minutes of an auction."

Early on in my eBay career I used one such sniping programme for a 1950s cupboard that I really wanted. Although it was successful, having never used the software before I almost had a heart attack in the last few minutes of the auction as I didn't know if it was even going to *work*, let alone whether my maximum bid would be high enough to win! Once you become more experienced at bidding you will develop enough nerve not to rely on specialist software although it can be very useful when you start out.

The downside to using sniping sites is that you are effectively handing over your username and password to a third party in order that they can bid on your behalf, so you need to make sure that they are legitimate sites. Don't respond to unsolicited emails inviting you to join a sniping programme as you cannot be sure of their authenticity. My own experience is limited to 'Auction Sniper', whose website is www.auctionsniper.com and which I found to be reliable and trustworthy.

After using a sniping programme it is probably a good idea to change your eBay password just to be on the safe side.

Once you've decided what to bid on there are two basic approaches to actually placing a bid which I have termed *Suck It and See* and *Lying In Wait*.

Suck it and see

This approach requires that you go straight in and bid your absolute maximum and then leave the auction alone. If you win, great; if you don't then you console yourself with the fact that the item went for more than you were prepared to pay.

This is a good approach to take if a) you haven't got the time to watch the auction and/or will be away when it ends and b) you are quite disciplined and won't be tempted to call in and raise your bid in the final minutes.

The disadvantage of this approach is that, as already mentioned, it shows your interest prematurely and, as such, may raise the bidding above the item's true value as other interested parties bid up in an attempt to guess your maximum. Although I have seen this method work on occasion, I must admit that its success tends to be limited to those with fairly deep pockets who can afford a maximum bid out of normal peoples' range.

Lying in wait

This is the second approach to bidding and one which I personally favour even though it demands more time and your focused attention. Dinners have burned and my son has been kept waiting for bedtime whilst I hawk over the last few seconds of an auction I want to win.

As previously mentioned, although this approach is, in essence, a form of sniping, it is a perfectly legitimate and effective way to bid. The first step with this method is to move any items that you are interested in over to the 'Watching' section of your My eBay page where you hang fire on the bidding until the last few minutes of the auction (the longer you feel able to leave it the better). This way, no one is aware of your interest and even though the seller will know how many 'watchers' an item has, usernames remain anonymous.

Even though you have yet to bid on the item, you do still need to have a maximum price in mind that you are prepared to stick to come what may. Quite a lot of people are now placing bids in the dying minutes of an auction so you do need to be on the ball, constantly refreshing the page to see where the current price is at. If, near to the end, the current bid is still lower than your maximum, go ahead and bid; obviously the closer this is to the end of the auction the greater your chance of winning (assuming that your maximum is greater than the next highest bidder's).

Bidding close to the end also prevents you from entering too many bids should you be unsuccessful with your first. It imposes discipline. I usually bid in the last 25 seconds of an auction which only gives me time for one or two bids at the most. My personal feeling is that if more people used this method of bidding, prices would generally be much lower on eBay.

Ready to bid

When you are finally ready to bid on an item click on the 'Bid Now' button on the item description and input your bid in pounds and pence. It always makes sense to bid in slightly uneven amounts, for example £5.87 or £3.52 as most people tend to bid in whole numbers and an extra penny here or there can make all the difference between winning and losing an item. (I recently won an old oak chest by the princely sum of 6p).

After you've placed your bid a new screen will ask you to check the amount and confirm it by clicking again; this theoretically safeguards you against inputting an incorrect amount, for example by misplacing a decimal point. If you do confirm your bid only to discover that you *have* made an error you can retract it as long as you then input the correct amount IMMEDIATELY. You cannot retract a bid simply because you have changed your mind about wanting the item. eBay takes its transactions very seriously and its sellers understandably regard with disdain time wasters who have nothing better to do than bid erroneously. However, genuine mistakes do occur and there are therefore some situations in which a bid *can* be legitimately cancelled. These are outlined below.

Bid retraction

Changing your mind about an item and wishing to back out of a bid is called Bid Retraction and can only be done if you satisfy certain criteria. This is to prevent unethical and unlawful activity occurring on the site, more about which can be found in the 'eBay Scams' section on page 253. It also protects sellers and other bidders who may be left disappointed or financially vulnerable. So, what are the circumstances in which you can retract a bid?

1. If you input a typographical error, for example, if you bid £999.00 instead of £99.90. In this instance you are permitted to retract the higher bid so long as you enter the correct amount immediately afterwards.

2. If the description of the item changes materially after you place your bid.

3. If you win the auction but can't reach the seller by email or telephone after getting their details through eBay.

4. If someone has impersonated you in order to make a bid.

5. If the item is subsequently found to contravene eBay's policies.

Bid retractions are also subject to some timing restrictions which operate as follows:

- If you place a bid before the last 12 hours of an auction you can retract before the last 12 hours if you can meet the criteria listed above. In this case you will eliminate all bids you have made on an item, but if the reason for the retraction was a typographical error you will have to bid again. You cannot retract in the final 12 hours of an auction.

- If you bid in the last 12 hours you may only retract within one hour of placing the bid and only if you meet one or more of the criteria above. When you retract in this situation, only your most recent bid will be eliminated. Bids placed prior to the final 12 hours will still stand.

- If you are not permitted to officially retract your bid because you do not meet the specific criteria, you can try and contact the seller and explain to them that you wish to cancel your bid. It will be up to the seller whether or not they permit this, although they would probably rather do so than risk a non-paying bidder situation.

The number of bid retractions made by you will be displayed on your feedback profile for others to see, and will be perceived in a negative light. eBay investigates all of these very carefully for signs of suspicious activity as the overuse of bid retractions can indicate a breach of policy or even fraud. In these cases you would risk suspension from eBay, something which is officially known as being NARU'D (No Longer a Registered User).

What happens after I bid?

After you place your bid you will either be met with a green tick congratulating you on being the current high bidder (see Fig. 20 below) or a red cross telling you that you have been outbid (see Fig. 21 overleaf). You will also receive a bid confirmation email from eBay to your registered address.

Fig. 20 – 'You are current high bidder' confirmation

Bid Confirmation

You are signed in   This item is being tracked in My eBay | Email to a friend | Printer Version

You are the current high bidder

Important: Another user may still outbid you, so check this item again in My eBay before it ends.

Title:	Baby bib for toddler, in pink	
Time left:		1 day
History:		3 bids
Current bid:		£5.51
Your maximum bid:		£7.98

Remember, if you are instantly outbid it does not necessarily mean that there is another buyer hovering over a keyboard who just happened to trump your bid seconds after you put it in. What it means, more often than not, is that another bidder put in a higher maximum bid than you *at some time* during the life of the auction, and that eBay's proxy bidding system is at work.

Fig. 21 – 'You've been outbid' confirmation

Bid Confirmation

You are signed in   This item is being tracked in My eBay | Email to a friend | Printer Version

✗ **You've been outbid. Bid again for another chance to win this item.**

> **Important:** Another bidder placed a higher maximum bid than yours, possibly **days or hours before**. To increase your chances of winning, enter the **highest** amount you would be willing to pay below.

Title: **Baby bib for toddler, in pink**

Time left: 1 day
History: 2 bids
Current bid: £4.41
Your new maximum bid: £ [   ]   (Enter £4.61 **or more**)

[Bid Again >]

If there is still some time to go before the item ends and you haven't yet bid your maximum, you'd be just as well advised to watch the auction and wait before bidding again.

If you *are* the current high bidder you'll be able to see how close you are to being outbid by seeing how high the current bid is to your maximum. For example, if you have bid a maximum of £10 and the current high bid stands at £9.50, the next person to bid will probably take over from you. If this happens, do question whether you really want or need the item enough to continue and never overstretch yourself financially.

10
COMMANDMENTS
of Successful Bidding

1. Thou shalt do thy research.

2. Thou shalt be aware that there is nothing so rare that it will not come up for sale again.

3. Thou shalt decide on a maximum bid and stick to it.

4. Thou shalt bid as late as possible.

5. Thou shalt ask questions if unsure about anything to do with the item.

6. Thou shalt check the postage costs and weigh this up as a total price against the true value of the item.

7. Thou shalt check the seller's feedback carefully.

8. Thou shalt read the item description in its entirety and ensure that thou can fulfil all the buyer requirements including method of payment.

9. Thou shalt ensure thou biddest the correct amount.

10. Thou shalt use a traceable/refundable method of payment for high value items.

After the auction

If you lose

If you were outbid before the end of the auction, eBay will already have sent you an Outbid Notification email inviting you to bid again before the finish. If you don't enter a new bid, and someone else wins the auction, you will be sent another email telling you that you didn't win (just to rub it in!), along with suggestions of similar items currently on the site which might be of interest to you.

Second chance offers

Even if you don't win the auction you may be sent what eBay calls a 'Second Chance Offer'. This occurs when the winning bidder has either been unable to complete the transaction or if the seller has another of the same item for sale. In either case you will be given the opportunity to buy the item at the *maximum that you bid*, not the actual winning price. It is completely up to you whether to accept this offer or not and you will have 48 hours from the time of the notification to consider before it expires. If you choose to accept you will be asked to click on a link in the email which will take you back to the item listing now showing a Buy It Now price for the maximum bid which you had previously placed.

By accepting a Second Chance Offer you are entering into the same binding agreement to purchase as you would have done if you had won the item in the original auction and you will also be able to leave and receive feedback on the transaction. You are also covered, where applicable, by the protection policies offered by eBay and, if you paid this way, by PayPal.

If you do not want to receive second chance offers for whatever reason you can specify this by changing your notification preferences in the appropriate section of My eBay.

If You Win

Each time you win an auction a confirmation message will be posted at the top of the completed listing.

Fig. 22 – Won Item screen

You will also be invited to do several things. If you know the total amount to pay and wish to do so by PayPal you can simply follow the link provided at the top of the page. The same link will also take you to a generic checkout screen where you can choose from all the available methods of payment and learn where it has to be sent (the seller's details).

If you're unsure of the total to pay, or if you have bought more than one item from this seller and want to see if you can get a postal discount, you can 'request the total from the seller' or 'contact the seller' using the links provided. Fig. 23 below shows an extract from a completed item listing pending payment.

Fig. 23 – Won Item screen: other actions

Other actions for this item:
You can manage all your items in My eBay and do the following:
- Request total payment amount from the seller.
- £ Mark payment sent for this item.
- ☆ Leave feedback for this item.
- ✉ Contact Seller about this item.

Additional Options:
- To view other items from this seller, view seller's other items.
- If this listing is similar to an item you want to sell, list an item like this.
- You may add this seller to your Favourite Sellers in My eBay.

Whichever method you choose to pay by it is courteous to do so as quickly as possible and certainly within a week of winning the item. Note that if you pay by cheque, eBay advises sellers to wait until clearance of funds before they dispatch your goods. Some sellers do exercise discretion on this point, however, and if you have good feedback may send you the goods as soon as they receive the cheque.

If you have any problems which mean that payment may be delayed, do contact the seller and let them know as soon as possible. For all they know you may have done a runner and they might end up leaving you negative feedback or opening a dispute with eBay as a result. Misunderstandings and ill feeling are almost always avoided by good communication with your trading partner.

Everything being equal, the transaction will proceed smoothly, the seller will send the item and you will be delighted when you receive it. If this is the case you should certainly leave feedback for the seller and they will probably return the favour if they haven't already done so. So what is feedback all about?

Feedback

The role of feedback

In a cynical and cut-throat world, the success of eBay is, when you think about it, an anomaly. Complete strangers agree a deal online, the buyer promises to send money, and the seller promises to send the goods. They know nothing about each other, may live hundreds or thousands of miles apart, and have very little recourse if the other party defaults. Yet, every week, millions of transactions are successfully concluded. How so?

'Feedback' has a lot to do with it. eBay's feedback system recognises that the only way the site works is if trading partners trust each other. To make it easy for users to know *who* to trust it enables each person to build up a reputation, based on ratings provided by other users, which is then displayed for everyone to see.

How feedback works

Basic feedback

A member's 'Feedback Profile' is composed of all the comments made by other buyers and sellers following their transactions. The grades are 'positive', 'negative' or 'neutral'. Whilst the first two are pretty self-explanatory, 'neutral' is generally used when one aspect of the transaction was favourable whilst another was less so. For example, if the item itself was good quality but the buyer had to wait four weeks for it to arrive or if the delivery was speedy but there was a small flaw in the item not mentioned in the listing.

Detailed ratings under Feedback 2.0

eBay has recently introduced 'Feedback 2.0'. This works in the same way as 'ordinary' feedback, but allows buyers to rate sellers separately for different aspects of the transaction. As well as the current 'positive', 'negative' and 'neutral' rating, buyers can score sellers on a 1 to 5 scale for each of item description, communication, delivery time, and postage & packaging charges. These are known as 'Detailed Seller's Ratings'. The average of all ratings is displayed on the seller's Feedback Profile page.

Who can see feedback?

Feedback comments made by and for a member can be viewed by anyone. This generates trust and increases the likelihood of other members wanting to conduct business with them. eBay users can keep comments made about them 'private' (i.e. invisible to others), but in October 2006 eBay introduced a new rule which says that if a user does this they are only allowed to buy on the site and not allowed to sell.

Aggregate feedback score

Each time someone leaves feedback for you a number will appear in brackets alongside your username. The higher the number the more feedback you have received and, by implication, the more transactions you have completed. Shown on the same page is the percentage of positive feedback that you have received. If you have never had anything other than positive feedback, this will be 100% If you receive negative feedback, the number alongside your name will reduce by 1, and your percentage will drop below 100%.

Fig. 24 – eBay feedback profile

Member Profile: (849 ☆)					
Feedback Score:	849	Recent Ratings:			
Positive Feedback:	99.9%		Past Month	Past 6 Months	Past 12 Months
Members who left a positive:	850	⊕ positive	17	199	537
Members who left a negative:	1	⊙ neutral	0	0	1
All positive feedback received:	945	⊖ negative	0	0	1
Learn about what these numbers mean.		Bid Retractions (Past 6 months): 0			

Generally speaking the higher the number beside your name, and the greater the percentage below it, the more trustworthy you are deemed to be by other members. By the same logic, when you are thinking about bidding on an item, check out the seller's feedback score and percentage rating to see if they have a good track record.

- If they have a high number and a 100% score, you can be confident that they will be good to deal with.

- If it's a low number and a 100% score, that's not a bad sign necessarily, but it does mean that they have not done enough trading to really establish a good reputation.

- If their positive feedback is below 95%, you need to take a closer look. You do this by clicking on the number in brackets after their username or, from an item description, click on the link to 'Read feedback comments'.

The screenshot below illustrates the summary feedback profile:

Fig. 25 – Sample of member feedback profile

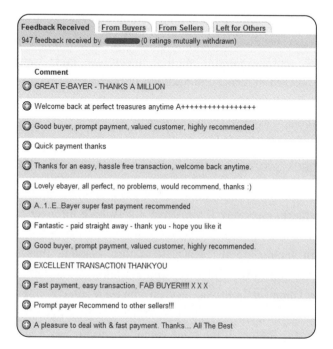

As you can see, this provides more detail on their feedback, and shows their recent performance.

How to leave feedback

Revisiting the item description after the auction has ended will give you an automatic link to the feedback page, like this:

Leave Feedback >

You can also follow the link under the 'My Account' view of My eBay to leave feedback for several items at once.

When you are directed to leave feedback you will be asked to select the type you wish to leave: positive, negative or neutral. You are limited to 80 characters only so choose your wording wisely. Try and be specific about the transaction; so rather than merely saying 'thanks' or 'not happy', elaborate on the features of the transaction that you found good or not so good. This helps develop future trade for good sellers and, conversely, warns others about bad ones.

If you are about to leave negative feedback you will be warned that this cannot be retracted once sent and asked if you wish to continue. Press 'leave feedback/continue' to proceed or 'cancel' to back out of the action. Do make sure that you have made reasonable attempts to resolve any problems with the seller in advance though, as mistakes do happen.

Interpreting feedback scores

Although all members would love to maintain a 100% positive feedback score this can be hard to achieve, especially if you have a very high turnover of transactions. It's just down to the law of averages, really, and the fact that some people are nigh impossible to please. It is also possible that a buyer/seller who has let you down will leave you retaliatory feedback in response to a negative comment from you, even if you have done nothing wrong. This is why it always pays to read the comments others have left rather than just rely on the figures. If the same complaint occurs again and again about a member then you should obviously take heed, but the odd grumble shouldn't worry you unduly.

The breakdown of each type of comment is shown on a member's profile, along with a timescale of 1 months, 6 months and 12 months. To access the non-positive comments you would see where they had occurred and then click on the appropriate period. If a member doesn't have that much feedback then it is just as easy to scroll down the page and look out for the negative or neutral comments which are designated by a red negative sign ⊖ or a grey dot ◉ respectively.

eBay operates a star rating system to reward members once they have accrued a certain number of positive feedbacks and for some people this acts as an added incentive to perform well as either a buyer or seller. When you first join eBay and have zero feedback or only a small number, a symbol like this will appear next to your username:

This tells other members that you are new to the site. If you change your username at any stage your new name will carry a symbol like this:

![symbol]

and other members will be able to check what other name or names you were previously known by and the feedback attributed to that former identity. This acts as a safeguard against those members who frequently switch ID in order to escape a bad feedback history. Of course, there are legitimate reasons to change one's ID; for example, if a seller wishes to delineate between different types of merchandise that they trade in on the site.

The right to reply

To ensure that the feedback process runs in a democratic manner, members are allowed to reply to any feedback they receive, be it positive, negative or neutral. This is relevant to you in two ways:

People you're thinking of trading with

If you are thinking of bidding on an item, and you notice that the seller has some negative feedback, check whether he replied to it and whether he made a convincing defence of the allegations. Not all negative feedback is justified, and after reading both sides of the story you may decide that the feedback was unjustified and that it is safe for you to bid. By the same token, be wary of sellers who don't reply to their negative feedback or do so in a really vague way. They may be trying to disguise their bad practices!

Your own feedback

Sometimes, when someone leaves *you* feedback, you may want to reply to it. If the feedback was positive, you may want to sign off the satisfactory transaction with a final 'thank you', Conversely, if the feedback was negative you may want to defend yourself by giving your side of the story. eBay gives you that opportunity.

To reply to any of your feedback, irrespective of its rating, simply scroll down to the bottom of your feedback profile page and click on 'Reply to Feedback Received'. You can then type in your reply, albeit in a limited fashion (the same 80 characters, so no novels).

A question of timing

There is always a lot of debate on eBay forums about the etiquette of feedback and *when* it should be left, especially by sellers. Some think that it should be left as soon as payment is made; others say they prefer to know that the goods have been received and the buyer is happy before they leave feedback. This, I can only assume, is to give the seller more of a right to reply should a buyer make a complaint and/or negative them and, as I say, some amount of retaliatory feedback does sadly occur.

> "The giving and receiving of feedback on eBay should be a matter of mutual self-interest, but is not compulsory."

Most legitimate sellers will do their utmost to avoid this situation, however, and as a buyer, you should follow the same etiquette by allowing them to remedy any potential problems before diving in with negative feedback. Do remember, too, that sellers will be much more inclined to help you *before* you've left them a nasty comment than after!

Having said this, if all reasonable attempts have been made to contact the seller and you have still failed to get a resolution to your problem then you should of course leave appropriate feedback as well as seek recourse through the proper protection policy channels where applicable. Even if you are afraid of receiving negative feedback in retaliation for your comments you owe it to the wider eBay community to warn others if a seller is dodgy or dishonest.

In over 900 transactions the one negative I received came from a seller who had sold me faulty goods and then refused to reply to my emails. I gave her the benefit of the doubt and waited three weeks for a reply but eventually left negative feedback. Her response, *the very same day*, was to negative me back even though I had upheld my side of the deal and paid for the item immediately.

Building up positive feedback

Although you may eventually want to trade on eBay as a seller, the best and quickest way to build up your feedback score is through buying. Of course you will want to ensure that you pay promptly and communicate well with your trading partner in order to start your profile off on the right foot. Nothing looks quite so bad as a low feedback score which already contains lots of negative comments and you couldn't blame anyone in this circumstance if they were unwilling to do business with you.

In a worse case scenario you can even get an overall negative feedback score which basically means that the number of negative comments received exceeds the number of positives. You don't see many of these and they usually belong to what eventually turn out to be scammers but some sellers (myself included) choose to automatically block buyers with this type of feedback. More information about how to block unwanted bidders from your auction listings can be found on page 311.

When you are new to eBay, you have no feedback at all, of course. Might people refuse to deal with you? Well, they might, but in general, other users know that everyone has to start somewhere on eBay and will cut you some slack. You will occasionally see an auction in which the seller specifies that he/she does not want to receive bids from 'newbies'. Don't be offended by this, and *do* comply with their wishes; it is, after all, their caution that safeguards you and others using the site. Even if there is no such restriction, it's a good idea, when you're brand new, have no feedback, and want to bid, to drop the seller a friendly email beforehand and let them know that your intentions are honourable. Usually that calms any nerves.

'Feedback exhortation'

The giving and receiving of feedback on eBay should be a matter of mutual self-interest, but it is not compulsory and not everyone does it. If you have forgotten to leave feedback for a member and they email you politely to ask if you will do so, the reasonable thing to do is to oblige their request – as long as you feel comfortable doing so. Everyone needs feedback to build up their profile especially if they are new to the site.

'Feedback exhortation' is a different and altogether more pernicious phenomenon which I have not experienced myself but which reputedly goes on. It happens when members (usually sellers) are threatened by buyers with negative feedback unless they perform certain actions; give a postage discount, lower the cost of the winning bid, change an item, etc.

If, as a seller, you know there was nothing wrong with the item and/or the buyer has taken months before lodging a complaint, something is definitely awry and you should stand firm and report the situation to eBay, copying them any correspondence from the party concerned. The culprit will most likely get a warning from eBay or may even be NARU'd which basically means getting permanently suspended from the site.

If, as a buyer, you are slightly unhappy with a transaction but the value of the item is too low to kick up a real fuss then the appropriate course of action is probably not to leave feedback at all. I once bought something from a seller and it arrived damaged. When I asked for the seller's assistance he basically said it was my own fault for not taking up insurance. Although I was annoyed I couldn't really argue against his case and, though he could have been slightly nicer in his response, I ended up not leaving feedback for the transaction (neither, might I add, did he). I also learned a valuable lesson in buying postal insurance.

'Feedback withdrawal'

Once you have left feedback it is very difficult to retract it although if both parties agree that their comments were made in error it is possible to do so through the mutual feedback withdrawal form. Withdrawing feedback in this way means that although the comments can still be read by others they do not adversely affect your overall feedback score.

Mutual feedback retraction must take place within 30 days of the original feedback being left or within 90 days of the transaction, whichever is longer. The downside to this system, obviously, is that it does require both parties to agree to the withdrawal and this can sometimes be tricky to negotiate. Incidentally, if one of the parties has not yet left feedback at the time the mutual withdrawal comes into effect they forfeit their right to do so. Should you need it, the link for the appropriate form can be found at:

pages.ebay.co.uk/help/account/withdraw-feedback.html

'Feedback removal'

There have to be fairly exceptional circumstances for feedback comments to actually be removed from public view. The most compelling is if a court order has been issued by one member against another for libel. The risk of libel is one reason why eBay urges members to stick to purely factual information when leaving feedback, (even though one person's fact might well be construed as another person's fantasy), and why eBay constantly stresses that your own words remain your sole responsibility.

Other circumstances where eBay might consider the removal of feedback is where there has been the use of profane or racist language, where the feedback includes confidential information about a member, where there are references to eBay or other official investigations, and/or when the feedback is from a member who has been NARU'd or should have been at the time the feedback was left.

Your own feedback score

As mentioned, your feedback profile can be accessed at any time by going to My eBay and scrolling down the left-hand margin to the 'Feedback' link (see overleaf). This is also where many other useful features of the site can be found and it's where we'll be going in the next section.

Exploring 'My eBay'

The 'My eBay' pages of the site are basically your personalised control panel from where you can watch items, leave feedback, check messages, change preferences and carry out a whole host of other useful tasks. A summary of all the 'views' accessible from My eBay is shown below. Clicking on any of them takes you to a more detailed window in that category.

Fig. 26 – My eBay views

My Summary

All Buying
- Watching (1)
- Bidding
- Best Offers
- Won (17)
- Didn't Win
- My Recommendations

All Selling
- Scheduled
- Selling
- Sold
- Unsold
Marketing Tools NEW!

Want It Now

My Messages

All Favourites
- Searches
- Sellers
- Categories

My Account
- Personal Information
- Addresses
- Preferences
- Feedback
- PayPal Account
- Seller Account
- Subscriptions

My Reviews & Guides

Dispute Console

Most of these views are pretty self-explanatory but we'll look at some of the most common ones here:

'Watching'

This is where you can keep track of all the items you are interested in but don't yet want to bid on. The watching section shows a summary of all the pertinent information, including the number of bids received (if any), the current price and the time remaining before the auction ends. The information appears in real-time, so whenever you load the page you are getting an up-to-date snapshot.

If you *have* already bid on an item and are currently winning, the price will be shown in green; if you aren't winning, the price will appear in red.

Items that you have chosen to watch will remain in this view even after the auctions have ended (unless you manually delete them). This can be useful: knowing what price a particular item has sold for in the past can help you to judge your own bid when a similar item comes up for auction in the future.

If an item ends with zero bids this obviously means that it received no bids and remained unsold at the end of the auction. In this instance, clicking on the item description will tell you whether it has been relisted.

eBay allows anyone to watch up to 10 items as a guest, although this number becomes limitless once you become a member. However, if you intend to bid on an item you will need to sign in with your member details or, if you have yet to do so, you will need to register.

'All Selling'

If and when you decide to start selling on eBay this is where you are able to keep tabs on all your items, checking how many bids have been placed, the current price and how many members are 'watching' the item.

You can also see summaries of items you have already managed to sell (with their total price), and items that you did not sell, with an option to relist them. This, along with many more details about selling can be found in Part 4 of this book.

'All Favourites'

This view allows you to save particular sellers, item searches or categories for easy future reference. These are updated daily to take into account any new inventory being listed. In addition, you can choose to be notified of any new items via email on a daily, weekly, or longer period.

'Best Offers'

This view shows you any items for which you have submitted a Best Offer (See page 187 for more details) along with a summary of the status of that offer (whether accepted, declined or pending).

'My Recommendations'

Based on the items that you have recently bought or watched, eBay selects other items from its current inventory that you may be interested in. If anything does take your fancy you can either bid on it or move it to your watching page by clicking on the item and then selecting the option to 'watch this item'.

'Want it Now'

This is a similar system to the want ads that you see in local newspapers. If you can't find what you need in the main part of eBay you can post a request on a designated message board which sellers check periodically. If someone has what you are looking for they can contact you directly. When posting a request in the 'Want It Now' section try to be as specific as possible, describing the colour, condition, features and price range of the item you are looking for.

'My Account'

From this view you can amend or edit personal information pertaining to your membership including credit or debit card details, email addresses etc. You can also access and customise preferences such as notifications (how eBay contacts you), selling, and general issues such as whether you would like recent searches to be displayed each time you visit eBay.

'My Messages'

Whenever another member contacts you in response to a question you have asked, about an item you're selling, or for any other reason, the message is displayed in the in-box of this view. The message view is also used by eBay to contact you for promotional reasons or to inform you that it's time to pay your seller's fees!

The interface is very similar to that of a regular email programme and also includes an archiving facility and a sent box for messages you have written to other members. As well as appearing in 'My Messages', all correspondence is also sent to your registered email address just in case you don't visit eBay every day.

From this view you can also find a member's contact details, although this will only be accessible if you have transacted with this member in the previous 90 days. eBay will also notify the other party that you have issued this request and will send your own email details by return. Both of these actions are obviously in place to safeguard other members' security.

'My Reviews and Guides'

From time to time, eBay members with a specialist field of knowledge, such as cars or modernist furniture, may choose to write a guide to assist other members looking to purchase in this area. For example, the Buyer's Guides in Part 2 of this book could have appeared in this section.

There are currently two types of guides: those written by eBay staff or eBay partners and those written by eBay members such as you or I. In order to differentiate the two, the former are always accompanied by an eBay logo.

'Dispute Console'

If you have had cause to open a dispute with eBay as either a buyer or seller the details will appear here along with its current status and any actions already taken. You can learn much more about disputes and how they can be resolved by going to the section entitled 'What To Do If It All Goes Wrong', starting on page 239.

'Items I've Won'

This view shows the list of items you have won at auction or bought on a BIN basis, and the total price you paid. From the drop-down menus in this view you can also check on both payment and dispatch status (as long as the other party has informed eBay of these).

Symbols used on My eBay

eBay uses a system of symbols to give a quick reference guide to whether items have been paid for and whether feedback has been left and received. Fig. 27 shows these symbols with their definitions.

Fig. 27 – My eBay symbols explained

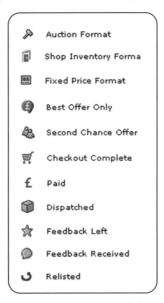

When these symbols are highlighted it indicates that the action has taken place whilst a greyed out symbol shows which parts of the transaction are still outstanding. If you pay for an item via PayPal the system is automatically updated to take account of this information; with other methods of payment you will need to manually select the option 'mark as payment sent' from the drop-down menu alongside the item description.

Advanced search techniques

Now that you've had some practice with browsing and perhaps even bidding we'll turn our attention to some advanced search techniques that can enhance your buying experience even more.

What advanced searching does eBay offer?

At the top right of most eBay pages you will find the search box and, directly beneath this, a link to the advanced search option.

Choosing this link will take you to a new page where you can search according to a wide range of criteria including *bidder, category, completed listings, country/region, ISBN, keyword, item number, 'My Favourite Searches', sellers* and *post code.*

The screenshot below shows you the 'Advanced Search' page.

Fig. 28 – eBay's Advanced Search page

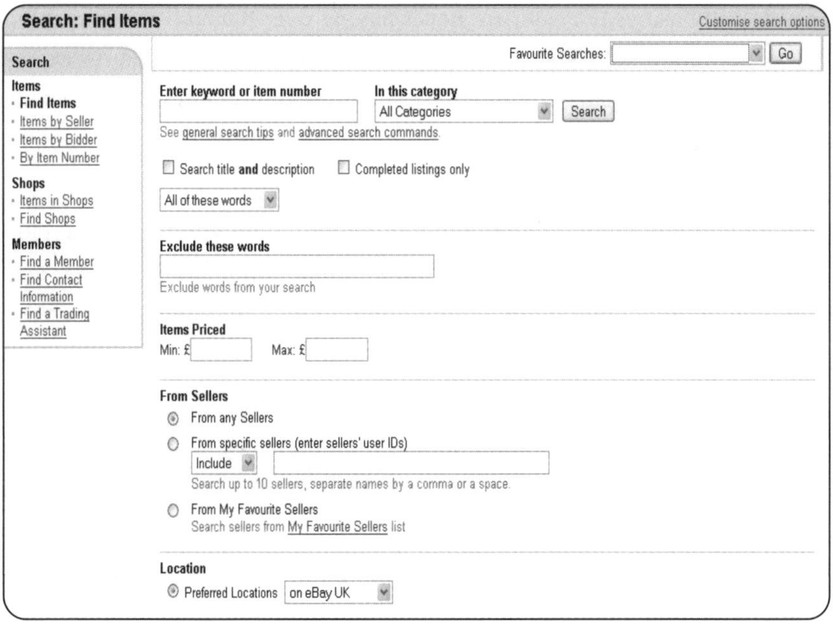

As you become more familiar with this page, you can experiment with different search criteria. For now, let's look at three of the most popular ways to use this facility.

Search by keyword

One of my favourite uses of this option is to compare the final sale prices of similar items that have been sold on eBay. As a buyer this can tell you what you can expect to pay and/or what not to pay, and as a seller you can see what sort of price you should charge and/or expect to realise should you sell something similar yourself.

To research items in this way, make sure that you tick the box labelled 'Completed Listings Only' once you have entered your search term. This narrows the search to auctions that have finished.

Once you have researched the price of items you are interested in you should make a note of them on the 'Items I'm Watching' view of My eBay. For example, if you are watching a particular pram you could add a note under the item listing to the effect of 'Usually goes for between £130 – £210'. Making notes in this way gives you a good ballpark figure within which to operate and ensures that you are never paying over the odds for something. If you get really keen you can even research which days of the week and which times of day tend to realise the highest/lowest prices. There are some hints and tips covering this last point in Part 4 of this book.

A spare hour spent browsing the site can be a lot of fun but sometimes you want to look for something quickly and specifically. For this purpose eBay has devised a special grammar which enables you to fine-tune your searching. This is achieved by using simple keystroke commands such as punctuation/quotation marks.

For example, when searching for an item containing certain words in a particular order you should use quotation marks; hence, a search for "Apple Green" will only return results containing the words 'Apple Green' in that order and not those containing the words 'Green' or 'Apple' on their own or the words 'Green Apple'. Fig. 29 opposite provides a concise summary of the search commands.

Fig. 29 – eBay's search commands

Search Commands

Search commands are ways of narrowing your search to get more specific results.

Note:
eBay searches are not case-sensitive, so whether or not you use capital letters, your results will be the same.

Your goal: You're looking for items where two or more keywords are all present.
Command: Just enter the keywords with a space between them.
Example search: Wedgwood cups blue
Returns: Items with all three words in the title in any order

Your goal: You're looking for items containing certain words in a particular order.
Command: Place quotation marks around the group of words.
Example search: "Gone With the Wind"
Returns: Items with titles containing Gone With the Wind, but not those just containing wind, gone or Gone With Wind

Your goal: You're looking for items that don't contain a certain word.
Command: Place a minus sign immediately before the word to be excluded (no space).
Example search: bib overalls -baby
Returns: Items with titles containing the words bib and overalls but not containing the word baby

Your goal: You're looking for items that don't contain several words.
Command: Place a minus sign before the list of words separated by commas (with no spaces) and put in parentheses.
Example search: Wedgwood -(black,green,purple)
Returns: Items with titles containing the word Wedgwood but not containing black, green or purple.

Your goal: You're looking for items where one word or another is present.
Command: Enter keywords in parentheses separated by commas. (No space after the commas.)
Example search: (Wedgwood,Lenox)
Returns: Items whose titles contain either the word Wedgwood or Lenox

Search for items by bidder

eBay's 'Items by Bidder' facility allows you to enter any eBay member's username and either see what they've recently won (by selecting the *completed items* checkbox) or what they are currently bidding on. This can be a very useful tool if you find yourself going head-to-head in various auctions against the same bidder. Looking at their completed items allows you to see what they have recently bought and what they were prepared to pay. There is a point to this seeming prurience and that is to determine whether you are ever likely to be in a position to outbid this person or whether they just have very deep pockets!

You can also see whether they are buying items in order to resell by doing the same member search but this time selecting 'Items by Seller'. If it transpires that this person is, indeed, also a trader, you can be pretty sure that they will always have the financial advantage – although as a pro they are more likely to bid with their head than their heart!

If you are still prepared to compete against them, click on one or two of their completed items and bring up the bidding history by clicking on the number of bids that were recorded. Next to each bid will be the time it was placed. Comparing this time to the time the auction actually ended will tell you this individual's bidding strategy, i.e, whether they demonstrate 'normal' bidding behaviour or whether they prefer to snipe in the closing seconds of an auction.

Another useful feature of the Items by Bidder facility is that you can check out what *current* auctions this member is bidding on. (When you do this remember to check the box labelled 'Even if not high bidder'). On quite a few occasions I have used this technique to find items I was interested in but hadn't found in the course of my own browsing. If you do find something you like you can simply add it to your watching section of My eBay.

Search for items by seller

If there is a seller whose inventory you watch on a regular basis, or who seems to stock things you are interested in, you can add them to a favourites list which then gets stored in My eBay.

When you do this, you can also add a note directly beneath their name, for example 'Good for nursery furniture' or 'Stocks a wide range of educational toys'. If, like me, you have quite a few sellers flagged in this way you can quickly forget what it is they specialise in; adding a note serves as a useful aide-memoire. The 'Add to Favourite Sellers' link can be found on the right hand side of any of their listings under 'Meet the Seller'.

Accessing your favourite seller's inventory can either be done via the appropriate section of My eBay or by doing an advanced search by seller. Simply type the seller's username into the advanced search box and hit return.

Another virtue of using this method is that you can also see recently completed sales simply by checking the 'Show Completed Listings' box. This means that if you see something which you missed you can contact the seller and ask them if they will have the item in stock again and whether they will mail you if/when they do.

Searching off eBay

As mentioned earlier, eBay is not *always* the best place for bargains so do be sure to check out the numerous price comparison websites now available. You will probably find items priced the same as or even cheaper than the Buy It Now prices advertised on eBay, and charging less or even zero postage. Plus, your consumer rights are more likely to be protected when buying from an established retail outlet.

Another tip for items such as music or books is to try somewhere that specialises in this type of merchandise. Often, the inventory will be much larger, thereby increasing your choice, and their specialisation means that they can negotiate bigger discounts with their suppliers which are then passed on to you. My favourites of these are www.ebuyer.co.uk and www.amazon.co.uk

Thousands of new items are listed on eBay every day and sometimes the most effective way of finding a bargain is to think in a non-linear fashion. What do I mean by this? Well, when searching for something to buy, most people type in the correct spelling of an item, brand name or product, but when listing items for sale hundreds of sellers don't! The consequence is that the buyers fail to find the items of the sellers, and those items, in some cases, sell very cheaply because of a lack of bids. What if there was a facility that could search on your behalf for every spelling permutation of an item, both correctly and incorrectly spelled? Believe it or not, such facilities really do exist.

My personal favourite is Bargainchecker, at www.bargainchecker.com You select the eBay site you want to search (in our case eBay.co.uk) and input your chosen search term making sure you enter the correct spelling. I have found that one-word searches or brand names yield the best results. Bargainchecker then searches for any and all possible permutations of that term (including or excluding the correct spelling). Sometimes this produces a staggering number of items, some of which have attracted few or even no bids because they were misspelled (and therefore unable to be found on normal searches). Of course, other eBayers may have stumbled across them in a description search but there is always likely to be less interest in badly spelled items and therefore some potential bargains to be had.

Other variations on this theme include www.fatfingers.com, www.ebay-typos.com and www.auctionfigure.com. The last of these sites aims not only to improve your search for bargains but to alert you to potentially dodgy sellers using their own developed criteria.

One important reality check to give here is that very few sellers will misspell the seriously high value items like Bugaboos or Stokke Xplorys. I guess there's just too much for them to lose to be so careless but hey . . . you never know!

What to do if it all goes wrong

Thankfully, most transactions on eBay take place without problems, both parties are happy, and positive feedback is exchanged. However, there are occasions when something goes wrong. This can happen for a number of reasons, the most publicised of which are scams. eBay *is* subject to scams from time to time and we'll be examining the most common types and how to avoid them a bit later. For now, however, let's turn our attention to the most frequent cause of complaint on eBay: good old human error.

Areas of complaint

The three main areas of complaint that eBay has to deal with are:

- Item not received (Buyer complaint)
- Item not as described (Buyer complaint)
- Unpaid item (Seller complaint)

For each of these there are certain steps which you should follow as a first port of call before involving the heavier guns of either eBay or PayPal's complaints procedures.

First steps

Check your facts

Before you complain it is always a good idea to make sure of your facts.

Item not received

If your complaint is that the item has not been received, check to see if the item is coming from abroad and, if it is, take the extra transit time into account. Then consider whether it may have been delayed at customs.

If enough time has passed, find out if the other party obtained a proof of posting certificate. This is issued free and contains the recipient's name and address and a postmarked stamp from the issuing post office.

If the item was valuable, and you fear that it may have been lost, check whether you asked for/took out insurance cover.

Item not as described

If you did receive the item, but it is significantly different from the way it was described, double-check the listing to check what the seller actually said, and whether there really was a misrepresentation. Did you read the small print? Could the description given be interpreted in several ways, such that what has occurred is a misunderstanding rather than misrepresentation? If a photo accompanies the listing, is it a photo of the product you have been sent, or a stock photo?

Send an email

The checks above are designed to stop you going in, all guns blazing, and then realising that perhaps the seller did not behave as badly as you first thought. Even if you decide that the fault is all his, your first move should not be overly aggressive.

In the first instance, email the seller and explain why you are unhappy. If you paid by PayPal you will have the seller's email address on your receipt. If you paid by another method, you can make contact through the link on the completed listings page.

Tell the seller politely that you would like to resolve the issue before feedback is exchanged and ask him to suggest an appropriate course of action. Give him a reasonable time to respond (perhaps 2-3 days) and then email again. Always keep your communications professional and non-threatening.

Fig. 30 – Specimen email for *Item Not Received* or *Item Not as Described*

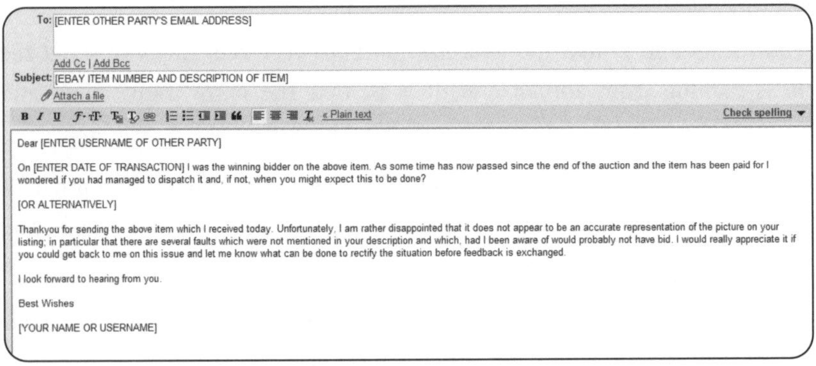

Unpaid item

If you are the seller of an item, and the dispute is over non-payment, contact the buyer and politely remind him that it has been X number of days since the listing ended and that by winning the auction they have entered into an agreement to complete the transaction. You can send your email using the link on the completed listings page.

Fig. 31 – Specimen email for *Unpaid Item*

If you get no reply

If you get no reply from the other party, ask eBay to supply you with their contact details and **make sure you are sending your email to the correct address**. They may also have a telephone number on file for them.

To request a member's contact information go to the 'Advanced Search' link, located under the search button in the top right hand corner of most eBay pages. From the members section on the left hand side of the page click on the link for 'Find Contact Information' and enter the member's username and the transaction number which you have in common. The member's details will be sent to your registered email address. As well as being informed of your request the other party will also be sent your contact information.

You should also **check your email spam filters** to make sure that a message from the other party hasn't accidentally been junked by your email program. If you have recently changed your own contact details check that these have also been updated on eBay's records.

- If, after reasonable attempts to contact the other party you are still unsuccessful you should then file a complaint with eBay under the appropriate heading (see 'eBay's dispute processes explained', below).

- If you have paid for your item with a credit card, either directly or via PayPal, you will probably be covered by your card issuer although some will only compensate for transactions over a certain value.

- If you paid via PayPal you can also file a complaint directly through them. This is covered more fully in the section on PayPal, starting on page 265.

Square Trade

Some sellers display a logo on their page which looks like this:

Square Trade is one way for legitimate sellers to demonstrate that they are committed to ethical and fair practices and have been verified by a third party. To retain this seal they must agree to participate in Square Trade's Dispute Process, have their identity verified by Square Trade and commit to Square Trade's standards for online selling. If you have a dispute with a seller displaying the Square Trade logo you can be assured that the seller will respond. Square Trade also guarantees all listings with a verified Square Trade seal for up to $250 compensation against fraud.

eBay's dispute processes explained

Out of over 900 transactions on eBay I have had only 9 which ended less than satisfactorily. These included (as a buyer): one damaged item, one not as described, five which never arrived and, (as a seller), two unpaid for by the winning bidder.

With the exception of the damaged item and the two items that were never paid for I managed to successfully liaise with the other party concerned to reach an amicable resolution. Most of the time I received a replacement but I have also had full refunds for items that were lost. There is no secret formula to this outcome; just a process of open, honest communication with the other people involved and a well-developed habit of checking feedback before even thinking about bidding. I also always make sure that as both a buyer and a seller, proof of posting is always obtained so that at least part of the financial burden for items lost or damaged will be shouldered by the mail company concerned.

If you cannot resolve a problem with your trading partner there are protection policies in place on eBay to help you. Each has its own steps which are outlined below.

Item not received / Item not as described

If you fail to receive an item which you have paid for, or if it arrives and is significantly different from what you thought you were buying, this is the process you need to follow. There are five steps in all which must be taken in the correct order:

Step 1. Open a dispute

You can do this anytime between 10-60 days after the transaction ends (the date of 'commitment' between buyer and seller). If the item was paid for by PayPal you will be immediately referred to the PayPal claims process. Fig. 32 shows the screen which you will be taken to when first opening a dispute.

Fig. 32 – Opening a dispute

Report an Item Not Received

It's rare for a transaction to go wrong on eBay, but sometimes problems can occur. If you've got a problem with a transaction the Item Not Received or Significantly Not as Described Process can help you resolve it.

Use this process when:
- You paid for an item but didn't receive it, or
- You paid for and received an item, but it was significantly different from the item description.

The most effective way to resolve transaction problems is direct and open communication between buyers and sellers. Once you initiate this process you will be able to communicate directly with your seller on the eBay Web site in order to resolve your problem.

Before you initiate this process, please make sure you have:
- Reviewed the item listing carefully.
- Emailed and called your seller.
- Ensured eBay has your correct contact information.
- Checked your spam filter for missed emails.

Learn more about the steps you should take before initiating this process.

You can begin this process at any time between 10 days and 60 days after the listing ended. Please enter the item number below and click **Continue** to get started.

Item number

| How do I find the item number? |

Continue >

Step 2. eBay contacts the seller on your behalf

eBay emails the seller to let them know that a dispute concerning them has been opened and encourages them to communicate with you. On many occasions this is as far as the official process needs to go as most reputable sellers will immediately try and remedy the situation privately with you.

Step 3. The seller responds

The seller is asked to choose from several responses which will determine the direction the dispute then takes.

In the case of an unreceived item, a seller selects from the following responses:

- *Payment has not been received, or has not yet cleared.*

- *I've already posted the item.* (The seller may need to provide proof.)

- *I'll offer a full refund.*

In the case of an item being not as described the seller can select from the following responses:

- *I've dispatched a replacement item.* (The seller may need to provide postage details to the buyer.)

- *I'll offer a refund.* (The seller may offer a full or partial refund.)

For both types of disputes the seller can also select:

- *I would like to communicate with the buyer.* (They will then post a message for you to review.)

Step 4. Mediated communication between buyer and seller

Both parties attempt to resolve things by communicating directly through eBay's online process.

Step 5. Closing the dispute

The buyer can close the dispute if the seller does not respond within 10 days, or anytime after the seller responds as long as at least 17 days have passed since the auction end. The buyer chooses from two options to close the dispute:

1. *My concerns have been resolved.*

    If the buyer chooses this option, no further action is taken against the seller and the buyer is <u>not</u> then eligible to claim under eBay's 'Standard Protection Programme'. Once closed, a dispute cannot be reopened so the buyer must be sure that they are entirely happy with this option. If a refund has been promised buyers are advised not to close the dispute until it has actually been received.

2. *I feel I have no other option but to escalate this to a claim.*

    When you select this option eBay's Trust and Safety Team is alerted about the transaction and if any suspicious activity is detected the seller's account may be restricted or suspended. If the transaction is eligible you may then file a claim under eBay's Standard Protection Programme where you can be reimbursed up to £105 (£120 minus a £15 processing fee). The safety team will then investigate the seller's account further and take any necessary additional action.

You should note that the reimbursement fees only cover the **final bid price** of the item/s in question and do not cover ancillary fees such as postage, packing and handling or fees incurred through additional services such as escrow.

A dispute can only be open for 90 days after the end of the auction. If a buyer fails to close the dispute after 90 days this will be done automatically. In these circumstances, the seller is not reported to eBay and the buyer becomes ineligible to submit a claim under the 'Standard Purchase Protection Programme'.

Feedback and disputes

NOTE

Buyers and sellers may still exchange feedback on items where a dispute has been opened and, indeed, eBay encourages this feedback for the information it relays to other members.

Participating in a dispute does not automatically alter a member's feedback score or profile.

Unpaid item dispute

If you go on to become an eBay seller you may have the misfortune of encountering a NPB or 'Non-Paying-Bidder' – in other words, a winning bidder who fails to come up with payment. After item not received / item not as described disputes, non-payment is the next most common cause of complaint amongst eBayers.

Sellers in this situation can open an 'Unpaid Items' dispute through eBay. As with the 'Item Not Received' process members are encouraged to try to solve the problem themselves first, by direct communication, but if this proves unsuccessful these are the steps you need to follow:

Step 1. Open a dispute

This can be done up to 45 days after the end of the auction. Usually you will have to wait at least seven days before filing the claim to give the buyer time to pay but this rule does NOT apply if:

- at the time of filing the buyer is No Longer A Registered User of eBay (i.e. they have been NARU'd); or

- the buyer and you mutually wish to withdraw from the transaction.

In both these cases you, as the seller, can file a claim immediately.

Under the first of these exceptions the buyer will receive an unpaid item strike and you will receive a 'Final Value Fee Credit (FVF Credit)' without any further action needed. The 'Final Value Fee' is the charge that eBay makes to sellers based on the final selling price of their items.

In the second of these exceptions sellers will receive a FVF credit but the buyer will not receive an unpaid item strike. Even if the buyer fails to respond to the dispute, it can be closed by the seller to the same effect.

Step 2. eBay contacts the buyer

Once the dispute has been filed, eBay will send an email notification to the buyer. Also, if the buyer accesses their eBay account within 14 days of the dispute being filed a pop-up message will appear. Both the email and the pop-up will contain one of the following:

- •. A friendly reminder to pay.

- • A link allowing the buyer to pay immediately or to respond to you directly.

If there is no response from the buyer within 7 days you can file for a FVF credit. You also become eligible for a free relist credit which, as the name suggests, allows you to relist the defaulted item free of charge.

If, during the course of the dispute you inform eBay that a mutual decision has been reached not to proceed with the transaction, eBay will contact the buyer to confirm that this is the case. If confirmation is received, you will receive a FVF credit and the buyer will not receive an 'Unpaid Item Strike'. If a buyer disagrees with this assertion, however, you will not receive a FVF credit neither will the buyer be penalised. In this second scenario the dispute is immediately closed and you would not be eligible to refile the dispute.

If the buyer fails to respond within 7 days, you are at liberty to close the dispute. You will receive a FVF credit and the buyer will receive an unpaid item strike.

Step 3. Mediated communication between buyer and seller

eBay presents the buyer with several response options:

1. *I want to pay now.*

   Paying for the item via PayPal will automatically close the dispute. If the buyer chooses to pay via any other means it is advisable to wait for payment to clear before manually closing the dispute.

2. *I have already paid.*

   If the buyer asserts that payment has already been sent for the item they may need to provide proof of this to you for review. It is then up to you whether you wish to close the dispute.

3. *I want to communicate with the seller.*

   You and the buyer can attempt to resolve the problem by communicating directly through eBay. eBay provides a dedicated message area for this exchange. From this message area the seller can choose to close the dispute at any time by selecting the appropriate option.

Step 4. Closing the dispute

As the seller you can close the dispute after the buyer has responded at least once or has not responded within 7 days. You have several ways to close the dispute:

1. *We've completed the transaction and we're both satisfied.*

   If you choose this option you will not receive a FVF credit and the buyer will not receive an Unpaid Item Strike.

2. *I no longer wish to communicate with or wait for the buyer.*

   This option becomes available on the 8th day of the dispute or once the buyer responds. With this option the buyer receives an Unpaid Item Strike and you receive an FVF credit and the item becomes eligible to be relisted for free.

3. *We've agreed not to complete the transaction.*

   This option is available after the buyer responds at least once. When you select this, the buyer does not receive an Unpaid Item Strike and you receive a FVF credit. The item is also eligible for a free relist.

A dispute can only remain open for 60 days after the transaction date. If you have not closed the dispute after this time it will be automatically closed. If that happens, you will forfeit your right to a FVF credit and the buyer will not have an Unpaid Item Strike made against them.

What happens regarding feedback in this situation?

If the buyer does not respond to an 'Unpaid Item Notification' and you close the dispute, with the buyer receiving an Unpaid Item Strike, they can still leave feedback for the transaction but any rating they leave will not appear and will not count towards your final feedback score. An administrative note by eBay will also appear underneath the buyer's feedback comment explaining that the buyer did not participate in the dispute process.

It is important to leave appropriate feedback for a wayward buyer in order to warn others. The risk of retaliatory feedback should not deter you from upholding the community spirit and is, anyway, easily recognised for what it is. Unpaid item strikes do not (sadly) affect a user's feedback score or member profile.

If, however, a member accrues a large number of unpaid item strikes within a short space of time (both to be determined by eBay), they may have their account suspended indefinitely. In some cases, limits may also be placed on the buyer's account in advance of the decision to suspend.

Compensation: eBay's Standard Purchase Protection

Whilst leaving feedback is all very good for the soul, most of the time you also want to be financially compensated for items which either don't turn up or are not what you expected. This is where eBay's 'Standard Purchase Protection' comes in: a process that reimburses eligible applicants for items purchased through the site. If you have not paid for your item by PayPal, this is the default choice for seeking compensation.

Who can claim?

Although most transactions on eBay will be covered by its Standard Purchase Protection there are a few conditions which govern whether your claim will be accepted. These are:

- You must have been the winning bidder on the item and completed the transaction through eBay.

- Both you and your trading partner must have a net feedback score of zero or above and not currently be the subject of investigation or suspension from the site.

- Your claim must have been filed within 90 days of the end of the auction.

- Your item must not contravene any of the criteria set out in eBay's User Policy, for example, it cannot be one which appears on eBay's list of prohibited items (see page 284).

- The value of the item must exceed £15, before postage costs.

- eBay makes an administrative charge of £15 for each claim, so a claim below that value is pointless. The £15 fee means that if you claim for an item costing £80 the most you will receive in compensation is £65. And the maximum that eBay will recompense for any item is £120 (£105 after its £15 fee). You should also note that eBay's Standard Purchase Protection only covers the winning price of the item in question and not costs incurred in postage and/or handling fees.

- You must not have claimed more than three times in the previous six month period.

- The item must not have been bought in an auction which had a reserve price and for which the reserve was not met. This is the case even if the seller eventually agreed to sell you the item for the closing price or below.

- You must have sent the seller money in good faith for the item and either never received it or received an item which was significantly different from the description. Items which have been damaged in transit are not covered and should be referred back to the mail/courier service in question.

Following on from this last point, if you receive a package via a courier service for which a signature is required, you should ensure that you sign for it as 'unchecked'. If the courier's form says 'Received in good condition', add a handwritten note on the manifest saying 'so far as could be ascertained from unopened package'. This will safeguard any future claim should the merchandise turn out to to have been damaged.

Items not covered by eBay's Standard Purchase Protection

- Any transaction paid for with cash or a cash equivalent service such as Western Union, Moneygram or Postal Order.

- Items that are picked up or delivered in person.

- Items not sold via eBay or for which you are not officially declared the winning bidder. This includes any listings which are completed off site or for reserve price auctions where the reserve was not met.

- Any item for which overpayment was received.

- Items where the buyer has simply changed their mind.

- Items that have been altered, repaired, discarded or resold. The item must be preserved in the condition in which it was received.

Filing a claim

With the above conditions in mind, if you think that you are eligible for eBay's Standard Purchase Protection you need to complete the following steps:

1. Complete the 'Item Not Received' or 'Significantly Not As Described' process (see above)

If you have already completed this step you should ensure that you close the dispute and select 'end communication with the seller'. If the transaction is deemed eligible you will then be taken to a link for the Standard Purchase Protection claim form.

2. Fill out the claim form

Fill out and submit the form. You can access this form from the dispute console view of My eBay: click on the relevant dispute and follow the link for 'View dispute'. Make sure you complete the form as accurately and as fully as possible.

3. Submit proof of payment

Within 14 days of a claim being filed, an eBay claims administrator may contact you via email and ask you to provide proof of payment for the item. If payment was made with a credit card but not via PayPal, eBay may require documentation from your card issuer confirming that they will not reimburse you for your loss. (eBay won't compensate you if you can get compensation elsewhere.) If you do not respond to eBay's request for this supporting documentation within 72 hours, eBay may close your case.

If you *have* paid for your item with a credit card be advised that there are alternative compensation schemes which may be offered, either through PayPal (if used) or through your credit card issuer directly. As the level of compensation offered by these alternative methods may be greater than that offered by eBay's Standard Purchase Protection I advise you to try these first. Instructions for this are covered in the section on PayPal beginning on page 265.

One born every minute: how to spot and avoid eBay scams

From *'That's Life'* in the 70s to *'Watchdog'* today, the TV schedules are filled with consumer programmes that demonstrate our weakness for scammers and confidence tricksters. No one, it seems, is immune; people from every walk of life can be successfully targeted and made a victim basically because everyone likes to think they can bag a bargain.

Not surprisingly, internet fraud has become one of the biggest areas of concern for both consumer and law enforcement agencies alike, and eBay, sadly, is a favourite target.

How much fraud is there on eBay?

Most of the transactions which take place on the site are conducted by well-meaning and honest individuals, but there is a small and highly dedicated group of fraudsters who operate within the community. New scams are constantly being devised and this section can only hope to scratch the surface.

eBay's official statistics put the incidence of fraud on the site at 0.01%. Put another way, for every million transactions, 100 will be fraudulent or have fraudulent intent. Anecdotally, the figure seems to be much higher and a Google search for eBay complaints throws up an alarming number of hits, including anti-PayPal sites, and forums awash with consumer complaints.

So, how do you protect yourself? My own view is that with a little bit of knowledge and common sense you can avoid becoming one of these statistics, and in my eight year history of using eBay I have only had three instances where I was a target of a scam. In each case I recognised the attempt for what it was and reported it immediately.

With its theoretical promise of bagging a bargain it is incredibly easy to be seduced into the clutches of a fraudster and it would be irresponsible of me not to include in this section a mention of the risks involved when trading on eBay.

Normal consumer protection law does not apply

The most important thing for you to know is that auctions, including internet auctions, are not covered by the consumer laws that prevail when you buy either from the high street or from on online retailer. The two most important laws in this regard are:

The Sale of Goods Act

This states that anything and everything you buy should be fit for its purpose, as it was described and of satisfactory quality. In addition that you should be entitled to a refund should the goods turn out to be faulty.

The Distance Selling Act

This covers purchases made through an online retailer and states that you should be entitled to return any goods which are not what you expected at the time of purchase.

For the vast majority of transactions which take place on eBay these consumer safe-havens are instead replaced with the caveat of *Buyer Beware*, the same principle which applies when buying, for example, a used car from an auction.

The one important exception to this is when goods are purchased on eBay Express, a speciality offshoot of eBay which only sells new items at a fixed price. The vendors of these items must be experienced eBay businesses who have met pre-approved criteria and who adhere to a strict standard of service. For these items, buyers are covered by the consumer laws detailed above which include the right to return an item for whatever reason within seven days of receiving it. In the case of items that are found to be misrepresented or faulty the refund must also include the costs of postage and handling. As with conventional retailers, however, there are exceptions to the returns policy, full details of which can be found at the following link:

pages.express.ebay.co.uk/service/about/checklist.html

The added level of security that eBay Express offers finds its disadvantage in the fact that prices are usually set close to the full retail price, a factor which most people looking for a bargain would probably find off-putting. For the rest of us, therefore, what safeguards are there when shopping via the conventional auction route?

- Firstly, I cannot stress enough the importance of checking both the feedback and selling history of potential trading partners. In particular, beware of sellers with high levels/disproportionate amounts of negative feedback. Read the comments carefully: are they all saying the same thing?

- If a seller does not respond to your questions or responds in a vague way, steer clear. There will be another similar item on the site soon.

- Be cautious of sellers suddenly trading in high value goods after building up lots of positive feedback selling much cheaper items. They may have used unethical means to falsify/build up their feedback in preparation for a big scam.

- If a seller has recently changed their username, check feedback from previous names to ensure they are not trying to escape a bad profile.

- Don't be tempted to buy items prohibited under eBay's rules or anything which potentially infringes copyright (bootleg computer games/DVD's etc). eBay maintains a list of items prohibited from the site. Not surprisingly it includes items such as satellite decoders, animals and lock picking devices. For a full list check out eBay's help section or see page 284 for more information.

Types of eBay scam

Below is a list of the most common type of scam being carried out on eBay at the time of writing:

1. Emails purporting to be from eBay, PayPal or its trading partners

Whenever money changes hands you can be sure that fraud is not far behind and if you are a member of eBay or its sister company, PayPal, forewarned is forearmed.

Perhaps the most common scam involves the sending of emails purporting to be from PayPal and/or eBay soliciting confidential details from you in order to 'update their records'. This is also known in the trade as 'phishing'.

Some of these emails are instantly recognisable because of their amateurish layout and appalling spelling. Much more dangerous are those which faithfully reproduce the design of the real site and, to all intents and purposes, look genuine.

The giveaway, however, is that they almost always begin with the line 'Dear eBay member' or 'Dear PayPal member'. True emails from eBay or PayPal will always address you by the name you entered upon registration and they will never ask for confidential details such as your credit card number, username or password to be forwarded via email. Beware, too, of those containing links or attachments which purport to redirect you to a safe place to update these details and which open a new window when opened. They are bogus.

On the rare occasions when eBay does request information from you (for example, when a seller has not been able to contact you because your details are missing or incomplete) you will receive a message alert via the My eBay section of the site. Always update such detail requests from the eBay interface itself; it's just safer that way.

If you suspect that you have received a fraudulent email forward it and any attachments to spoof@ebay.co.uk where it will be thoroughly investigated.

2. PayPal pyramid scheme

This scam is as old as the hills and one which I was asked to participate in no less than three times in one month.

Someone with whom I had recently traded sent me an email containing what I can only describe as a glorified chain letter and asked me to forward it on to ten other eBayers with whom I had conducted business via PayPal. In addition I was asked to deposit the sum of £3 into the account of the person named at the top of the list. The idea was that every time one of these contacts perpetuated the chain my name would move higher up the mythical pyramid until it reached the top; money beyond my wildest dreams would then follow.

It sounds ridiculous that anyone would ever be caught out by such a scheme, but the email itself was quite plausibly written. What actually prevented me from falling for the trick (apart from my inbuilt bullshit radar) was the appalling breach of trust my participation required, trust that is implicit in all transactions on eBay. I reported the scam without naming names and also emailed the sender of the email warning them against using my details lest I report them to eBay. If this had happened they would almost certainly have been NARU'd by the site.

Incidentally, contrary to the reassurances contained within the email, these types of schemes are completely *illegal.*

3. Fraudulent sellers

It's worth emphasising that the majority of sellers on eBay are trustworthy individuals looking to make an honest living and, providing you do the security checks outlined here and elsewhere in this section, you should rarely have cause for concern. No global business, however, is free from those who seek to exploit a situation for financial return and so I present below the most common scams that you may have the misfortune to encounter during your eBay career.

The basic fraud

The basic, common or garden, fraudulent sale is one where the seller advertises something for sale, takes your money, and then fails to send you the item, or sends you something materially different from that which was advertised e.g. counterfeit goods. One of the virtues of the feedback system is that it can quickly flag up people who engage in this type of fraud. Hopefully this ensures that dishonourable sellers don't stay in business for very long, although many try to avoid detection by changing their usernames.

As well as checking out feedback scrupulously, you should also be careful if you come across sellers who purport to be trading 'on behalf of a well-established company'. Do a Google search on the name of that company and/or email them to see if the seller is genuine.

The method you choose to pay by is important when it comes to damage limitation. Remember that if you pay by cash, postal order or cheque you have little recourse if the transaction is fraudulent. You do, however, have some protection if you pay via PayPal or by credit card. For high value items you should always endeavour to pay via PayPal; that way, even if the fraudsters do a number on you you'll still be protected. And, if you use a credit card like Visa or Mastercard you may, depending on the card issuer's terms, benefit from additional (and some say, even better) protection.

The long game

This is a variation on the basic fraud described above and can be one of the hardest scams to detect as the sellers involved often go to great lengths to cover their tracks. The classic method is to build up lots of positive feedback by selling low value items, then, once a sense of trust has been established over the course of several weeks or even months (the long game), the seller starts to offer items of much higher value. The unsuspecting bidder, reassured by the feedback score, buys those items which are then never received. By the time an investigation is launched the seller has disappeared.

The best way of avoiding this type of scam is to browse the feedback comments carefully. You can also use the advanced search facility to have a look at the seller's completed items in order to see whether they have recently changed trading direction. In other words if, after selling a large number of cheap items, they have suddenly switched to selling expensive ones. (Conducting advanced searches is covered on pages 233-238). Of course, there may be perfectly honourable reasons for the change, but you should be wary.

One-day auctions

The fact that something is for sale on a one-day auction does not automatically mean it is an attempted scam, but your defences should be raised.

One-day auctions are a favourite hangout of fraudsters because the time constraint works in their favour, as there is less time for bidders to ask awkward questions. When the auction end approaches and there has been no response to a question some bidders may decide to take a chance and bid anyway; this is what the fraudster relies on.

My advice with these auctions is to proceed with extreme caution. Ask yourself why the seller would want to hold a one-day auction when they are much more likely to get a good sale price by holding it over a longer period. There *can* be good reasons – for instance if the item being sold is a ticket to a concert happening in the next few days – and I discuss some of these more fully in Part 4 of this book. But more often a one-day auction makes no sense, and for that reasons you should be sceptical.

If you are in any doubt don't bid, don't pay and certainly don't excuse the lack of a reply to a pertinent question. As already mentioned, there will always be another day and another item; save your money until you're sure it's the right one.

If it looks too good to be true

One of the more recent scams to emerge on eBay involves the selling of highly desirable consumer durables such as iPods for unbelievably low prices.

When you click on one of these listings you are told that what you are actually paying for is not the item itself but information on, or a link to, a website where you can buy the item for that price. This in turn involves, at best, spending hundreds of pounds on other consumer goods in order to receive a discount on said iPod – some deal! At worst, you could find yourself paying for a dead link to...you guessed it...nothing at all.

As my dear old mother always says "There's no such fat goose lying in the road". If it looks too good to be true, it probably is.

Multiple User IDs

Although it is not against eBay regulations to have more than one username it *is* against the rules to allow these IDs to interact on each other's auctions or to leave each other feedback. This would tend to indicate 'shill bidding' (see below) which is not only against eBay's own rules but also illegal under the Fraud Act 2006.

Shill bidding

Shill bidding occurs when sellers use multiple usernames, or the usernames of friends/relatives, to artificially bid up an auction price. Although you might think that this would be hard to detect (how on earth can you know that Bidder Bob is a mate of Seller Simon?), a dodgy pattern of bidding can usually be picked up by looking at the seller's completed listings. If you see the same bidder cropping up on a seller's listings, but that bidder never seems to win, that indicates a potential ringer.

Buyers can also be involved in shill bidding by using a second username to put in a ridiculously high price in an attempt to scare off other bidders. Meanwhile they use their regular username to put themselves in the position of *second* highest bidder. Towards the end of the auction, or even after it, they retract their ridiculously high bid, allowing the second username to win the auction.

At the beginning of this year, the Sunday Times ran a lead article about shill bidding, suggesting that it is much more widespread than eBay admits. It cited several high profile sellers who admitted that they routinely enlist friends to bid up the price of items they are selling, and criticised eBay for not doing enough to combat the problem. eBay responded by saying that it thoroughly investigates suspicious bidding activity and anyone caught shill bidding risks a permanent ban from the site.

Not strictly fraud, but...

There are other offences which, although not technically fraudulent, can earn you a sharp slap on the wrists from eBay officials and, in serious and persistent cases, can get you NARU'd.

Auction spoiling

Spoiling someone's auction can take many forms. One way is for a bidder, who, by virtue of their location, feedback or payment method is not entitled to bid on an item, to do so anyway, putting in a high bid which then has to be cancelled by the seller. If the anomaly is not detected until after the auction has ended, the seller is then forced to relist the item or offer a lower second chance offer.

Another method is for phantom members (people who create bogus usernames with no intention of buying anything) to club together and submit ridiculously high bids for items. You can see this happening every day of the week on listings for consumer durables such as mobile phones. After they 'win' the auction, they obviously never pay. Although they would probably disagree, this type of spoiler is not unlike the self-styled auction vigilante who exists merely to sabotage auctions which they believe are unethical.

Examples of items the saboteurs love to wreak havoc on are tickets for music festivals, charity events, and football matches. Their justification is that they don't believe people should make a profit by selling these sorts of tickets at a mark-up. As the spoilers usually have zero feedback they look like new eBay members. Agree with their ethical stance or not, they don't do much for the reputation of eBay as an honest marketplace.

Soliciting bidders away from a sale

I have never encountered this myself, but I know several people who have received emails from one seller warning them off another seller's items. The tactics are all variations on a particularly nasty theme; saying that the other seller's goods are dangerous, for example, whilst trying to entice you to their own items for sale.

The best defence in these cases is to report the offending party to eBay along with copies of their correspondence to you.

Soliciting sellers to end an auction early

Some bidders may email a seller and attempt to get them to end the auction early for a certain price. They may also disguise this request by asking if the seller would be willing to sell the item on a Buy It Now basis, in itself a legitimate selling tool but only under certain conditions.

If there are no bids yet placed on an item a seller *can* add a BIN price to the listing but they are not allowed to cancel bids already placed in order to then sell the item off eBay. Although this is not illegal, sellers who are found to continuously withdraw their items for no apparent reason may be flagged and disciplined by eBay. In addition, you should remember that if you do choose to conduct business off the site you will not be covered for any loss or damage that you subsequently suffer.

I mentioned earlier that I have been the target of three scam attempts on eBay. One of them employed a variation on the "will you end your auction early?" theme. It happened like this:

I had decided to sell a fairly desirable mobile phone which I had received but didn't need. As a precaution, I set in place certain criteria which blocked bidders who did not match my requirements (see page 310 on how to do this). I also set a Buy It Now price of £150 on the phone. Within 3 hours of the listing going live I received a message via eBay from a member in Nigeria offering to buy the phone for £300 if I would take it off the site and deal with him by email only. He went on to say that the money was waiting to be sent via Western Union Money Transfer.

This of course rang alarm bells for all sorts of reasons; firstly, I only wanted £150 for the phone so why offer £300? Secondly, he did not want to transact through eBay but requested my personal email and bank account details. I reported the matter to eBay who later told me that this was indeed a favourite scam used by professional fraudsters. Sadly, the lure of the money is too much for some sellers who pass on their details to the fraudsters and then find that their bank accounts have been emptied some days later.

Another variation involves cheques which 'accidentally' overpay the seller for an item. The seller is then asked to send their own cheque back to the buyer in order to reimburse for the overpayment. The seller sends the reimbursement only to discover that the original cheque was fraudulent all along . . .

Since this scam, eBay has outlawed the use of Western Union Money Transfers as a form of payment on their site. I doubt it will be too long, however, before another vulnerable area becomes ripe for exploitation.

Extortionate postal charges

Again, although not technically fraud, this certainly features high on my personal list of eBay cons to avoid.

It involves sellers offering goods at ridiculously cheap prices, many on a Buy It Now basis, but then charging extortionate amounts to post them. I have seen £1 items with £10, £20 and even £30 postage costs being listed which clearly goes beyond the realm of reasonable. However, there is method to this particular madness: eBay charges sellers a fee for listing (which depends on the start price of an item) and a final value fee (which depends on the end price of an item, not including postage). Therefore, if bidding starts and ends at 99p, the seller will have to pay virtually nothing in fees to eBay and the excess postage charge becomes pure profit.

It is interesting to note that although eBay does not prescribe the actual costs that a seller may charge for postage, packing and handling, it does have what it terms an 'Excessive Postage and Packaging Charges Policy'. In practice this means that a seller may add additional costs to the actual costs (in order to cover his own time, etc) as long as these costs are reasonable. Sellers may not, however, charge more than the actual cost of any insurance and/or any applicable taxes including VAT.

The problem with this policy, of course, is in the interpretation of the word 'reasonable' – one person's *reasonable* is another person's *extortionate*. Listings which seem to charge unreasonably high amounts based on the size, weight and country of origin of an item can be reported to eBay who will make the final decision as to whether that listing should be removed. Persistent offences by the same seller may result in them being subject to certain sanctions, including having their account suspended.

If you find yourself in the unhappy situation of having won an item only to be stung by the postage costs don't expect eBay to be overly concerned. Anecdotally, at least (judging from the forum debates), eBay regards it as the buyer's responsibility to check all the small print of a listing before bidding and, if the listing is silent or vague on the question of postage charges, to ask the seller for clarification. Things may, however, be about to change. In January 07 eBay announced: "We're taking a stronger stance on reinforcing our policies in areas that provide bad buyer experiences, such as when sellers charge excessive postage." We shall see.

In the meantime, if you find yourself on the wrong end of excessive postage charges, and feel that you really can't go through with the transaction, you should email the seller to tell them. Be completely honest about your reasons and they may agree to mutually withdraw from the sale. If not, however, you may find yourself the subject of an unpaid item dispute which may earn you both negative feedback and an 'Unpaid Item Strike'. Although the latter is not too serious on a one-off basis, too many can result in your account being terminated.

The best advice is to make sure that you read the entire item description carefully for any charges of this nature (hidden or otherwise). If postage costs are not clearly defined ask the seller via the link on the listing before you bid rather than being stung after the auction has ended and you have what you think is the bargain of the century.

PayPal surcharges

In the course of browsing eBay you may come across some item descriptions which end with the legend: "Pay with PayPal, I don't charge my customers extra!" or similar wording.

This dates back to the time before eBay acquired PayPal when it was legitimate and common practice for sellers to levy a surcharge on anyone who chose to pay by PayPal. The justification for the fee was that it covereed the charges which PayPal made to sellers for handling the money transaction.

PayPal still makes these charges but eBay has now amended its policy and prohibits sellers from passing them on to the bidder. To my mind this is a good thing, as some sellers of old were in the habit of levying surcharges that far exceeded PayPal's fees. Now that eBay has outlawed the surcharge any sellers who try to pass it on to you are breaking the rules and should be told so.

Sellers who do not want to accept PayPal's charges can opt out of accepting credit/debit card payments but for me, the speed, convenience and relative security of transacting in this manner would make opting out both an annoyance and ultimately a false economy.

In fact, I will now *only* accept PayPal for my own items and am happy to absorb the costs because of the time it saves me trying to chase up other forms of payment. It's a personal choice.

PayPal is such a huge part of transacting on eBay that it deserves a chapter all on its own so this is where we'll be going next.

PayPal

Introduction

PayPal is an electronic payment system, now owned by eBay, which allows members of eBay and anyone else with an email address to send and receive secure online payments using either their credit card or bank account. Perhaps understandably, eBay now recommends that transactions carried out on its site use this payment method.

Once you have completed the registration process, having an account with PayPal is (at least in theory) much like having any other online bank account. Funds can be sourced from a number of places: if you sell items on eBay and take payment through PayPal, the buyer's money flows into your account and you can then use these cash 'reservoirs' to pay for purchases, either from eBay or other online merchants who accept PayPal. Alternatively, you can transfer funds into your PayPal account from your high street bank account (as long as you have the cash available!) or, if you register your debit or credit card with PayPal, use it to fund purchases.

eBay sellers displaying this logo are telling buyers that they accept PayPal as a form of payment, sometimes to the exclusion of any other method. PayPal is popular because it is such a safe and time-effective way to conduct business. It is by no means an absolute defence against fraud, however, and it also makes quite hefty charges for providing its services. For this reason, some eBay members actively choose *not* to accept it, preferring an alternative service such as the smaller Nochex or BidPay in addition to cheques and postal orders.

At the time of writing Google is trialing its own online payment method system, called 'Google Checkout'. Given Google's brand recognition and internet dominance, this may yet prove to be a serious rival to PayPal.

As an integral part of the eBay experience, however, PayPal cannot be ignored and this chapter will hopefully give you some insight into its basics as well as enabling you to draw your own conclusions.

PayPal: a brief history

One of the defining features of a successful transaction on eBay is a quick turnaround of payment and delivery. Indeed, when buying online generally, the ability to use a quick and reliable online payment system is crucial.

The phenomenon that is PayPal was begun in 1999 and, although not initially devised to deal with auction payments, this was quickly recognised as its most useful and powerful application. Even in its infancy, it had close to 12,000 users but by 2002 when eBay finally acquired it for $1.5 billion, this figure had sky-rocketed to close on a million. That figure is now closer to *40 times* that number and continues to grow every day.

The UK version of PayPal arrived in 2003 and has now become the *de facto* online payment method for many users, just as eBay has become the only online auction site worth browsing.

Registering with PayPal

To register with PayPal for the first time you need to go to its UK homepage, at www.paypal.co.uk and click on the 'Sign Up' tab at the top right corner.

Fig. 33 – PayPal's home page and sign up tab

Note that you must be over 18 to hold a PayPal account. You will need to decide which type of account you want to register for (see below) and fill out some personal details such as name, address, phone number and country of origin. These details must match those that appear on your credit card and/or bank account.

You will then be asked to supply your email address and choose a password which will be used as your account log each time you access the site either through eBay or independently. Your email address will also be the contact other members will use when sending or requesting money.

For the purpose of password recovery PayPal will ask you to choose two security questions and their answers. You will also need to read and agree to the 'User Agreement' and 'Privacy Policy' and finally, as an added security measure, to verify some disguised characters that appear on your screen.

After this is completed, it will take a moment for PayPal to check your details; any problems such as incomplete information will take you back to the application screen with the potential errors/omissions highlighted in red for you to correct.

What happens next?

When you first sign up PayPal offers you the chance to register a credit or debit card. Although you are not obliged to do this straightaway you will be limited as to what you can do with your account if you choose not to. For example, although you will be able to *receive* payments you will only be able to buy items using the available balance in your account.

Once you have gone through this process you will be taken to a final page where you will be told that an email has been sent to your registered address. Once you access this email and click on the link your registration can be completed and your account made active.

In order to check that you are the rightful owner of the card that you have registered, PayPal will deposit a small amount of money (a penny or two) into your card account and ask you to confirm this amount when you receive your next statement. Once you have carried out this verification process you will be what's known as both a confirmed and a verified member.

Types of PayPal account

PayPal now offers three types of account, each designed for and targeted at different kinds of user. They are:

Personal Account

Personal accounts are only available to individual users and although free, they cannot be used to receive credit or debit card payments. This can be a disadvantage because it means you cannot accept payment from buyers who want to pay that way. If, however, you think that your eBay career will be limited to buying only, it is the account you should go for, at least initially. It offers all the core features of PayPal, including:

- The ability to send money.
- The ability to request money.
- Website payments.
- Virtual debit card.
- Account insurance.
- Downloadable activity log.
- Email-based customer service.

Premier Account

This is the account that I have as it enables me to both buy and sell on eBay *and* accept credit card payments from buyers who want to pay that way. It is suitable for people who have a high transaction volume, who need to accept credit card payments and/or would like access to PayPal's special features. Premier accounts may operate under an individual name as well as a business name. They include all the core features detailed above, plus others, including:

- The ability to do business in your own name, a corporate name or a group name.
- The ability to accept unlimited credit/debit card payments.
- ATM/debit card.
- Multi-user accounts for business account holders.
- Advanced downloadable activity log.
- 7-day-per-week free customer service.

Business account

As the name suggests, Business accounts are reserved for businesses only and are therefore aimed at people who make at least part of their livelihood trading on eBay or other web-based companies. They include all of the features of both Personal and Premium accounts but Business accounts can only operate under a company or group name.

If you are unsure which account is right for you, play it safe and go with a Personal one to begin with. The main reason for this is that if you choose to have either a Premier or Business account you will be charged a transaction fee equal to a small percentage of any payment received irrespective of how that payment was funded. A copy of the fee schedule is shown below.

Fig. 34 – PayPal's fee schedule

Fees

PayPal charges Premier and Business accounts to receive payments. Personal accounts are free, but may not receive debit or credit card payments.

	Personal Account	Premier/Business Account
Open an Account	Free	Free
Send Money	Free	Free
Withdraw Funds	Free for £50.00 GBP or more, £0.25 GBP for £49.99 GBP or less to bank accounts in the UK Fees for other banks	Free for £50.00 GBP or more, £0.25 GBP for £49.99 GBP or less to bank accounts in the UK Fees for other banks
Add Funds	Free	Free
Receive Funds	Free	1.4% + £0.20 GBP to 3.4% + £0.20 GBP
Multiple Currency Transactions	Exchange rate includes a 2.5% fee*	Exchange rate includes a 2.5% fee*

* If your transaction involves a currency conversion, it will be completed at a retail foreign exchange rate determined by PayPal, which is adjusted regularly, based on market conditions. This exchange rate includes a 2.5% spread above the wholesale exchange rate at which PayPal obtains foreign currency, and the spread is retained by PayPal. The specific exchange rate that applies to your multiple currency transaction will be displayed at the time of the transaction.

Quoted fees are inclusive of all applicable taxes; however, other taxes or costs may exist that are not paid through PayPal or imposed by us. You are liable for any telephone charges and any charges made by your internet service provider or similar or associated charges as a result of the use by you of the PayPal Service.

How do I receive money using PayPal?

Once you have set up your PayPal account, you are in a position to accept payments into the account from buyers on eBay. All the information they need to deposit money into your account is embedded in the eBay auction system. They just click on a link on the auction page, confirm how much they want to send you, and the money is immediately transferred. You receive an email confirming how much has been received, and who the sender was. And your account is updated to show the new balance. It's fantastically easy.

"PayPal is not just for eBay. You can also accept payments into your account from other people, people who have nothing to do with eBay."

But PayPal is not just for eBay. You can also accept payments into your Paypal account from other people, people who have nothing to do with eBay. All you do is tell them the email address you use for your PayPal account. They go to the PayPal home page, click the 'Send Money' tab, type your username into the 'Recipient's email' box, and instruct the transfer. It's a doddle.

How do I send money using PayPal?

If you want to pay for an item that you have won on eBay, and are already registered with PayPal, simply follow the 'Pay Now' link on the completed item listing or the link on your My eBay page under the 'Items I've Won' view. Both will take you to a page where you can select PayPal as your method of payment and from there be redirected to the PayPal site to log in and complete the transaction.

To pay for non-eBay goods or services, go to the PayPal home page at www.paypal.co.uk, log into your account, click on the Send Money tab, and then on the 'Pay Anyone' sub-tab. A page like the one opposite comes up:

In the screenshot you can see how the drop-down box invites you to classify your payment under one of five categories. Select the last option ('Quasi-cash') to send money to someone for anything other than an underlying service or goods.

Note that if you use your credit card to fund this type of transaction, rather than drawing the money from your PayPal cash balance, your card issuer may make an additional charge for what they classify as a cash advance. PayPal has no control over this and you may therefore wish to use an alternative payment method in this instance.

Fig. 35 – PayPal's 'Pay Anyone' tab

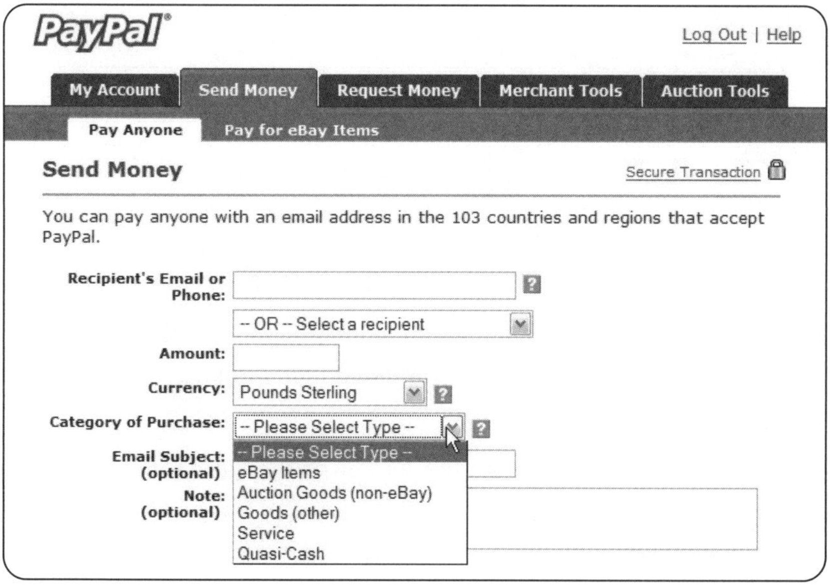

Tracking payments

PayPal members can access a full history of their account activity online, and can also download the history from the website as a comma-separated text file or spreadsheet. This can be useful if you need to print off the information for tax purposes etc.

To track your payments you just log in to your account, click on the My Account blue tab, then on the 'History' sub-tab, and you see a table of your 'Recent Activity' – i.e. money coming in and money going out of your account – similar to a bank statement. Fig. 36 overleaf shows such a page, and how you can choose the time period covered by the statement.

Fig. 36 – PayPal's History tab

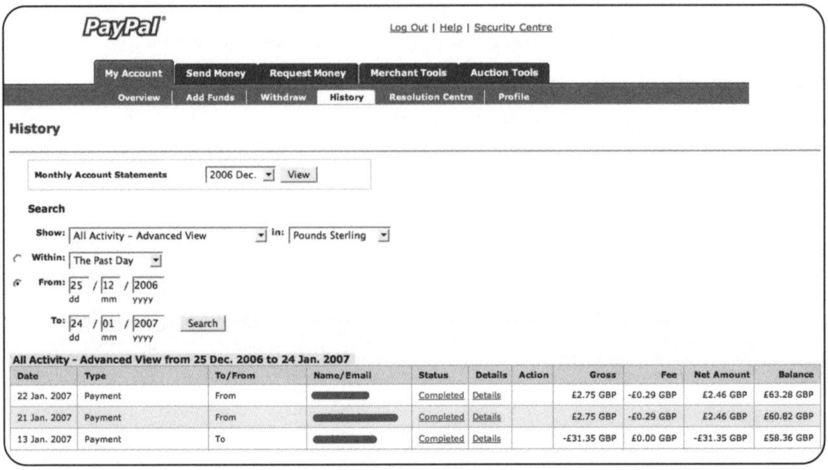

The boxes in the top half of the screen allow you to set various parameters for your report. By adjusting the date boxes, for instance, you can call a shorter or longer report as required.

To see more information about any *one* transaction, click on 'Details' in whichever line it is you want more information on.

Withdrawing money

If you make a few sales on eBay, and the buyer uses PayPal to pay you, the balance in your PayPal account will start to build up. You can leave the money in the account, or you can use it to pay for your purchases on eBay, or you can withdraw it.

In order to withdraw money, you need to have registered your bank account with PayPal. Once you have done that, you simply go to the 'Withdraw' sub-tab under the My Account section, and click on the 'Transfer funds to your bank account' link.

It is always a good idea to empty your fund whenever it has accrued a substantial amount as fraudsters who target PayPal find easy pickings in raiding these reservoirs of available cash. Whenever I have built up money through my eBay sales, I either use the balance on my PayPal account to fund new purchases or withdraw it immediately, depending on the volume of funds present. Another reason to keep this reservoir low is that it is PayPal's first port of call if, for whatever reason, they try to recover funds on behalf of someone who has opened a dispute against you.

Adding funds

In order to add funds to your PayPal account you need to have sufficient money in your registered, confirmed bank account. Once you have executed a transfer to PayPal you can check when the funds are likely to be available by logging in to your PayPal account, clicking on the 'History' sub-tab, then clicking the 'Details' link of the transaction in question. Looking under the 'status' heading will give you the expected clearing date.

Unfortunately, once a transfer request has been made from your bank account to PayPal it cannot be cancelled. You will need to wait until the transfer is complete before transferring the funds back again. There is no charge for this.

Upgrading your account

If you think your eBay activity will be limited to buying, there is probably no need to ever have anything other than a Personal account. If, however, you decide to start selling and it becomes more than an occasional hobby, you may want to upgrade to a Premier account. The advantage of this is that it allows you to accept payment from buyers with a credit or debit card, meaning that your auctions will be more likely to attract interest than if you only accept payment by cheques, postal orders, etc.

The downside to accepting card payments, of course, is that PayPal will charge you for every transaction made using this method. At the time of writing this costs between 1.4% to 3.4% of the total transaction value plus 20p. Not only this, but once you have a Premier or Business account, the charge applies to EVERY future transaction, not only those funded by a card.

If, after upgrading, you decide that it really isn't worth your while paying these charges as you don't sell enough to justify them, PayPal will allow you to revert back to a Personal account, but only once.

How does PayPal make money?

PayPal makes its money in two main ways: the first is by effectively acting as a 'holding dock' for the cash which members have in their accounts but not paying interest on it. The second is by allowing members to pay for goods and services using their credit and debit cards and then charging Premier and Business account holders fees for processing these transactions.

PayPal protection

As we have already seen, when you pay for an item on eBay you are protected to a certain degree by eBay's own safety policies (see page 250). If you use PayPal as your method of payment, there are two further levels of protection available: The **PayPal Buyer Protection Policy** and the **Buyer Complaint Process**. The efficacy of both of these has been called into question over the years but before considering the alternatives we'll look at each in turn.

1. PayPal Buyer Protection Policy

This policy exists to help buyers recover funds when sellers do not send the goods that were purchased or when they deliver goods that are significantly different from those advertised. If your claim is successful PayPal say that they will reimburse you for losses up to £500 sterling, payable in the currency of the original payment.

- If the item is worth more than the maximum £500, PayPal will still only reimburse up to that amount. Under its policy, it promises to make reasonable efforts to recover any deficit from the seller although this cannot be guaranteed. Critics of the system complain that the term 'reasonable efforts' is deliberately open to interpretation and therefore denial.

- If you make a single payment for multiple items from the same seller you will be eligible to claim the maximum amount for each listing separately as long as you make no more than three claims per year.

- If you purchase multiple items from a single listing you are only eligible for the payout on the entire listing.

When you buy goods on eBay look for sellers displaying the PayPal Buyer Protection logo:

With this logo you know that they have satisfied the criteria set out by PayPal to qualify for this service. The current criteria are divided into those which have to be satisfied by the seller and those which have to be satisfied by the buyer. They are:

Seller criteria

1. The seller has achieved a feedback rating of at least 50 feedback scores AND at least 98% of this is positive. The percentage calculation for this purpose will include multiple feedbacks from the same user and may therefore be higher than the unique feedback percentage as shown on eBay.

2. The seller is a registered PayPal member in one of 19 designated countries, including the UK.

3. The seller has a verified Premier or Business account.

4. The seller's PayPal account is in good standing.

5. The item must have been listed on one of 13 designated eBay sites, including eBay.co.uk

6. PayPal must be selected as an accepted payment method at the time of the listing and the PayPal email address given must be correct. This is wholly the seller's responsibility.

7. The item listed must be a tangible physical item or goods which can be sent in the mail. Services, quasi cash, gift certificates, e-book downloads, motor vehicles and live auctions are all ineligible. In addition, items prohibited in the PayPal Acceptable Use Policy are ineligible.

It is worth noting that a seller's eligibility to display the PayPal Buyer Protection Policy logo is determined by eBay at the time of the item listing and not necessarily determined by past performance or history.

Buyer criteria

1. The buyer has sent a single PayPal payment for the full price of the item to the PayPal account specified by the seller on the listing.

2. The payment must be associated with the eBay listing in question, i.e. it must be linked to an eBay item and correspond to the item number as it appears on eBay.

3. The claim must be filed within 45 days of the date of payment.

4. To ensure that these criteria are met PayPal advises that buyers 'check out' of the auction using the 'Pay Now' button on the item listing which will ensure payment is sent to the correct account.

5. If PayPal Buyer Protection is not offered at the time the seller posts the listing the decision cannot be appealed. Remember: if your seller's listing does not carry the PayPal Buyer Protection logo, the item is NOT covered by this policy.

When to claim

Subject to all the above criteria being met by both buyer and seller, a buyer may file a claim if:

- The seller did not deliver the promised goods; or

- The item delivered was significantly different from that described in the listing.

For the purposes of a claim through PayPal it is not enough to simply be disappointed in the item. Nor will a claim under 'significant difference' succeed just because the description could have been reasonably misinterpreted by the buyer, for example, if there was a slight discrepancy in the shade or tone of colour. The decision as to whether a difference is 'significant' rests with PayPal, and its decision is final and binding.

Buyers cannot claim more than three times in a year under this policy although, if necessary, additional claims will be dealt with under the Buyer Complaints Process (see next section). Recovery of funds is not guaranteed, however, under this latter scheme.

Before filing a claim the buyer is encouraged to wait a reasonable time (say, 7 days) for the item and then to contact the seller in order to try and resolve the issue. Only when these avenues have been exhausted are buyers expected to make a claim.

What will PayPal do on receipt of my claim?

On receipt of your claim PayPal will contact the seller to investigate the matter. If the claim is for non-delivery the seller must provide proof of posting to the buyer's address. If the claim is upheld, PayPal will reimburse you up to the maximum £500 and if this is less than the item's sale value, will endeavour to recoup the excess from the seller's account.

If the transaction was funded partly or wholly by a credit card, PayPal will reimburse you up to the maximum through your credit card with any additional monies recovered going into your PayPal balance.

Buyers are expected to fully cooperate with this process including fulfilling any requests for information from PayPal. Failure to respond to these requests will result in the claim being cancelled.

If you have filed a claim under the 'Item Not as Described' clause you will generally be required to return the item to the seller at your own expense although you may alternatively be asked to return it to PayPal or their agents. Once PayPal has confirmed that the item has been returned (or, perhaps, destroyed in the case of counterfeit goods) they will process your claim.

Sellers are also required to comply with PayPal's requests for information and forfeit any right to appeal if they fail to do so.

2. PayPal Buyer Complaint Policy

For buyers, sellers and item listings that do not qualify for PayPal Buyer Protection alternative redress may be possible through the Buyer Complaint Policy. Whilst this covers the same areas of dispute as PBP, buyers will only be able to receive a refund if there are adequate funds in the seller's account. This may mean that only a partial recovery is possible and, in some cases, no recovery at all.

The Buyer Complaint Policy is only available where the purchase involved physical, tangible goods which were sent in the post. Again, if you choose to claim under the 'Item Not as Described' clause you must be sure that the seller misrepresented the details of the item so as to affect its value or suitability.

Under the BCP procedure, PayPal automatically applies eBay's Standard Purchase Protection Programme meaning that the maximum recoverable amount is £105 (£120 minus the £15 processing fee).

When should you claim?

You should make a claim under this policy only if you are not eligible for PayPal Buyer Protection and you have already made reasonable efforts to liaise with the other party in order to resolve the issue.

What will PayPal do on receipt of my claim?

PayPal will initiate the same steps as for the Buyer Protection Policy outlined above although the recovery of all or even part of the claim is not guaranteed.

When I made a claim for an item not received last year, I was forced to go through this process as the seller did not fulfil the more stringent criteria for the Buyer Protection Policy. I claimed for a £30 item but in the end only received a £5 recovery, which was all the seller had in his account at the time the claim was upheld. The case was closed by PayPal with an assurance that they would try to recover more money. Needless to say, I am still waiting 11 months later. The shortfall in compensation, and the fact that it took a month to receive £5 left a bitter taste and from talking to other people who have been through the same process, my experience was not exceptional.

The alternative?

One of the most common complaints about the processes described above is that neither eBay or PayPal are proactive enough in recovering the full amount of money lost by buyers. And the reason for this?

Well, conspiracy theorists maintain that because it is ultimately the sellers and not the buyers who keep the money rolling in they are the ones that both sites want to protect. Although this makes one kind of sense to me, I am not sure it makes good *business* sense since buyers are surely an integral part of the equation? Without us, eBay would simply not exist or would at least have half a dozen reasonable competititors.

Whatever your particular take on the subject, it is important to know that there *is* an alternative to both eBay and PayPal's protection policies, however much both companies discourage you from using it. If I were to get stung again for a higher value item I would not hesitate to go this alternative route, known in the trade as 'Chargebacks'.

Chargebacks

Whenever you use your credit card to carry out a transaction your card issuer provides a level of automatic protection that far exceeds eBay's own anti-fraud and protection policies.

If you fail to receive your item or it turns up faulty in any way you are entitled to ask your credit card issuer (e.g. Visa, Mastercard) to initiate a 'chargeback' on your account. This basically means that your bank will take back the money charged by the merchant (in this case, PayPal) and refund it to your account.

Although PayPal has no choice but to comply in this situation it would understandably much rather you did not initiate the chargeback procedure. This is because the money refunded to you has to be stumped up from PayPal's own coffers in the first instance and *then* PayPal has to try to recover the same amount from the seller's account. This shifts the risk of loss from you onto PayPal. If the seller's account does not have enough in it to cover the refunded amount, PayPal might be the one left short.

Because of this, and because it makes better business sense generally, PayPal urges buyers to use its own complaints procedure rather than chargebacks. However, for high value items, especially those not covered by the more reliable Buyer Protection Policy, I would never hesitate to initiate a chargeback just for the reassurance of getting the full total of my money back.

If you find yourself in this position you should know that PayPal, by its own admission, strenuously tries to protect its sellers against chargeback claims so it is not something you should go into without the proper preparation. Similarly, your credit card issuer will need to see documented evidence of your claim, whether it was for an item not received (they will require proof of both purchase and payment), or because the item was materially different from what you expected (you may need to show them the item so keep it in the condition received). There are a couple of other reasons that a chargeback can be initiated; if, for example, you have been charged twice for a transaction, or if your card was used without your authority/knowledge. In any of these cases, the final decision rests with the card issuer.

Although PayPal has no choice but to cooperate with chargebacks they don't have to like them and, in their own words, they "reserve the right to terminate or limit account access privileges of any buyers [who demonstrate a] consistent failure to pursue PayPal's Buyer Complaint Process before processing any alternative reversal process provided by the buyer's issuing bank . . ."

To me, this seems overly harsh but it's up to you to decide whether such a policy is justified. If you think not, you can simply choose not to use PayPal.

How to (Re)sell on eBay

Money for old rope

If you've already spent some time browsing and perhaps bidding on eBay you will be aware not only of the vast number of items on the site but also the incredible variety. It might also have crossed your mind that there's money to be made by selling things you no longer need, use, or even like. That's what Part 3 of this book is all about.

As mentioned at the start of this book, most of us in the developed world live incredibly materialist lifestyles and as a consequence our possessions have a life span that would have appalled previous generations. When it comes to baby items, this is even more so, partly because the little devils grow so quickly, and partly because our own fickle tastes and fashions change so much.

Short life span is one reason why eBay makes perfect sense when buying for our babies and it is also a great reason to resell. If you keep your items in relatively good condition, especially those at the higher end of the market, it is not unfeasible to make back a good 50% of what you paid for them, and sometimes much more.

The downside to selling is that it involves a lot more effort and responsibility. When you buy, your only concern is to settle payment and await delivery. Selling, however, involves many stages, from sourcing, listing and collecting payment, to packing and dispatching. This has to be done in a timely and professional manner if you want to achieve the best possible price and ensure that your 'customers' are happy at the end of the day.

Having said that, selling can also be deeply rewarding and the financial benefits, although sometimes modest, undoubtedly come in handy. I made my first sale about a year after my buying career began and now find it gives me greater satisfaction than buying. Even though I only resell my own unwanted stuff I make enough to offset the more indulgent purchases for my son. I would estimate that my time on eBay is now roughly divided 50:50 between buying and selling.

If you think you might like to have a go at selling your unwanted or excess possessions this section will take you through every step of the process, from what to sell and how to price it, to opening a seller's account and writing great item listings that spark the imagination and get bidders buying.

If you really get a taste for selling and consider doing it full time, or as a business, there is also information on the legal position, including tax implications, at the end of this section. I hope you have a great time and make a mint!

What can I sell?

The short answer to this question is 'practically anything,' although as this book is aimed primarily at parents and parents-to-be we'll limit ourselves to that area.

The knowledge that you are expecting your first child (or adding to your family) can provoke many strange impulses, including the nesting instinct, which generally kicks in during the final weeks of pregnancy – although if you're anything like me starts at around conception. It manifests itself as an urge to rid your abode of its clutter in preparation for the new arrival(s) and is a fantastic excuse to gather together items of value to sell on eBay. Furniture and clothing are worthy finds; husbands and partners less so, but whatever you decide to sell it should first be subjected to the following test: *Is it worth my while?*

Is it worth my while?

Amongst the more bizarre things I have seen sold on eBay one of the strangest has to be a used matchstick which reached the princely sum of £3.50. Admittedly, this was very early on in the site's existence when novelty alone guaranteed a sale. Before going to the trouble of listing your similarly trivial items you should ask yourself if the price you are likely to achieve will justify the time you spend selling it. For example, if an item starts and ends at 99p you will not even make minimum wage so you'd probably be better off giving it to charity. If, on the other hand, you have a vast unwanted collection of mint Clarice Cliff knocking around the attic you can be sure of hitting a substantial return, especially if you photograph and list it beautifully.

Thinking ahead to the time after your little bundle of joy arrives you'll probably discover that they go through clothes quicker than a dose of salts and, if you're particularly blessed(!) may even find they never wear any of the smaller items at all. If this is the case you can either save them for the next baby (ahem), or sell them in order to finance all the bigger stuff you're going to need.

Designer baby clothes, or those at the higher end of the market, seem to hold their value remarkably well, especially if you've kept them in good condition. Accordingly, t-shirts with 'plasticized' logos should be washed inside out on a gentle cycle with non-biological powder. I also recommend avoiding the tumble drier if you want to prevent the logos cracking altogether. Another tip is not to remove the retailer's tags from items until you're ready to use them. For obvious reasons, clothes with their tags still attached tend to attract many more bidders and have higher resale values than those without.

There are, of course, some items specifically prohibited from sale on eBay and though these probably won't concern you I have included an abridged list below purely for interest.

What *not* to sell

Whenever you list an item for sale on eBay, the site goes to some lengths to remind you that you are responsible for ensuring that the item is both legal under statutory law and does not infringe eBay's own rules.

There are currently three categories of item where the selling boundaries are either a clearly defined "no" or a more vague shade of grey. For a full list visit eBay's help pages. Below, however, is a taste of what you can expect to see: some of them may surprise you!

Prohibited items

Items that may not be listed on eBay include:

- Animals
- Aeroplane tickets
- Credit cards
- Counterfeit goods
- Lottery tickets
- Recalled products
- Satellite digital and cable TV decoders
- Unlocking software

Questionable

Items which may only be listed under certain conditions, include:

- Autographed Items
- Batteries
- Used medical devices and knives

Strangely, used clothing is also listed under this category which may initially seem to sabotage 90% of your and everyone else's potential sales. However, as long as the items are listed as clean and free from 'stains' they are permissible. Listings for *used* undergarments, however – notably briefs, boxer shorts, pants, etc. – are not permissible and will be removed by eBay, as will items listed with 'inappropriate' descriptions. I can only imagine that this ruling was made after the almost mythic tale of a scorned boyfriend who tried to auction several items of his ex-girlfriend's used underwear along with photographs...! The mind boggles.

Potentially infringing: Copyright and Trademark

This refers to items which may infringe certain copyrights, trademarks or other rights. These include:

- Academic software
- Brand name misuse
- Downloadable media
- Promotional items & unauthorised copies

If your listing violates any of these policies it is liable to be removed. If that happens, eBay will notify you via email and explain why. In some cases you will have your listing fee re-credited to your account. Obviously, consistent misuse of these policies can and usually will result in your account being suspended and/or your membership being terminated (NARU'd).

Your eBay seller's account

Even if you are already registered as a buyer, selling items on eBay requires a separate account, so this is what you will need to do next. You can either use the ID you already have (and therefore capitalise on any feedback already accrued) or create a new one to specifically handle your selling activities. For simplicity, I recommend that you use the same ID.

As with your initial registration, creating a seller's account is free, although you will need to provide information to verify your identity and select how you intend to pay your seller's fees to eBay. Verifying your identity is done by providing credit or debit card details and, in some cases, details of your bank account. This information is kept strictly confidential and encrypted by the industry standard SSL technology. It is important to note that neither your credit card nor your bank account will be charged unless you authorise them as a means of paying your fees. These **fees** are charged whenever you list or sell an item and can be paid through any of the following methods:

- PayPal (monthly and one-time payments).
- Direct debit from your bank account (monthly and one-time payments).
- Credit card (monthly and one-time payments).
- Cheque or postal order (one-time payments only).

To create a seller's account go to the 'Sell' link at the top of any eBay page and follow the prompts.

Building your reputation as a seller

Feedback

In order to sell regularly and successfully on eBay, reputation is everything. Bidders want to feel confident in you and your items and the best way to achieve this is to build up your positive feedback. Most people do this, initially, by buying from the site, ensuring that they pay promptly, reciprocate on feedback and practise good communication with their trading partner. Then, once they've got some feedback, and a 100% positive record, they start to sell.

The 'About Me' page

Another way of instilling confidence in your potential audience is by creating an 'About Me' page on the site. About Me is a service provided by eBay which allows members to create a page detailing their interests, hobbies, and other personal information. If you feel comfortable with HTML and web design, you can really go to town creating an attractive and informative page but if you're design-illiterate the custom templates provided by eBay are perfectly adequate.

There are no golden rules about what to put and what not to put on your About Me page. Anything that makes prospective bidders feel more confident about buying from you is worthwhile. If you are selling baby products, that may include brief information about you and your family – though there are obviously privacy issues to be considered.

Beyond personal information, it can help to tell people about any specialist knowledge or interest that you have. For instance, if you have expertise in restoring furniture, old cars, etc, and this is the type of item you are selling, it makes sense to advertise this skill on your About Me page and so attract more bidders. In general, buyers like to feel that you know and love what you sell and aren't simply out to make a quick buck.

Perhaps the biggest advantage of creating an About Me page, however, is that it gives you a sense of permanence in the eyes of other members. It shows that you are not a fly-by-night seller or buyer who's likely to do a runner or go AWOL on a transaction.

Once you've designed and published your info a symbol like this –

me

will appear next to your user ID. This symbol links to the page you have created.

If you're interested in setting up an About Me page, click on the 'Help' link at the top of the home page, then click on the A-Z Index in the left-hand menu bar, and you'll see that the very first item is 'About Me Page: Creating'.

Of course, at the end of the day, the best way to keep the bidders coming back for more is to ensure that your items are of good quality, well and honestly described, and dispatched promptly. If you don't give your buyers any reason to complain about your goods and services how can they help but give you positive feedback?!

We will be covering the finer points of making a good sale in more detail later, but for now, let's *prepare* to sell.

Preparing to sell

Once you have decided what you want to sell on eBay, there is a fairly straightforward series of steps to get your items listed.

You can either use eBay's standard 'Sell Your Item' form or, for more advanced users, there are selling tools such as Turbo Lister. Turbo Lister, which can be downloaded free from eBay, includes features and templates which can make your listing more attractive to buyers. It also allows you to create multiple listings and upload them in bulk to the site.

In early 2007 eBay revamped its Sell Your Item form, making it more intuitive and easier to use than ever. Although the steps for all these methods are fairly similar, we'll concentrate on this new version for our examples below.

Step 1. Choose a category and subcategory

Once you have registered your 'Seller's Account', go to the eBay home page, log in, then click on the Sell tab at the top of the page.

The first thing you will be asked to do is enter a rough description of the item you wish to sell. Let's, for the purpose of our example, imagine we want to sell a cot bumper. Enter the words 'cot bumper' into the box then click on the 'Sell It' tab. Fig. 37 opposite shows what you see next.

eBay automatically lists what it thinks are the most appropriate main categories and subcategories for your item, and orders them by degree of relevance. If you don't agree with the suggestions, you can click on the 'Browse Categories' tab and make your own selection, or the 'Recently Used Categories' which will show categories used on your other sales.

In Fig. 37, we can see what eBay suggested for our cot bumper:

- *Baby>Nursery Bedding>Cot Bumpers*
- *Baby>Nursery Bedding>Bedding Sets*

In each case, *Baby* is the main category, and the words on the right are the subcategories. The first is accorded 67% relevance, the second 18%. So eBay is strongly suggesting you go for the first. Before deciding let's have a brief reminder of the difference between Secondary Categories and Subcategories.

Fig. 37 – eBay's Select a Category interface

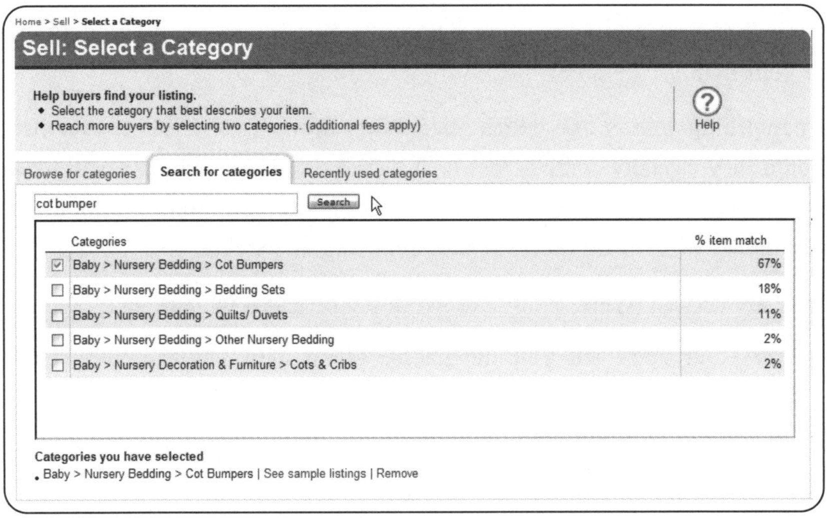

- **Secondary categories** are useful if you have a fairly high-value item that you want to be as visible to buyers as possible. Choosing a secondary category means that it will appear in two different places on the site making it more likely to be found by different keywords. We could, for example, choose both: Baby>Nursery Bedding>Cot Bumpers and Baby>Nursery Bedding>Bedding Sets. If you decide to use a secondary category eBay will charge you double the insertion fee and listing fee, although not double the final value fee.

- **Subcategories**, on the other hand are subsidiary to your main category and are free. Their purpose is to refine your listing and thus improve its visibility. Again, in the example above, the subcategories are Nursery Bedding>Cot Bumpers and Nursery Bedding>Bedding Sets.

Let's decide to go with the highest percentage match and choose *Baby>Nursery Bedding>Cot Bumpers*. As it's a comparatively low-value item, we won't bother with a secondary category. If you want to have a look at other items on eBay that also went into this category click on the 'See Sample Listings' link at the bottom. Otherwise tick the box next to your selection and click 'Save and Continue'. What's next?

Step 2. Choose a title

You will then be asked to choose a title and, for an additional fee, a subtitle for your item.

A compelling title is one which encourages browsers to explore your item should they casually come across it. A clever title is one which ensures that your item is found as a result of keyword searches. Your objective should be to come up with a title that is both compelling and clever.

There are certain styles of title *not* permitted on eBay, including:

- Titles that don't tell you the nature of an item, for example, "Great bargain. Look Here".

- Titles containing web addresses (except auctions for domain names), email addresses, phone numbers, etc.

- Titles which contain obscene or profane language.

- Titles which use sensationalist adjectives such as 'prohibited', 'banned', and 'illegal' and/or including anything which raises questions regarding the legality of the item being listed.

- Keyword 'Spamming'. This means the inclusion of brand names not related to the item being sold but to elicit more interest or to deceive a bidder. Examples of this would be the use of phrases such as 'Similar to' 'Identical to' etc. I have been caught out on this one myself and have had listings removed, even though my intention was one of clarity rather than deception! I have, however, noticed that many sellers intentionally try and get around this by introducing the word 'not' before a popular brand name even though this too is a breach of eBay's rules.

Conversely, there are a number of things you should definitely include in your title:

- Descriptive keywords that convey what you are selling, including the condition and size, where applicable.

- The brand name or designer of a piece or the period from which it originates.

- A literal description of what the item is.

Titles are limited to **85 characters** so don't waste them or muddy your title with words that buyers don't generally use in their searches such as 'Wow!' or 'Look!'

In all cases it pays to think about the sort or words or phrases which buyers would be typing into the search box and, where possible, to include them in your title.

Step 3. Upload a photo

It goes without saying that the inclusion of a good photo with your listing will improve its chances immeasurably. Unless you are selling a well-known item such as a recent DVD or CD most people will not take a chance on an item which is not accompanied by a photo.

When listing on eBay you are given the chance to upload one photo free of charge. There is a fee for additional photos (currently 12p each) which is worth paying if your item is valuable or if buyers would benefit from seeing it in more detail.

How to create a good photo

Lighting

Make sure that your item is well lit from all sides. Try and take the picture against a plain, uncluttered background. Some sellers use a piece of black or white fabric or even the inside of a bathtub! Items such as jewellery definitely need a plain background to avoid loss of detail. Plain carpets and wooden floors are also a good option for clothing, etc.

Resolution

If using a digital camera set it to at least its medium resolution (1024 x 768 pixels). This will give you clean, crisp results that won't take an eternity to upload. Some photo editing programmes such as Picasa (available free from Google) will automatically resize your pictures when you export them to eBay. If you routinely photograph on a very high resolution you will definitely need to resize prior to uploading as the current maximum image size accepted by eBay is 2MB.

Clutter

Try to avoid getting the whole world and its mother into the shot. Zoom in as close as possible to the item and erase any unnecessary clutter from the edges using the cropping tool from your photo editing programme. If scale is an important factor use a familiar object such as a coin for comparison.

Flash

Using flash photography can cause flare on an image but without flash the image can sometimes be blurred due to decreased shutter speed and increased aperture settings. If this is the case consider using a tripod. Note that flash shouldn't be used to photograph reflective surfaces such as glass or mirrors.

Copyright

One big no-no is to simply copy and paste another seller's photographs without their permission. If you really need to use someone else's picture you should message the seller and ask them. Some sellers will report you to eBay for unauthorised use of their pictures and request that your listing be removed.

Editing

Once you have transferred your photos to your computer you should consider doing some basic editing to make it as clear and as appealing as possible. Often it is enough to use some simple corrections such as cropping, rotating and resizing.

Saving: Format

Save the picture file in one of the following formats: jpg, gif (including animated gif), bmp, tif, png. You should only save the finished article in these formats and avoid re-editing them, as subsequent saves will cause the image quality to deteriorate.

Saving: Location

Make sure that you save the edited picture to a place on your hard drive that you will be able to locate again before Doomsday – for example, your virtual desktop. You need to know where it is, and what the file is called, in order to upload it to your eBay listing. If you are doing a lot of selling consider setting up a documents folder called 'eBay Selling' and file your photos in there, giving them clear names. For instance:

`McLaren_Buggy_20.06.07`

tells you what the item is and the date on which you created the listing.

How to upload using eBay's picture service

Once you have created your photo and saved it to your hard drive, you can upload it to your item listing.

eBay offers a picture service which will host your item's photo for the duration of your listing. If you have a personalised webspace you can also use this to upload your pictures to eBay but for beginners, eBay's service is the easiest place to start.

To upload your picture, click on the 'Add Picture' button on the Sell Your Item form. A pop-up window will appear inviting you to find the image you want by browsing on your hard disk. Fig. 38 illustrates.

Fig. 38 – eBay's Upload a Picture screen

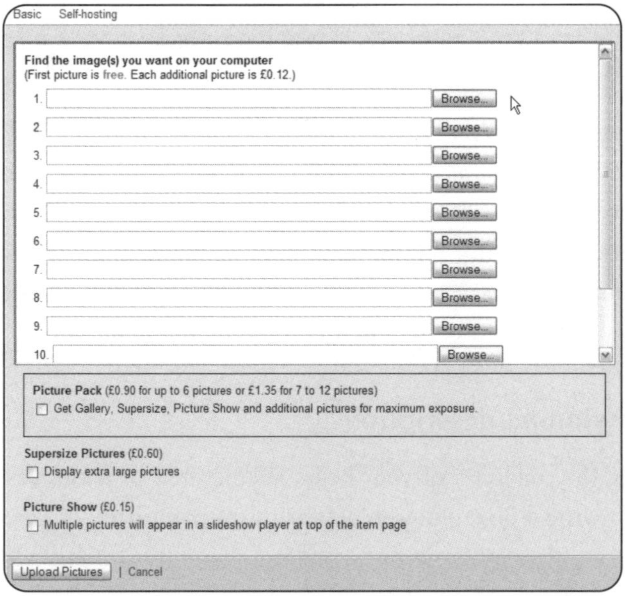

You will also be asked whether you want to enhance your listing by choosing features such as a 'Picture Pack', 'Supersized Picture' or even a slideshow, called 'Picture Show'. Once you are happy with your choices and have located your photo, click 'Upload Pictures'. Depending on the size of your image it should appear fairly quickly.

Back on the main form you will also be asked if you want to take advantage of eBay's 'Gallery Feature'. This means that a small version of your picture will appear on the search results page and can sometimes help buyers decide whether or not to investigate your item further. The cost for this is currently 15p. If you forgo this option, an icon of a camera will appear on the page instead, denoting that there is a picture which can be viewed on the full-page listing.

As already mentioned, the first picture with this service is free and, subject to the fees outlined above, you can add an additional eleven pictures if you need to. eBay's servers will retain standard-sized pictures for up to 90 days after a listing has ended so you can automatically reuse them if you have to relist an unsold item or sell a similar one at a future date.

If you use eBay's picture service you will not be able to edit your pictures online. However, as this service is supported by most web browsers it is a good all-round option to choose, especially if you have access to your own photo-editing software to do all the fixes beforehand.

eBay also offers an enhanced picture service to users running Windows 98SE or later and with Internet Explorer version 5.5 or equivalent as their web browser. The enhanced service allows you to upload images up to 4MB in size, preview pictures prior to uploading, and edit them in a more comprehensive fashion. If you decide to use this service don't do any editing prior to uploading as this may result in a deterioration of image quality.

Step 4. Write a winning description

As well as indicating the condition of your item (whether new or used), you will now be asked to write a description to appear in the main body of your listing.

Looking through any item's description on eBay tells you a lot about its seller. There are some sellers who provide long and effusive descriptions.

They are obviously enthusiastic about their items and are taking the trouble to provide you with all the helpful information they can think of. There are others for whom even a cursory line or two seems a little too much effort. I know who I would rather buy from – what about you?

Writing a thorough description can really enhance your chances of selling success and prevent misunderstandings with your buyers. Some things you may want to include are:

- The name, or type of item.

- Its size and/or dimensions.

- When it was made and the name of the manufacturer or designer, if appropriate.

- Its general condition, including whether it comes with its original packaging, tags or guarantees.

- Any notable features, or, conversely, flaws. Don't be tempted to lie or deceive bidders about the condition hoping they won't notice. They will, and will probably complain mightily about it, too.

- An item's provenance. In this context, 'provenance' can simply be where you bought the item, eg. Mamas and Papas, or, for more highly-valued items, such as antiques, provenance can also indicate an object's history, such as previous owners, etc. For example, 'Walking stick as owned by Charles Chaplin' or 'Genuine letter from Winston Churchill'. Again, in these latter examples, don't be tempted to embellish the truth as most buyers will require some documentation to authenticate your claims.

As an addendum to this last point you should always include an accurate and detailed description of an item's condition, especially when dealing with collectibles such as records, CDs or ceramics, all of which have their own grading systems. Using the correct terminology will instil confidence in your buyers meaning you will more likely end up with a better sale price. If you know nothing about grading you can find this information from a Google search or similar.

Alongside these facts and figures I like to include more abstract comments such as why I am selling the item and some suggestions as to who might be interested in it, such as "Would suit a style conscious mum" or "ideal for retro homewares lover". Always try and sell a lifestyle with your item; that way, bidders who either identify with or aspire to that lifestyle will automatically have their imaginations piqued. Sell benefits and not just features to get bidders needing what you've got!

Finally, you may want to include the 'nitty gritty' of an item including any terms of sale (TOS), postage and packaging details and a reminder to buyers to ask questions prior to placing a bid if they are unsure about anything. You would be amazed how many people don't read listings in their entirety and then complain about something which was there in black in white. By including everything in the main body of the description, even at the risk of being repetitive, no-one gets any nasty surprises. Once you've written your description and are happy with it, check it for typos.

For some items you will also be asked to fill in something called 'Item Specifics'. This may ask for clarification on things such as size, colour and condition (for clothing) or for specific functions and features (for prams or electronic items such as cameras or mobile phones).

Listing with pre-filled information

For certain items, such as books, DVDs or CDs, eBay can assist you in your listing with pre-filled item information. It does this by cross-referencing your item's unique identifier (such as an ISBN or EAN) with items already on its database. When it has this information certain details can be added automatically, for example, the book's title, genre and year of publication. It can also fill in reviews where applicable. You can even get a stock image of the item to save you more time.

When using the pre-filled item information don't forget to add your own details to give the most honest account of your item – for example, telling potential bidders its actual condition plus any extra features, unusual details, etc. You should also make it clear if you have used a stock photo to avoid any accusations of mis-selling your item if yours isn't as pristine as the photo suggests.

Pre-filled item information can only be used when the item you are selling has standardised criteria. If you select a category where this applies you will automatically be given the opportunity of using the information on eBay's system. If, whilst using such information, you spot any errors or omissions, you should notify eBay using the 'report and error' link on the titles and descriptions page.

If, after completing your description, you fancy 'jazzing' up the way it looks on the page you can use the 'Listing Designer' feature (currently 7p per listing). This embellishes your description with pictures and motifs such as baby clothes, animal prints, etc. It's not essential, but some people like it.

Step 5. Choose an auction format

Here's where you decide whether you want to sell your item through an online auction or at a fixed price i.e. Buy It Now. (Note that if you want to offer the choice of a BIN alongside the usual auction you should choose the former). Fig. 39 shows this detail from the Sell Your Item form.

Fig. 39 – Choosing an auction format, start price and duration

How you're selling

Get ideas about pricing by searching completed listings.

Selling format ⑦

| Online Auction | Fixed Price |

Starting price ✳ ⑦   Reserve price (fee varies) ⑦
£ [   ]   £ [   ]

Buy It Now price (fee varies) ⑦
£ [   ]

Quantity ✳ ⑦
[1   ] items

Duration ⑦
[7 days ▾]

Private listing ⑦
☐ Allow buyers to remain anonymous to other eBay members

Scheduled start (£0.06) ⑦   Donate a percentage to charity ⑦
[▾] [01.00 ▾] GMT   [No charity selected ▾] [Select % ▾]

Although this may seem like a fairly straightforward choice to make there are some considerations you might like to bear in mind.

Firstly, it's worth remembering that most sales on eBay are auction sales. Fixed price sales (i.e. BIN-only items) account for quite a small percentage as, for the most part, the prices listed are generally equal to or very close to the normal retail value. Since most people go onto the site in search of a bargain they aren't usually tempted by BIN prices. The exceptions tend to be seasonal items, with Christmas presents being a notable example. These can sell well as BINs, especially if you are offering the latest must-have toy or gadget.

Another reason to offer a BIN is when you have something that has just arrived on the market but which will, in a short space of time, be as common as mud. Clearly, you will want to get rid of it before its value starts to deteriorate. This is often the case with so-called 'Limited Edition' items such as DVDs, etc. which soon transpire to be not so limited after all. By the time another ten or twenty sellers have got their listings up you'll be fighting not to get undercut. The moral of the story, therefore, is to get in quickly.

> "Since most people go onto the site in search of a bargain, they aren't usually tempted by BIN prices. The exceptions tend to be seasonal items."

An alternative to the BIN-only option is to offer a Buy It Now price *in conjunction with* a conventional auction. This is attractive to bidders as they can either purchase the item immediately, or try their luck in the auction. Sometimes they will make the right decision and sometimes the wrong one. I personally have had sales in which the bidders took a chance and ended up paying more at auction than the original Buy It Now price.

Note that once a bid has been placed on this type of listing, the BIN option disappears and the auction proceeds as per usual. Placing a pre-emptive bid with the sole intention of removing the BIN option for others is known as 'stomping' and often occurs when the BIN price is way above the start price. Because of this activity, eBay charges sellers a flat fee for the BIN option and not one based on the actual Buy It Now price.

Step 6. Choose a start price

Doing your research

There are a number of factors that can help you decide where to start your auction price-wise. What you need to remember, however, is that pricing your item always comes down to a balance between how much you are hoping to make and what bidders are prepared to pay for it. These two elements are sometimes quite far apart and you need to be realistic. If the item has real value to you emotionally but is unlikely to be highly valued in monetary terms by others, consider whether it is worth putting up for auction at all.

Knowing what start price to set for your auction is partly a matter of doing your research. By doing a 'completed items' search from the advanced search link you can see the start price set by other sellers for similar items and the final sale price that they eventually realised. The item listing itself will tell you where the bidding started. In Fig. 40 below, the item began at £5.00 and ended at £28.50 after 12 bids.

Fig. 40 – Completed item listing showing Start Price and Final Price.

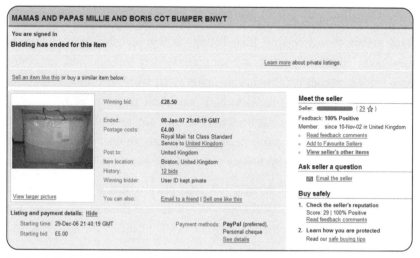

Be careful of pricing yourself out of the market by setting the start price too high; it is far better to set a lower start price and allow the competitiveness of an auction to carry the bids upwards than to set a high start price which deters bidders and robs the auction of momentum.

Antiques and collectibles

If you intend to sell antique or collectible items, eBay is still one of the best places to judge the current market as most bidders will have done their homework and will have bid no more than the going rate. Again, looking at the final sale prices of completed items will give you a good idea of what to expect from your own listing.

The exception to this is if you are lucky enough to interest a 'completist' and happen to have the missing piece from his collection. Then the price can race upwards, particularly if two or more bidders engage in a bidding war.

Another way of gauging prices for this type of auction is to purchase one of the many collectors' guides now available, although do make sure that you buy the most up-to-date edition that you can. Not only are these guides useful for pricing, they can also be a goldmine of information when it comes to writing your item's description.

The Advantages of a 99p start price

Many sellers choose to start their listings at 99p and this has a couple of advantages. Firstly, it tends to attract more bidders early on and, generally, more bidders overall because people believe that with such a low start price their chances of winning the item at a reasonable price are higher. And of course, once their interest has been piqued, they are more likely to stick with the auction, sometimes going head-to-head with another bidder until the bitter end. Remember – psychology plays a large part in all this.

The second advantage of using a low start price is that it keeps down the initial listing fee which eBay charges. We will look at these in detail later, but for now it's worth noting that a start price below £1 incurs the minimum 15p fee.

Using a reserve

If you like the idea of generating more interest with a low start price but are worried that the auction may fail to take off and that you might end up actually selling at that low price, you can place a reserve on your item. This is a figure which you specify and which is the lowest figure that you are willing to sell at. **Until the reserve is met by a bidder you are not obliged to sell the item** and a message saying 'reserve not met' appears on the listing. The reserve price is not shown to bidders but if a bidder asks you what that price is you should tell them as it does no-one any favours to keep it a secret.

At the current time, eBay only allows reserves of £50 and above to be used so it's only worth it for potentially high-value items. Although reserve price auctions do attract an additional fee (based on the actual reserve figure) this fee is refunded to the seller if the item goes on to sell as there will then be a final value fee to be paid based on the final selling price.

Personally, when I am buying I avoid reserve price auctions, and research seems to show that buyers in general find them off-putting. A far better solution, to me at least, is to start the auction at the lowest price you would be prepared to sell the item for. I think this makes the process far more transparent and in addition is a win-win situation for the seller.

Fixed price listings (Buy It Now)

If you decide to sell your item at a fixed price you will need to select this option at the time of listing and enter the 'Buy It Now Price' you are offering. You can also add a Best Offer feature if you wish (see page 187 for more details).

Step 7. Choose the auction duration

At the time of writing eBay offers the choice of listing your item for 1, 3, 5, 7 or 10 days. As with every other aspect of your listing it helps to get inside the mind of your target audience before deciding which one to go for.

One-day auctions are the best choice for items that have a finite life span such as concert or match tickets. These auctions obviously have to end with enough time before the event to ensure delivery of the tickets to the recipient.

One-day auctions are also a good choice if you need the money quickly although you should be aware that for non-urgent items they tend to attract fewer bids.

By and large, the one-day listing is of most benefit to high-volume sellers who deal in large quantities of identical items. This is because with this type of listing, eBay's rules specify that you can offer up to 70 listings a week (a maximum of ten per day); with a three day listing you will be limited to only 20 per week (with the same allowance of 10 per day).

Apart from the special circumstances outlined above I recommend that you go for the longest auction duration possible. It gives you more time to attract bids and, other things being equal, should result in a higher sale price.

If you make a mistake or change your mind after your listing has gone live you can revise it, subject to certain provisos. To do this you will need to go to the listing and click on the link for 'Revise My Items'. We'll be examining the subject of revisions a little later on.

Step 8. Choose a start and end time

When you list your item using eBay's Sell Your Item form, the auction will begin immediately unless you have opted to use the scheduled listing option (see below).

Listings on eBay.co.uk correspond to GMT or BST depending on the season and are run according to eBay's 'Official Time', whose link can be found at the bottom left hand corner of any page. It is important to watch this, rather than relying on your own clocks and watches, especially if you are a buyer hoping to put in a last-minute snipe.

Listings end in whole day increments meaning that if your item begins at 5:00pm on a Monday and is scheduled to run for 5 days, it will end at 5:00pm on the following Saturday. Obviously, if you have chosen to list an item as BIN-only or a combination of BIN and auction and the BIN option is taken up by a buyer, the listing ends immediately.

Although start and end times may seem arbitrary and even unimportant, there is plenty of evidence that they do have an effect on final sale values. To get the maximum interest in your auction you need to end it at a time when your target audience is likely to be browsing the internet and, conversely, not to end it when they are likely to be elsewhere. To use an example, if your auction ends at 4 o'clock in the morning, the number of people still awake to bid in the crucial final minutes will be very low.

The best way to approach this is to think of your own browsing and bidding habits. When are you most likely to be at your computer with time to browse? Do these times hold true for the audience your items are aimed at? If so, time your auction to end in one of these 'sweet spots'.

Remember that parents of babies and young children are more likely to be browsing in the evening after the kids have eaten and have perhaps gone to bed, or during the day at scheduled nap times. Some people on the other hand, only have access to their computer during work hours – what sort of items are they likely to be interested in?

Think also about the best times of the week to start and end a listing. Some people say that spanning your 10-day auction to cover two weekends is a good idea as lots of people browse the internet at the weekends. There's also a school of thought that believes you should end your auction late on a Sunday evening when people are at home preparing for the week ahead but simultaneously trying to make the weekend last a little longer.

Bear in mind that if your target audience is at the younger end of the market then it is unlikely they'll be around on a Friday night or early on a Saturday. It may seem like a cliché but there is an element of truth to it.

If you are prepared to sell your item to an international bidder think, too, about the time differences involved across different continents and give bidders a fair crack of the whip, especially on collectibles which tend to attract a huge audience in the US and Japan. Listing at midnight GMT tends to allow them to be up and at their computers. If the thought of listing your items at midnight seems too much to bear, fear not; eBay has thought of this and come up with something called 'Scheduled Listings'.

Scheduled listings

If you know that you are going to be away from your computer at your preferred start time you can use the scheduled listing option at a current rate of 12p per listing. This allows you to write your listings at your leisure but hold off on them going live until such time as suits your purposes, up to three weeks in advance. If you're a really prolific seller you can do this for up to 2,999 other listings!

The scheduled listings option can be selected from the pricing and duration section of the Sell Your Item form. Simply click on the option for 'Scheduled Start' and then, when prompted, enter a start date and time for your listing to begin. Complete the rest of the form as normal and eBay will take care of the rest. Your scheduled listings will appear in the 'Scheduled' section of the My eBay 'Items I'm Selling' view.

Using Turbo Lister to schedule a listing

Another (free) way of scheduling a listing is to use Turbo Lister, eBay's free downloadable selling tool. All you need to do is prepare your listings and move them to the upload page but hold off on the actual uploading process until you're ready. It's then simply a case of pressing a button. If you are actually going to be away from your computer at the preferred listing time, however, you will probably have to swallow the 12p fee.

Up until the time when your listings go live you can amend the scheduled start time. Simply go to the 'Scheduled' section of the 'Items I'm Selling' view in My eBay and select 'edit' from the drop-down menu alongside the appropriate item.

Step 9. Choose payment methods

The next step is to decide which method or methods of payment you are willing to accept. Your choices are PayPal, personal cheque, postal order/banker's draft, direct card payment, escrow and other. 'Other' can include direct bank transfer or well-concealed cash, although rumour has it that this latter option has now been outlawed by eBay for security reasons and is no longer permitted on item descriptions.

As a busy working mum I only accept PayPal funded by a bank account, credit card or PayPal funds, but what you choose to accept is entirely a matter for you.

Step 10. Decide how buyers can contact you

By default this is set to email, but you can now also choose to be contacted by voice through eBay's new VOIP (Voice Over Internet Protocol) service Skype. Skype is free and if you choose to use it will need to create a username when prompted. For more information about Skype and what it offers go here:

http://pages.ebay.co.uk/help/account/managing-skype.html

Step 11. Choose countries and set postage costs

When you list an item for sale you will be asked to specify which countries you are prepared to ship to and the costs of postage. If you select the UK only you may still get enquiries from non-UK residents asking if you will make an exception to the rule. This is your call at the end of the day. I tend to exercise my discretion by checking out their feedback and projecting what I think my item will eventually realise. If you decide to make the exception you may need to go back into your 'Buyer's Preferences' and revise your settings so that international bidders are not blocked.

If you are selling more than one item, consider offering a postage discount for multiple wins. This may attract greater interest in your less commercial items than might otherwise be the case.

Postage costs can be expressed either as 'Seller's Standard Rate' or by quoting a particular service such as First or Second class, Recorded Delivery etc. Seller's Standard Rate is sometimes used by sellers as open season to hike up the true costs of postage so make sure as a buyer that you agree with the figure quoted before committing yourself to the sale. If you decide to offer insurance on an item be aware that you can only charge the actual costs incurred.

If postal insurance is not included in your postage costs, for example, through Recorded or Special Delivery in the UK, it is important to obtain a Proof of Posting Certificate from the post office at the time of sending the item. This is a free service and the certificate is required if you subsequently claim for loss or damage to your consignment against the postal service.

For items that are valuable or fragile you would do well to offer the buyer the option of taking out a premium service such as Special Delivery. This is because Royal Mail only offers limited compensation for items sent via the ordinary mail which are lost or damaged and none if the package contains money or jewellery.

Complications when selling outside the UK

On the face of it you might think that as you have to go to the Post Office anyway it doesn't make much difference whether you are sending a parcel abroad or within the UK. In reality sending abroad throws up a host of potential issues which sometimes harden into problems. Briefly, these are:

Knowing what shipping charges to quote

When you list an item for auction and allow international bids you don't have to quote international shipping costs but you can do so and many buyers prefer to see them before bidding. If you do quote a shipping cost you will be bound by it so it's important to get it right.

But how do you know how much to quote? Well, both the Royal Mail and Parcel Force publish online rate cards and if you know the weight of the item it's relatively easy to look up the cost.

www.royalmail.com
www.parcelforce.com

The problem is – until you've packaged an item you don't know how much it weighs and until you know how much it weighs you don't know the possible sending methods and their costs.

For a light item like a baby's bib this isn't such an issue as it needs only basic wrapping. This means that its shipping weight will be close to its actual weight, say, 200g. You can easily work out the cost.

For big, awkward, fragile items it's a different matter. Wrapping and protecting a fragile item can require a lot of bubble wrap, cardboard and boxing and easily add a kilo to the weight. And while a 1.95 kilo parcel can be sent by the relatively inexpensive 'Small Packet' method, a parcel just 100g heavier at 2.05 kilos has to go by the more expensive 'International Standard'. This is before you even consider the dimensions limit on Small Packet parcels.

See what I mean?

If you decide not to quote charges for international shipping you should include the item's dimensions and weight (if known) in the main body of your description so that bidders can make their own estimate. Another option is to tell interested parties to email you via the 'Ask Seller a Question' link so you can find out if necessary. This way, if someone in Japan expresses an interest you can research the costs and get back to them.

Although reasonable to charge a little extra for packing materials and the time spent posting an item don't try and rip off your buyers by adding exorbitant extra charges. Buyers have been known to leave negative feedback for this very reason and you can't really blame them. Transparent, honest costs serve you and your buyers best.

Form filling

When you get to the Post Office with your parcel for Hong Kong, you will have to fill in forms. Oh yes! There's one for Small Packet, and another for International Standard, and another for Airsure and another for International Signed For. Then there's the customs form for non-EC countries.

None of it is rocket science and, if you're sending a lot of parcels abroad you'll get used to the forms and can even complete them at home, but it's still a hassle. And it takes time: once you've completed the forms you've got to stand in the queue at the Post Office (is anyone else's worse than our own??) and wait whilst the assistant fills her own documentation. Now picture yourself in that queue. With a hungry baby, who wants the one toy you didn't bring. The joy of international selling can quickly evaporate...

Transit time

When you send an item by first class post within the UK you can be fairly sure it will arrive the next day or the day after that.

When you send an item abroad there is no such certainty. Whatever transit time the Post Office quotes should be treated as a guideline only. You may be lucky and your parcel to the USA, sent by Small Packet, might reach is destination in 5 days flat, or it may take 13. Or 23. I once sent an item to New Zealand that took 4 MONTHS (count 'em) to arrive. That carrier pigeon sure deserved a medal though . . .

All this time the buyer is waiting, wondering if you are a fraudster, sending you increasingly testy emails, and mentally preparing negative feedback for you. Bad karma all round.

The risk of non-arrival

Even worse than a delayed shipment is complete non-arrival. International parcels don't go missing that often but it happens. It's worse for some countries than for others. My experience has been that Western Europe is fine, Eastern Europe a bit risky, America reasonably reliable, Hong Kong and Australia very reliable, South Africa very risky. This, of course, is only my experience. It is based on a small sample size and other sellers may tell a different story altogether. But the obvious point is that the risk of non-arrival is higher with international shipments than with UK ones.

Customs

Some countries levy customs duty on imported goods. Within the EC there are no duties but outside it there often are. In theory this is not a problem for you, the seller, as customs duties are the responsibility of the buyer. In practice it can be a problem in two circumstances:

- If a buyer is not expecting customs duties he will probably resent paying them and feel that he has got a 'bad deal' from his eBay purchase. Even though it was nothing to do with you he may take out his frustrations in the form of negative feedback, or ask you why you didn't tell him about the customs charges (as if you were supposed to know!).

- Parcels sometimes get stuck in customs. I have had situations where a buyer has asked me why he has not received his item only to find out that it was held up in customs. There is no way that you, as a seller, can anticipate these delays or alleviate them. But still, the flak comes your way.

Don't forget to check the prohibited and restricted items list to become familiar with import/export restrictions or visit eBay's Global Trading Community at www.pages.ebay.co.uk/globaltrade/index.html for lots of excellent advice.

Payment methods and international shipping

It's important when deciding whether to sell internationally that you consider the issue of payment methods. We look at this in more detail on page 321 but generally, for international sales, PayPal is the only way to go. You don't want to be mucking around with cheques or bank drafts and nor does the buyer.

If you have a PayPal account all these complications are ironed out. Assuming the buyer has one too, he can simply make a transfer to your account quickly and easily. And, if you have a Premier or Business PayPal account you can accept credit card payments from 38 different countries including Japan, New Zealand and Ireland. That's convenient for buyers and makes it more likely that you will get bids.

For more information check out the help pages on PayPal's website at www.paypal.co.uk

The risk of fraud

One of the arguments against trading internationally is that it is a favourite target of the professional fraudster. Indeed, eBay UK has now prohibited the use of instant money transfers as a form of payment due to their vulnerability to fraud. You should also note that the risk of fraudulent cheques, international or otherwise, rests with the seller. If you accept a cheque as payment, send out goods and the cheque bounces, you may find it very difficult to get redress. Only if you have yet to send out an item will you be able to make a claim under eBay's 'Payment Not Received' policy. You have been warned.

Escrow

One way of defending yourself against fraud is to use an 'escrow' service which can be used for both local or international transactions. An escrow service effectively acts as an impartial third party to a transaction, holding a buyer's payment in trust until the seller sends the item to them. The buyer has to be both in receipt of the goods and 100% happy with the transaction before authorising the escrow to release the funds to the seller. The seller also has the comfort of knowing that the buyer has produced funds ready to satisfy the purchase price.

The problem with escrow is that it costs money. Due to its high fees and charges it is only really suited to high-value items – eBay currently recommends its use for purchases over £250 in value.

If you would like to know more visit: www.escrow.com, a site independent of eBay but recommended by them.

Communicating with overseas buyers

When selling internationally you have to get your head around certain things not encountered with purely domestic sales; namely, time differences, currency differences and potential language differences. One way in which eBay helps is that bids and prices on an item listing are automatically displayed in the currency you specify and the currency pertinent to the site your bidder is viewing the item from. A buyer can also convert all prices to their local site by clicking the 'show all prices in local currency' link in the 'show' box of the search and listings page.

If you do not speak the same language as your buyer/bidder, try one of the free internet translation sites such as Babelfish (www.babelfish.com) in order to facilitate communication both prior to and on completion of a sale. Bear in mind, however, that the automatic translations are not always 100% accurate.

Step 12. Set 'Buyer Requirements'

You can choose not to set any buyer requirements for your auctions, which means that anyone in any location with any feedback record will be able to bid, or you can choose to restrict bids to people who you think will be easy to do business with.

Buyer requirements are eBay's way of allowing you to prohibit unwelcome bidders according to certain criteria. The screenshot opposite shows the options.

Whether or not you set buyer requirements is a completely personal choice and one which will probably be guided by your own level of experience. As a seller who has experienced non-paying bidders in the past, I choose to block buyers who:

Fig. 41 – How to set Buyer Requirements

To add buyer requirements to your listings:
1. In My eBay, under the My Account column, click the "Preferences" link.
2. In the Seller Preferences section, click the "Edit" link. The Buyer Requirements page opens.
3. Select your buyer requirements. These include blocking buyers who:
   - Are registered in countries to which you don't post to
   - Have a feedback score of -1,-2,-3 or lower
   - Have received 2 Unpaid Item strikes in the last 30 days
   - Are currently winning or have bought '1-100' of your items in the last 10 days
   - Do not have a PayPal account
4. Click the **Submit** button to save your requirements.

- Have a feedback score equal to or lower than -1.
- Have received 2 unpaid item strikes in the last 30 days.
- Have a feedback score of 0 or lower and no credit card on file.

In order not to alienate the genuine members who have yet to acquire any feedback I also add a note on my listings to the effect that any new members who wish to bid can email me in advance.

eBay used to offer another 'Buyer Management' tool called 'Pre-Approved Buyers'. This allowed sellers to create a pre-approved bidder/buyer list for any item and only allow the individuals on the list to bid for or buy it. Anyone not on the list had to contact the seller by email if they wanted to place a bid. In a sense, PAB was quite similar to the 'Buyer Requirements' feature, but more specific. As of January 2007, eBay eliminated the PAB feature on the grounds that "sellers who use it are often less reliable and it is often used to support off-eBay trade which is not safe."

Step 12: State your returns policy

The final thing for you to consider is whether you are prepared to offer a returns policy on items that buyers are unhappy with, for whatever reason. My personal opinion is that if you are completely honest in your description buyers should really be aware of what it is they are buying and should therefore have no reason to return an item. My exception to this is when I have omitted to mention a flaw in an item which materially affects its condition and/or value, in which case I welcome a dialogue with the buyer in order to negotiate a partial or full refund.

A natural question which arises from this last point is who should bear the cost of returning an item. Although eBay states that buyers are wholly responsible for postage costs it is less clear whether this should be the case when an item is faulty or has been misrepresented. Although this has yet to happen to me I like to think that I would bear the brunt of these costs if the error was made at my end.

Once the auction begins

Tracking your sales

Even as an eBay veteran, watching an auction's progress still excites me. You've researched your item, taken your photos and composed your listing. Now, if you want, you can just sit back and watch the fun.

Personally, I take a more active approach. I like to track each item's progress through the Selling view of My eBay. This tells you the time left to run on the auction, how many bids have been received, the current price and how many 'watchers' your item has. Fig. 42 shows an extract from my own selling pages.

Fig. 42 – Selling view of My eBay

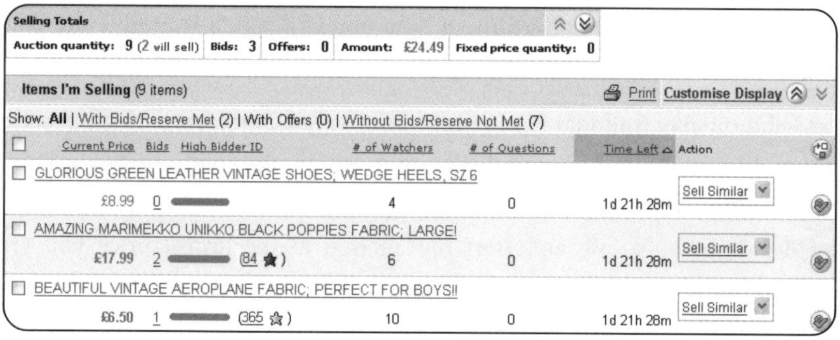

At the top of the 'Selling' view is a summary of your entire catalogue of listings. This tells you how many (if any) of your items will sell (i.e. have already received at least one bid) and how much you are currently 'earning' on them. In the example above, you can see that of 9 listed items, 2 are currently going to sell for a combined total of £24.49, not including postage.

Don't be disheartened if, for the first few days, your items don't generate any interest. Remember that as the novelty of eBay has worn off over the years, buyers have become shrewder and no longer rush in to make a bid. Instead they may choose to sit on the sidelines, watching an item until near the end of the auction, so as not to artificially inflate its price. And then they pounce.

Bidding tends to be infectious, so if there is some interest in your item, the first bid usually spurs the other interested parties into action. You should also bear in mind that most bids tend to be placed in the final hour or so of the auction meaning that even if there are no bids in the first 9 days, you can sometimes be pleasantly surprised by an item's eventual price.

One way of gauging the interest in your item is to track the number of watchers it has. This can also be seen from the 'Selling' view of My eBay. In the example given above, one of my items has 4 watchers and no bids, and the others have 6 and 10 watchers respectively. Be realistic about what these figures mean: a high number of watchers doesn't necessarily mean that the item will skyrocket in price, just as a low number or no watchers doesn't mean it won't sell. I've been in both positions numerous times and been disappointed and elated respectively. Think of your own browsing habits: quite often I will watch an item, not with any intention of bidding but simply to see what sort of price a certain type of item is making these days. Other times I am only half interested in an item and will watch it to give me time to make up my mind about bidding.

You will probably find that items with a relatively low start price attract more bids early on. The bidders gradually thin out as the item reaches a more realistic price until only the most interested bidders remain. Conversely, if you decide to play safe and start the auction at the lowest price you are prepared to accept, bidders will probably leave bidding to the very last moment unless they are exceptionally keen or suspect that there will be a lot of competition.

If you get unduly concerned by the lack of interest in your item(s) you can think about revising them. Read each part of the listing again, including the title and subtitle. Ask yourself:

- Are you selling your item in the best possible light to bidders?
- Does your photo do justice to the item?
- Have you set a realistic price, including postage charges?
- Are other sellers of similar items doing something that you're not? Are they describing the items better, or using better photos, or listing them in different categories, or choosing a different start price, or setting a different auction duration?

Revising your listing, mid-sale

If you decide that your listing would benefit from some pruning or additional text, simply locate the item and click on the 'revise your item' link at the top left of the page. This will take you back to a link similar in appearance to the original Sell Your Item form. Alternatively you can use the drop-down menu alongside the item in the 'Selling' view of My eBay and click on the link for 'edit'.

It's important to note that the degree to which you are allowed to edit a listing that has already gone live is dependent on the amount of time left before the auction ends. It is also dependent on whether you have already received bids on the item or, in the case of multiple item listings, any sales. Generally speaking, you cannot change the format of a listing, i.e, from fixed price to auction or vice versa, although you can add a 'Buy It Now Price' if no bids have yet been placed.

As a rule of thumb, if you don't see a link to either 'add' or 'edit' alongside a particular section of your listing this means that you will not be able to make changes to that part of your listing. eBay offers an excellent table-style guide to allowable revisions on both auction and fixed price listings which is reproduced overleaf in Fig. 43 and Fig. 44.

From these tables you can see that the less time there is remaining on an auction the fewer revisions can be made, especially if a bid has already been placed. With less than 12 hours to go you cannot alter the basic item description and any comments you wish to make will be applied to the end of the description and signposted by eBay as added information.

Cross-promoting your items

Whenever you have more than one item for sale, eBay gives you the opportunity to promote your additional listings whenever someone makes a bid or wins an item from you.

If you go to any of your current auctions you will see a link at the top of the page to 'Change your cross-promoted items'. Clicking on this link will show you which of your other items eBay has linked by default to this listing.

Fig. 43 – What you can revise – Auction listing

Time left before the listing ends	Did the listing receive bids?	What you can revise
More than 12 hours	No	• Revise any information except the selling format. • Remove the following optional features only: Buy It Now, eBay Picture Services, Reserve Price, 10-day listing • Add optional features to increase your listing's visibility (for example, bold). • Add or change a Gallery picture. • Add or change pictures using eBay Picture Services.
More than 12 hours	Yes	• Add a second category. • Add to the item description. • Add pictures using eBay Picture Services. • Add optional features to increase your listing's visibility (for example, bold).
Less than 12 hours	No	• Change the category and add Item Specifics. • Add to the item description. • Add optional features to increase your listing's visibility (for example, bold). • Add page view counters. • Add or change a Gallery picture. • Add pictures using eBay Picture Services. • Add new payment methods and post-to locations.
Less than 12 hours	Yes	• Add optional features to increase your listing's visibility (for example, bold). • Add or change a Gallery picture. You cannot add to your listing description in this circumstance.

The number of linked items is set at four so if you are selling four items or fewer they will already be linked to each other. If you are selling more than four items, however, you may wish to change the other items linked to a particular listing.

For example, if you are selling a vintage desk and have a matching chair for sale in another auction it would make sense to cross-promote these two items in the hope of enticing the same bidder for both. Similarly, if you decide to sell baby clothing, think about which items go together and which may appeal to the same buyer interested in a particular look or brand. When you

Fig. 44 – What you can revise – Fixed Price listing

Time left before the listing ends	Has an item from the listing been sold?	What you can revise
More than 12 hours	No	• Revise any information except the selling format. • Remove optional features. • Add or change a Gallery picture. • Add or change pictures using eBay Picture Services.
More than 12 hours	Yes	• Add to the item description. • Add pictures using eBay Picture Services. • Add optional features to increase your listing's visibility (for example, bold).
Less than 12 hours	No	• Add to the item description. • Add pictures using eBay Picture Services. • Add Item Specifics and Gift Services
Less than 12 hours	Yes	• Add optional features to increase your listing's visibility (for example, bold).

cross-promote in this way, consider offering buyers a postage discount if they buy more than one of the items. Not only is it 'fair' to do so, as posting two items together costs less than posting them separately, but it will also incentivise buyers to make multiple purchases.

If you don't want to go through the cross-promotion process or are happy with eBay's default choices don't forget that bidders can also view all your other items in one go by clicking on the 'View seller's other items' link on any of your listings. The cross-promotions facility is free of charge, however, so it is worthwhile making the most of it.

Answering buyers' questions

If you have been a little perfunctory in describing an item, or there are some points that need clarification, a buyer may send you a question using the link on the item listing. The question will appear in the 'In Box' of 'My Messages' and a copy will also be sent to your registered email address to improve your chances of seeing it.

Some buyers do this very late into the auction so you need to be vigilant. Try to answer promptly and accurately whilst being polite and courteous. Thank a buyer for their interest and never forget that they may be the person to make the difference between a sale or a non-sale.

When a buyer sends a question you have the option of posting both it and your response at the bottom of the listing for others to see. If you think that it will benefit other potential bidders by, for instance, clarifying the measurements of the item, the best policy is to include it in the listing.

One of the questions you may get is whether you would be prepared to end the listing early and/or sell it 'off eBay'. As mentioned earlier, although not technically a scam, selling items off-site is strongly discouraged by eBay as it leaves you vulnerable to fraud with no form of redress from the official channels. If the buyer seems genuine, by all means have a discussion about price and then, so long as there are no other bids, add a Buy It Now price to the listing. You could synchronise a time with the bidder when this will be added, so that they can be ready to take up the BIN offer. Be cautious though about mails from abroad offering to buy your item for a ridiculously high price. This is a classic sign of the overpayment scam mentioned on page 262 and any such correspondence should be reported to spoof@ebay.co.uk

Ending your listing early

If something unexpected happens and you find yourself unable to complete on an auction you can choose to end it early. If there have already been bids on the item you will also need to cancel these.

Rules about cancelling a listing

Valid reasons to end a listing early include:

1. The item is no longer available.
2. There is an error in the start price or reserve.
3. There is an error in the listing.
4. The item gets lost or broken.

Note that eBay will still charge its insertion fee in this situation so you may want to think carefully about whether you cannot simply revise your listing as opposed to ending it.

If there are 12 hours or less to go on a listing and it already has a winning bid you cannot end the listing unless you are selling to the high bidder. This rule is designed to avoid lots of buyers being disappointed by cancelled auctions, which would erode trust in the whole eBay experience.

How to cancel a listing

If you still decide that you want to end a listing early you need to access the 'End my listing early' form from eBay's Help pages or use the command from the item's drop-down menu in My eBay. If bids have already been placed you will be given two options:

1. Cancel bids and end the listing early.
2. Sell to the high bidder and end the listing early.

Once you have selected the appropriate option the listing will be ended by eBay and any bidders will be notified via email that their bids have been cancelled. Anyone who has been watching the item who attempts to access the listing will see a note at the top of the listing page explaining that the item has been ended.

Whilst eBay gives you the option to end a listing early it does not expect you to exploit this process for illegitimate ends, for example, pulling a listing which does not look like it will make as much as you had hoped. This process is known as 'reserve fee circumvention' and is much frowned upon. If a pattern develops of you overusing the end item early process it will be flagged by eBay and an investigation made.

After the auction ends

If you are online at the time one of your auctions ends, it can be quite exciting to watch the final moments. Items you had given up on selling may attract a last-minute bid, whilst others may rise in price as canny bidders get their snipes in. Of course, it's unusual to sell absolutely everything that you list, and I generally work on a selling ratio of anywhere between 50% – 80%.

As soon as a listing ends it moves from the 'Selling' view to either the 'Sold' or the Unsold view of My eBay. If the item has sold the listing will be telegraphed with a "Congratulations! Your item sold for £££ [the winning amount]". You will be able to see the number of bids placed and the user ID of the winning bidder. There are now a couple of things you have to do.

Step 1. Send an invoice

Most buyers don't pay immediately, even if they bid right at the end of the auction, so you should email them an invoice as soon as possible.

You don't have to create an invoice yourself – eBay does it for you. The link can be found on the drop-down menu alongside the item listing in My eBay. The invoice will tell the buyer how much to pay in total, including postage and packing and how and to whom to make payment. If you need to add any more information or specify a postal discount for multiple wins you should amend the invoice accordingly and add any additional instructions in the box provided. Don't forget to preview the final invoice before sending it to the buyer.

If your total price has not been made clear from the item listing, or if the buyer needs to get in touch with you for any other reason, they may 'request the total' from you via eBay. In this case you will receive an email with this request and should respond as quickly as possible.

It never hurts to add a personal salutation to the end of your invoice/communications such as 'thanks for your business' or something similar. These things all help build a rapport with your buyer and give them the confidence to buy from you again.

If a buyer is paying with a cheque or postal order you should make it clear that goods will be dispatched on receipt of cleared funds. i.e. when the cheque or postal order has cleared and not just when it has been received. Some sellers are willing to send goods before a cheque has cleared if they have dealt with a buyer before or the buyer has consistently good feedback but this is a matter purely for your discretion and is generally not advised.

Once you receive a cheque, however, try not to take too long to deposit the funds as this will only prolong the delay and possibly annoy the buyer into the bargain. If calamity strikes and you cannot get to the bank, email the buyer and explain the situation. Most people will understand as long as the line of communication is kept open.

If you have stipulated payment via PayPal you should expect the buyer to send the money within three days of the end of the auction although some sellers allow up to a week. A week gives the buyer time to transfer money from his bank account into his PayPal account, should he not have sufficient funds already deposited with PayPal.

As soon as payment is received, PayPal will notify you by sending an email to your registered email address. It really is an instant payment which is why so many eBayers, myself included, prefer it to other methods. The funds are held in your PayPal account and can either be transferred to your bank or held in trust by PayPal until you transfer them or use them to fund future purchases.

If you choose to withdraw the funds from your PayPal Account there is a small charge (at the time of writing, 25p) for amounts of £49.99 and below when they are transferred into a UK bank account. For amounts over £50 the transfer is free, irrespective of the type of account held. If you wish to transfer funds into an account outside the UK you should consult PayPal's help pages for the relevant charges.

Step 2. Pack your item

After the auction is over and assuming the item has sold, you will need to pack it to ensure it reaches its destination undamaged and in the condition described.

- Before packing, give it **one last look over** to ensure that it is clean/ironed/in the condition that you described. Buyers are generally willing to overlook a few creases in transit but smells, especially cigarette and pet smells not pointed out in the listing, are a definite no-no and will almost certainly result in complaints from a disgruntled buyer.

- When wrapping and packing, remember that postal carriers are notoriously heavy-handed. It is best to **assume that your package is going to be thrown around**, dropped and treated like a football throughout its journey. Protect it accordingly!

- Good packaging scores points with buyers and is often referred to in feedback, so **it pays to make an effort**. You can buy padded envelopes and bubble wrap from high street stores, from the Post Office or from storage centres, but another option is to buy on eBay – there is a whole category of sellers on eBay who trade solely in packing materials.

- For items of clothing, a layer or two of **acid-free tissue paper** and a tamper proof self-seal bag have always worked for me and can be bought in bulk at reasonable cost. For smaller items, such as CDs, DVDs, etc, a padded envelope is sufficient, although if you are selling vinyl records you will need to encase the sleeves between rigid squares of cardboard in addition to marking them as 'fragile'.

- For **larger fragile items** you should play safe with a combination of bubble wrap, foam chips, newspaper and even boxes within boxes to protect individual components from coming into contact with one another whilst in transit. Use your common sense and you can't go wrong.

- Just **make sure that the buyer doesn't need a chain saw** to open the various layers as overkill can be just as annoying as inadequate packaging. You should obviously ensure that any protrusions or sharp edges are well padded to prevent accidents and injury.

- **Include the printable receipt from PayPal** or a copy of the item listing so that the buyer knows who the item has come from. Some people are prolific buyers and can lose track of their purchases! Giving them a reference will also enable them to leave appropriate feedback.

- Make sure that you address the package clearly, adding a return address to the reverse. For bulkier items use strong parcel tape at least three inches wide and include with the package a print out of the item listing or your printable receipt from PayPal if applicable.

Step 3. Send the item

Whatever form of payment is used, once you have received the money you should aim to send the item out promptly.

- When you send the item, remember to get a **Proof of Posting certificate** if you are not using a trackable delivery service. The certificate will only cover goods to the value of £30 and doesn't include jewellery or money, but it is still important if you need to claim compensation or to prove to the buyer that you have dispatched the item.

- For **larger items**, such as articles of furniture, you can either specify that the buyer collects (although this does tend to attract fewer bids) or you can check out a service such as ParcelForce 48 which offers a door-to-door courier service. You can also suggest that buyers find and fund their own courier service or offer them a choice from the various individuals and companies currently doing the rounds on eBay itself. Some of the names have been around longer and are more prominent on eBay than others, and it is probably wise to stick to them. You may be able to negotiate preferential rates if you intend to use their services more than once or twice.

- For valuable items going abroad, I recommend a service called 'Pharos'. It offers the speed, reliability and trackability of a courier (in fact it uses UPS's network), and whilst not cheap, it is less expensive than DHL, UPS or Fedex. You don't have to have an account with them; you can simply go to their website, key in the weight of the parcel and its destination, and get an immediate quote. If you like it, you fill in your address, your credit card number, and the date you want it collected, and lo and behold – a UPS van turns up!

  Pharos can only really be justified where you're selling a valuable item to an overseas buyer, and where the buyer is happy to pay the charges, but if you're in that position, I recommend it. www.pharos-international.co.uk

- Hopefully, your parcel will arrive on time, the buyer will be delighted and will leave you glowing feedback. If you haven't already done so you should return the gesture as soon as possible by leaving feedback for the buyer.

What if the transaction goes wrong?

If you have followed all the advice thus far, very little should go wrong that is your fault. However, in the real world, problems do occur so you should be prepared for them. Here are the most common ones:

Buyer unhappy with item

If a buyer emails you after receipt of the item and says that he is unhappy, resist the temptation to fire off an angry or indignant response. Instead, read the points carefully and see whether any of them relate to faults that could be attributable to you. For example, if the buyer complains that the item does not fit but you have measured and listed it correctly then that is their fault, not yours. Similarly if they have since decided that it doesn't suit them/they don't like it, that in itself does not constitute an immediate right to a refund.

On the other hand, complaints about condition, smells, flaws, etc, not mentioned in the listing should be taken seriously. Reply to the buyer asking what he would like you to do. Offering a full or partial refund usually does the trick, although whether this should also include the cost of postage both ways is your call. eBay's position on this point is that it is the buyer's responsibility to cover postage costs although it is not clear whether this should be the case when the seller is at fault.

At all costs avoid a situation where things get nasty or aggrieved with a buyer, especially if you are threatened with negative feedback. As long as you are confident that you are acting correctly you should stand your ground and respond to any negative feedback received with your right to reply. People aren't stupid and will generally understand that even eBayers with exemplary records can sometimes receive negative feedback if they encounter an unreasonable buyer.

Item not received

If you look through any number of eBay listings you will see quite a few sellers who now make a point of saying that they will not be held responsible for items that get lost or damaged in the mail, although they will co-operate in filing a claim with the carrier. In fact, it is only the seller that can claim for these losses – something which many buyers are not aware of.

If a buyer says that the item has not been received and it was sent out a while ago, check with Royal Mail's online portal. If you have used a trackable service, such as Recorded Delivery or Registered Post, you can check the parcel's progress by inputting the 13 digit reference number at the bottom of your receipt.

If the item was sent through the normal post you will need to wait around 15 days from the date of posting before Royal Mail will acknowledge it as probably lost. You will then be able to make a claim and will need to provide the Proof of Posting Certificate in support of your claim. Note that it is up to you as the seller to do this.

Communicate with your buyer and let them know the situation. As the contract for delivery is between you and the Royal Mail, assure the buyer that you will be filing a claim for compensation and that you will issue a refund to the buyer as soon as you have received your compensation. If the buyer agrees, great; if not and they leave negative feedback, there isn't much you can do. Some people would also argue that in this instance there isn't much incentive for the seller to then claim or to refund the buyer, but I'll let your own conscience be the guide on this!

The important point to remember here is that you must get documented evidence of sending your items to stand the best chance of receiving compensation from the Post Office or, in the worst case scenario, to be able to defend any claims made against you through eBay from the buyer.

Non-paying bidder

This is every seller's nightmare but, generally speaking, still accounts for only a tiny percentage of failed transactions on eBay. Again, most of the time this can be resolved with a friendly reminder sent via eBay's messaging system.

Don't forget that people have busy lives, get ill etc, so don't immediately fear the worst if they don't pay straight off bat.

If three days have passed however, with no payment and no communication you should either email the buyer or re-invoice them. Keep things polite and just mention that you were hoping to send the item as soon as possible and could they let you know what they intend to do regarding payment. Most of the time a friendly message gets the ball rolling again and everything proceeds smoothly.

If there has been no communication after another two days have passed you should send a firmer email instructing the buyer that the next stage will be to report the situation to eBay and leave negative feedback. If the buyer has no intention of paying you'll probably not hear from him again in which case you should go ahead and start proceedings for a non-paying bidder (see "What To Do If It All Goes Wrong", beginning on page 239).

Although horrible when it happens (and it's happened to me twice) this is still a rare occurrence and you should generally have confidence in eBay's safety procedures.

What if the item doesn't sell?

Sometimes, you will list items on eBay and receive no bids at all. The auction will run its course and end without a sale. Unsold items, surprise surprise, appear in the Unsold view of My eBay.

If the non-sale is as a result of a non-paying bidder, the item will appear as if sold until you activate the process for non-payment. If you take this step you can, if you wish, use the 'Second Chance Offer' facility in order to try and sell the item to the next highest bidder (assuming there was more than one bid). You must ensure, however, that you have given the winning bidder ample opportunity to either pay or communicate their intention to you before taking this course of action.

When an item remains unsold for any other reason one option is to relist it and, under certain circumstances, this can be done for free.

Free relisting

The free relist policy works by refunding the insertion fee to your account if your relisted item sells the second time around. This means that you will be charged for the insertion initially but will receive a credit post-sale.

In order to be eligible for this credit you must use the official 'Relist' feature, accessible from the drop-down menu in the 'Unsold' view of My eBay. There will also be a link to this facility on the completed item listing. You cannot simply copy and paste the item description into a new listing as eBay will not be able to recognise it as the same listing and will not process the refund.

There are some other conditions attached to the free relist policy. In brief, these specify a time limit between a first and second listing of 90 days, the starting price has to remain the same, and both the original and subsequent listing must be for single auction-format items only.

If you are applying for a relist credit because your winning bidder did not pay you must make sure that you file an unpaid item dispute for the original listing and request a full final value fee credit for that listing. This credit must be posted to your account before you can receive the insertion fee credit. For more details on how to file an 'Unpaid Items Dispute' refer to page 246.

An important point to note is that if you had extra features on your original listing such as Bold, Gallery Featured, etc, these will NOT be included in the relist credit. Only the basic insertion fee is covered. Note too that if your relisted item sells the second time you will be charged a final value fee.

The free relist policy only applies to the second listing of an item and not to any subsequent attempts to sell. If your item doesn't sell second time round, think about the merits of continuing to flog this particular horse; it may be better to give the item to charity or keep it in storage for another time. Vintage items, in particular, go in and out of fashion, and if you have the patience, it pays to hold on to them until they are in back in favour. Just check on eBay to see if similar items are rising in value.

If you do decide to relist, don't forget to have a good look at your description and see whether it can be made more appealing to potential buyers. Once you have relisted using the official 'Relist' feature you can revise your item as normal and still be eligible for the credit.

7
DEADLY SINS

WRATH
Going way over your budget because
someone dared to outbid you.

AVARICE
Buying 26 baby blankets and having to resell 23
of them. At a loss.

GLUTTONY
Comfort spending in the belief that you're saving
money. Fatal to your wealth.

SLOTH
Paid £50 for a £12.50 toy? Someone needs
to do their homework...

ENVY
Yes, your neighbours pram is very nice.
But do you really need another one?

(FALSE) PRIDE
Can you not just buy something
new for a change...?

LUST
"I love it. I want it. I need it." Get a grip.

All about fees

eBay's fees are, of course, where it makes the bulk of its profit – all $1.1billion of it last year. That money has to come from somewhere, and when you look at your monthly statement, you begin to realise where!

It can sometimes be a bit of a surprise to see how the fees have added up, especially if you have done quite well on your listings. To be fair to eBay, their fees are very transparent, so there is no reason why you should be surprised.

Whenever you list an item on the site you are charged both an insertion fee and, if the item sells, a final value fee. These two amounts become the total cost of selling on eBay.

Insertion fees

The insertion fee charged when you list an item is based on the starting price which you set for the auction. The table below shows how the fee rises in levels from a minimum of 15p to a maximum (for single listings) of £2.

Fig. 45 – Insertion fees

Insertion Fees	
Starting or Reserve Price	Insertion Fee
£0.01 - £0.99	£0.15
£1.00 - £4.99	£0.20
£5.00 - £14.99	£0.35
£15.00 - £29.99	£0.75
£30.00 - £99.99	£1.50
£100.00 or more	£2.00
for multiple item listings in £100.00 or more tier	£3.00

If you set a reserve price for your item, it, rather than the starting price is used to determine the insertion fee.

For multiple item auctions (i.e. Dutch Auctions) and BIN listings, the insertion fees are based on the starting price or fixed price multiplied by the number of items. For items above £100 you will never be charged more than £3.00.

The insertion fee is non-refundable. In other words, even if you don't sell the item, the fee has to be paid. (As noted on page 327 you may be able to re-list an unsold item free of charge.)

Free Listing Days

Occasionally, eBay will notify you of special selling promotions such as free or reduced-price listing days. If you are new to selling, or have a few unwanted items which are unlikely to fetch a high final price, these days can be a good opportunity. As you can imagine, other sellers will do the same thing, so you tend to find that a whole load of dross goes through eBay's pages on free listing days!

As with every other sales promotion, internet-based or otherwise, there are terms and conditions attached to free and reduced-price listing days and you would do well to read these before going gung-ho and listing everything you can lay your hands on.

Generally, the free or reduced listing price will only apply to the basic insertion fee and not to optional extra features such as bold, highlight, etc.

It also does not include the final value fee which has to be paid on every item that you sell.

Speciality sections, such as eBay motors are also generally excluded from these promotions and have their own specific offers.

My advice is not to be seduced into selling stuff you would normally throw away or give to charity, as the chances are they won't be attractive enough to make it worth your time, effort or money. In addition the final value fees may come as a nasty surprise when set against your actual revenue.

Final Value fees

Final value fees are the fees that you pay if you sell an item, whether in an auction or in a Buy It Now listing. If you don't sell the item, you don't have to pay a final value fee. Like insertion fees, final value fees are charged on a sliding scale, based on the amount your item sold for. The table below shows the levels. You don't have to work out the percentage yourself – eBay does it for you – but it is important to be aware of what you're going to have to pay.

Fig. 46 – Final Value fees

Final Value Fees	
Closing Price	Final Value Fee
Item not sold	**No Fee**
£0.01 - £29.99	**5.25%** for the amount of the high bid (at the listing close for auction-style listings) up to £29.99
£30.00 - £599.99	**5.25%** of the initial £29.99 (£1.57), plus **3.25%** of the remaining closing value balance
Over £600.00	**5.25%** of the initial £29.99 (£1.57), plus **3.25%** of the initial £30.00 - £599.99 (£18.53), plus **1.75%** of the remaining closing value balance

There are some circumstances in which the calculation of final value fees is a bit more complicated.

- On Dutch Auctions it is calculated by taking the final value fee of the lowest successful bid and multiplying it by the total number of items sold.

- For multiple items on a Buy It Now listing, the fee is calculated on a per sold item basis, taken from the final sale price.

- If you have used a reserve price on your listing this will incur an additional and separate fee. As explained previously, the fee eBay charges the seller in this instance is determined by the amount of the reserve. At the time of writing, reserve fees range from £1.50 for reserves under £99.99 and £2.00 for items over £100. Again you should note that reserves can only be set at £50 or above. If the item goes on to sell, this fee is refunded to the seller as they will then have to pay eBay a Final Value Fee.

- Special rules apply to some listings created in Turbo Lister or Selling Manager Pro. If you use these tools, read the terms & conditions carefully.

- Special rules apply if you sell property (i.e. real estate) on eBay.

All fees include VAT calculated at the current rate of 17.5% and will be shown on your monthly invoice.

eBay's billing cycle

eBay invoices sellers on a monthly basis, using two billing cycles. Your billing cycle is determined automatically by the date on which you created your seller's account and will either be:

15th of the month
If your account is running on the 15th day cycle, eBay will calculate the fees which you owe for each monthly period from 16th of month to 15th of the following month, and will email you an invoice between the 16th-20th.

Last day of the month
If your account is run on the last day cycle, eBay will calculate your fees from the 1st day to the last day of each month, and will email you an invoice between the 1st-5th of the following month.

Paying eBay's fees

Your invoice needs to be paid by the next invoice date. So if you are invoiced on 4th April you need to have paid by the 30th May. If you have set up an automatic payments process via your credit card, bank account or PayPal your fees will be deducted automatically and the invoice will only be sent for information purposes.

You can pay in various ways:

- PayPal (for both monthly and one-time payments).
- Direct debit from your bank account (for both monthly and one-time payments).
- Credit card (for both monthly and one-time payments).
- Cheques and postal orders (one-time payments only).

When you first register with eBay, you will be invited to select one of these options. If you change your mind, and want to pay a different way, you can do so through your 'Seller Account' view of My eBay.

If you decide to pay by direct debit it will take around 19/20 days for your bank account information to be approved and automated for monthly payments. Fees will be debited by eBay 7-10 days after it sends your monthly invoice. If your direct debit payments are ever declined by your bank eBay will administer an additional £5 charge to your account (this is on top of your own bank's penalties for defaulting on a direct debit, so be warned!)

Credit card payments are also taken approximately 7-10 days after the date of your monthly invoice.

If you decide to pay your fees by cheque, eBay requires between 7-10 days for clearance after which time your account will be updated. As you need to have paid by the next invoice date you should take this into account when sending payments by this method. Don't forget to write your invoice number and eBay User ID on the back of the cheque to facilitate this process.

Payments by both cheque and postal order should be accompanied by a printed payment coupon which can be downloaded from eBay. The address to send your payment is printed on the coupon, along with all the relevant instructions.

What happens if you don't pay?

Non-payment of your eBay fees may result in your account being suspended and may make you liable for additional collection costs.

If your seller's account is suspended by eBay for any reason, any outstanding payments must be paid immediately. If you have an automatic payments process established eBay reserves the right to charge any amount outstanding to that payment method.

If you do not pay your balance by the due dates you will become liable for a late payment charge PLUS you will be charged interest the day after the payment due date each month until the debt is paid. For accounts over 180 days late eBay reserves the right to deduct the amount owed from your PayPal account balance where applicable.

If you do not have an automatic payments process established you will not be allowed to exceed £15.00 in seller's fees. In this situation eBay may prevent you from listing more items until these fees are paid.

You can view your 'Account Status' including a full invoice history by looking up your Seller's Account on My eBay.

eBay and the taxman

For many eBayers, the auction website is an entertaining way of making a bit of extra money out of unwanted goods, and being green at the same time. The process is fun, satisfying, and modestly remunerative.

For others, eBay is much more than that. What starts out as a hobby turns into a business, and they find that as well as getting a buzz out of being an eBay entrepreneur, they are also getting a steady income.

You may find yourself falling into this second group, and if you do, you'll be in good company: it is estimated that several hundred thousand people now make at least a significant percentage of their income from trading on eBay. Without the overheads of retail property rental and extra utility bills to consider it is an attractive business model. Just don't fool yourself that it's easy. There is a lot of hard work involved in researching, sourcing and listing items and ensuring that your business runs as a smooth and efficient unit behind the scenes as well as front of house.

Unfortunately there are also tax implications to selling on eBay, the full range of which are beyond the remit of this book. As a general rule, occasional buying and selling on eBay is not something that the Inland Revenue is concerned with, so if you buy and sell baby goods on eBay and use them for your own purposes, you won't be expected to declare the income in your tax return.

However, internet trading is subject to the same tax rules as any other form of trading, and this means that at some indefinable point, small irregular trades that don't have to be declared become more regular, more significant trades that do.

How do you know when you've crossed that line? Partly it is a matter of the value of the trades you are involved in. The rules for self-assessment clearly state that the taxpayer is legally obliged to declare any income beyond the Individual Capital Gains Tax Threshold (set at £8,500 for 2005/6) and all taxable business profits. However, the sale of your own second hand goods or 'chattels' is exempt from Capital Gains Tax. Even if you sell things on eBay on behalf of a relative or friend these are regarded as 'safe' transactions as they are perceived as domestic rather than commercial endeavours.

The other factor is the frequency and underlying purpose of your trading. If you trade very frequently, and the reason you are doing it is to make a profit, then your activity is, in effect, a business, and you need to tell the Revenue. If, however, you are buying baby goods, using them for your family, then selling them on second hand, that is not – other things being equal – a business. What matters is your intention when you originally bought the goods. It is really a question of common sense.

Don't assume, however, that the Revenue will always see things the way that you do. It will consider the facts in each case and in some situations the relevant case law.

There are undoubtedly a number of people who make substantial amounts of money from eBay but who do not declare these earnings. From a tax point of view they are sailing perilously close to the wind as, despite appearances, eBay is not technically part of the cash economy. As most sales are paid for by cheque, postal order or by one of the virtual credit card payment methods such as PayPal or escrow, a record of any and all transactions does exist.

Theoretically, at least, this means that the Inland Revenue, if it wanted to, could request a list of registered users on eBay and ask for details of transactions going through a particular account. If there is a detectable and consistent pattern of sales as well as purchases, this could be used to prove that trading is occurring.

Don't forget that if a trading pattern is suspected there may be implications for other matters such as tax credits and State benefits.

If you are at all interested in the idea of turning your casual eBay pursuit into a business, or suspect that you already have (!), get some advice from an accountant or other tax expert. There are some excellent books on the subject now available, some written by eBay PowerSellers. Be aware, though, that American books on the subject will focus on US tax law, not UK tax law, and cannot therefore be relied on.

Conclusion

This book has been a joy to write; both from the point of view of sharing a passion and from the knowledge that it may benefit others who, like me, might otherwise have struggled to manage the financial aspects of childrearing.

Like many new mothers, I have often found myself overwhelmed by the choice of baby products available and the powerful moral imperative to do the best that I can for my child. However, whilst there are undoubtedly some amazing products out there, it is also important to remember that much of what we are told our children need is, in fact, driven by consumerism and not necessity. I know from first hand experience how easy it is to get carried away with the excitement of a new baby but I also know that materially speaking they actually want for very little beyond the basic.

Having a baby is hard work, the hardest, most responsible work that most of us will ever have the privilege of doing. It is also one of the most rewarding but frustratingly undervalued jobs out there, and one which makes any income, whatever its level, soon dwindle. This is why any inside information as to how to make our lives both easier and cheaper is so valuable.

Learning to use eBay is one such insider's 'tool' and, much like the old proverb about teaching a man to fish, once you know the rudiments of eBay you have a tool which can last you beyond pregnancy and birth to when your child is 5, 10 and beyond.

You should also gain some satisfaction from the knowledge that you are making a contribution to the recycling movement, and sharing with other mums and dads things which you have found useful in your own parenting career. Throw into the mix the small financial gains which you may make as a result of selling your unwanted items and you have a great recipe that will serve both you and your family well.

I hope that you find this book, and the information it contains, a useful addition to your parenting library. I wish you all the very best for your new lives together!

Wiz Wharton

Glossary

A

About Me **me**

A page which you create on eBay that gives other members information about you such as hobbies, interests and specialist areas of knowledge. Once created, a special logo will appear alongside your user ID that anyone can click on to view.

Auction-Style Listing (Online Auction Format)

The most common way of selling items on eBay. Items are listed for a fixed duration, after which time the highest bidder wins.

B

Best Offer

A listing feature used by sellers that allows potential buyers to make a financial offer for an item.

Bid Cancellation

The cancellation of a bid by a seller during an auction-style listing either at their own discretion or (occasionally) when mutually agreed with a bidder.

Bid Increment

The amount by which a bid must be raised in order for it to be accepted in an auction-style listing. The bid increment is determined by the current price of an item.

Bid Retraction

The cancellation of a bid by a buyer during an auction-style listing.

Bidder

A member who bids on an item on eBay.

Bidder Search

Technique which allows you to search for items that another eBay member has bid on or which you yourself have bid on in the last 30 days.

Block Bidders/Buyers

A list that you create naming individual eBay members who are not allowed to bid on or buy items you offer for sale. Any member on your list will be blocked from ALL your listings until you choose to remove them.

Buyer

member who buys an item from a seller on eBay.

Buy It Now
A listing feature that lets a buyer purchase an item immediately for a price the seller has set.

C

Category Listings
The method by which items are organized for sale on eBay, for example, Baby, Women's Clothing, Antique Furniture, etc.

Changed User ID Icon
Indicates that a member has changed their User ID in the past 30 days.

Completed Listings (Search)
Search technique which allows anyone to look for items that have ended in the previous 15 days. This can be very useful in determining the current market value of a particular item.

D

Discussion Boards
Virtual arena created by eBay where members can post messages, ask questions, or simply "hang out" with other users.

Dispute Console
Managed through My eBay, the Dispute Console allows members to check on the status of any disputes relating to their transactions on eBay, for example during the Item Not Received process.

Dutch Auction (Multiple Item Auction)
A listing in which a seller offers multiple identical items for sale and where bidders specify the number of items they want and the price they are prepared to pay per item. Because winning bids are determined by their overall value Dutch Auctions can have multiple winners.

E

eBay Motors
A specialist division of eBay dedicated to the buying and selling of vehicles, their parts and accessories.

eBay Stores

Special pages on eBay featuring all the items offered by an individual Store seller. These virtual shop fronts can often offer many unique items not available through the usual auction listings.

eBay Time

The official time of day at eBay headquarters in San Jose, California.

Escrow

A (payable) service in which a third party holds a buyer's payment in trust until the buyer receives and approves the item from the seller. Recommended for higher value items bought on eBay.

F

Feedback

The bedrock of the eBay community, the Feedback system allows members to rate their buying or selling experiences with other eBayers using a grading of positive, negative or neutral. In addition, members can leave a short written comment.

Feedback Score

A shorthand indication of a member's reputation on eBay. Members receive points for ratings as follows: +1 (positive), 0 (neutral), or -1 (negative). The feedback score is the sum of all the ratings a member has received from unique users.

Feedback Star

An additional scoring system which indicates that members have achieved or surpassed a certain amount of feedback ratings. Different colours are used to indicate different levels of feedback, for example, a yellow star indicates a rating of between 10-49 feedback points.

Final Value Fee

A fee eBay charges to a seller based on the closing price of a completed item listing. Where the item remains unsold there is no FVF.

G

Guides

Virtual pamphlets written by eBay members or its staff which share information on a specialist area of interest or knowledge. The Buyer's Guides in Part 2 of this book would qualify as such.

H – I

Insertion Fee

The fee eBay charges to a seller for listing an item. This fee varies by the type of listing and is non-refundable.

J – K , L – M

Member

A buyer or seller who has registered with eBay and has their own unique User ID and password for accessing the site.

Member Profile

A page showing all of a member's feedback information, including ratings and comments from people they have transacted with on eBay.

My eBay

A member's personal control panel within eBay from where they can manage all of their activities including buying, selling, feedback and account preferences.

N – O

New Member/User Icon

Used where a buyer or seller has been registered with eBay for 30 days or less.

P – Q

PayPal

An efficient and secure payment method with which to complete your eBay transactions. Payment to a seller is funded via a credit card or bank account via your registered email address.

PayPal Buyer Protection

A buyer protection program that offers up to $1,000 of free coverage for buyers who pay with PayPal on qualified listings. As with all compensation schemes, however, terms and conditions will apply.

Picture Icon

Indicates that the listing has a picture of the item in its description. This icon appears in browse and search result lists.

PowerSeller

An experienced seller on eBay who has demonstrated that they have provided a high level of service to their buyers by maintaining a positive feedback score of 98% and above.

Private Auction Listing

A listing in which the User IDs of bidders remain anonymous. Sellers can choose to make their auctions private at the time of listing but eBay may also replace User IDs with more anonymous information ("Bidder 1", "Bidder 2", etc) when an item's value exceeds a certain amount.

Proxy Bidding

Process by which eBay automatically bids on the buyer's behalf, up to the maximum amount they set.

R

Registered Member/User

A person who has registered with eBay by providing basic contact information.

Relisting

Listing an unsold item for sale again. If the item sells on its second attempt eBay automatically refunds the relisting fee.

Reserve Price

The lowest price at which a seller is willing to sell an item in an auction-style listing. If the highest bid does not meet the reserve, the seller is under no obligation to sell the item.

S

Second Chance Offer

Process by which a seller can make an offer to a non-winning bidder when either the winning bidder has failed to pay for an item or the seller has a duplicate of the item.

Secure Sockets Layer (SSL)

An industry-standard encryption protocol that is used to transmit users' personal or credit card information securely and privately over the internet. As used by eBay.

Safety Centre

The central place on eBay for members to report problems as well as learn techniques for trading safely on the site and elsewhere on the internet.

Sell Similar Item

A feature that lets sellers easily list new items based on the information they've previously entered for another item.

Seller's Return Policy

A seller's criteria for returning goods bought from them on eBay as specified in their individual item listings.

Seller Search

Technique allowing members to search for items being sold by a specific seller by inputting the seller's unique User ID.

Shill Bidding

The deliberate placing of bids to artificially raise the price of an item.

Skype

A free bit of software you install on your computer to communicate with other eBay members. Skype lets you make free calls over the Internet from your computer using speakers, a microphone or headset.

Sniping

Placing a bid in the closing minutes or even seconds of an auction. Though disliked by some members this is a perfectly legitimate tactic.

Starting Price

The price at which a seller wants bidding for an item to begin in an auction.

T

Title Search

A method of finding items on eBay by entering keywords that match the title of the items.

Turbo Lister

An advanced eBay selling tool available free to download that helps sellers create multiple listings quickly and easily on their computer.

U – V

Unpaid Item Process

The dispute resolution process used by sellers when they have not been paid for their item.

User Agreement

The terms under which eBay offers its members access to eBay services. All registered members must agree to these terms before they can bid on or list items, or use any other eBay service.

User ID

The unique name used to identify yourself on eBay. Your User ID is chosen as part of the initial registration process.

W - Z

Want It Now

eBay's virtual noticeboard which allows buyers to tell sellers exactly what they are looking for via a written description. Sellers periodically review these messages and, where applicable, respond to buyers with items they are selling on eBay.

Index

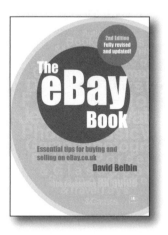
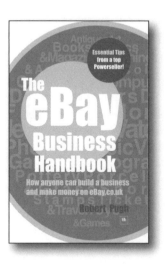

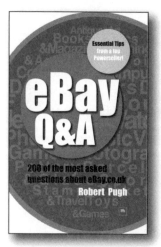

The eBay UK Bulletin

FREE weekly email newsletter

www.ebaybulletin.co.uk

*From the author of the best selling eBay Business Handbook comes a **free** weekly email bulletin packed with essential hints and tips.*

 Why not sign up for my free weekly email newsletter and keep up-to-date with the latest developments for eBay sellers. Each email contains hints and tips for eBay sellers, technical developments within eBay, a reader's letter in 'Ask Molly' and other essential information. HTML issues are also covered, with explanations of when and how to use additional codes to drive your profits even higher. Plus, keep tabs on new sales techniques and advice for moving with the markets.

It's not all hard work and no play. There are always strange and crazy things happening on eBay and in my 'Trader's Tales' section, I will share some of the more amusing moments from the world of sales. Like the guy who bought 'half a kilo of Lego' and then was disappointed with the amount! Not to mention the weird and wonderful auctions that take place online – how much would you bid for an 'air guitar'?

I will also keep you up-to-date with my own eBay career as I share my experiences, both good and bad. Hopefully you'll pick up some useful tips or at least avoid repeating any of my mistakes.

To sign up to my free newsletter, visit: www.ebaybulletin.co.uk – or if you'd like some advice or want to share a story why not send me an email: mollybol@ebaybulletin.co.uk.

Happy eBaying!

Mollybol (aka Robert Pugh)

Win a year's supply of Babylicious food!

Harriman House has teamed up with **Babylicious** to offer readers a very tasty prize.

The award-winning baby food company have a year's supply of their nutritious range up for grabs.

Just visit **www.babylicious.co.uk** for full details of how you can win this amazing prize.

Babylicious meals give your baby and toddler delicious, healthy, 'home made' food without you being chained to the kitchen. Hoorah!

Life is tough enough with little people, without stressing over what to feed them. Babylicious and Kiddylicious Snap-frozen™ cubes are little dishes of delicious, REAL food.

No artificial this and added that. No jars. No packets. Just naturally wholesome ingredients turned into tasty, healthy meals for little tummies.

So your kids can eat good food right from their first bite.

See www.babylicious.co.uk for full terms and conditions.